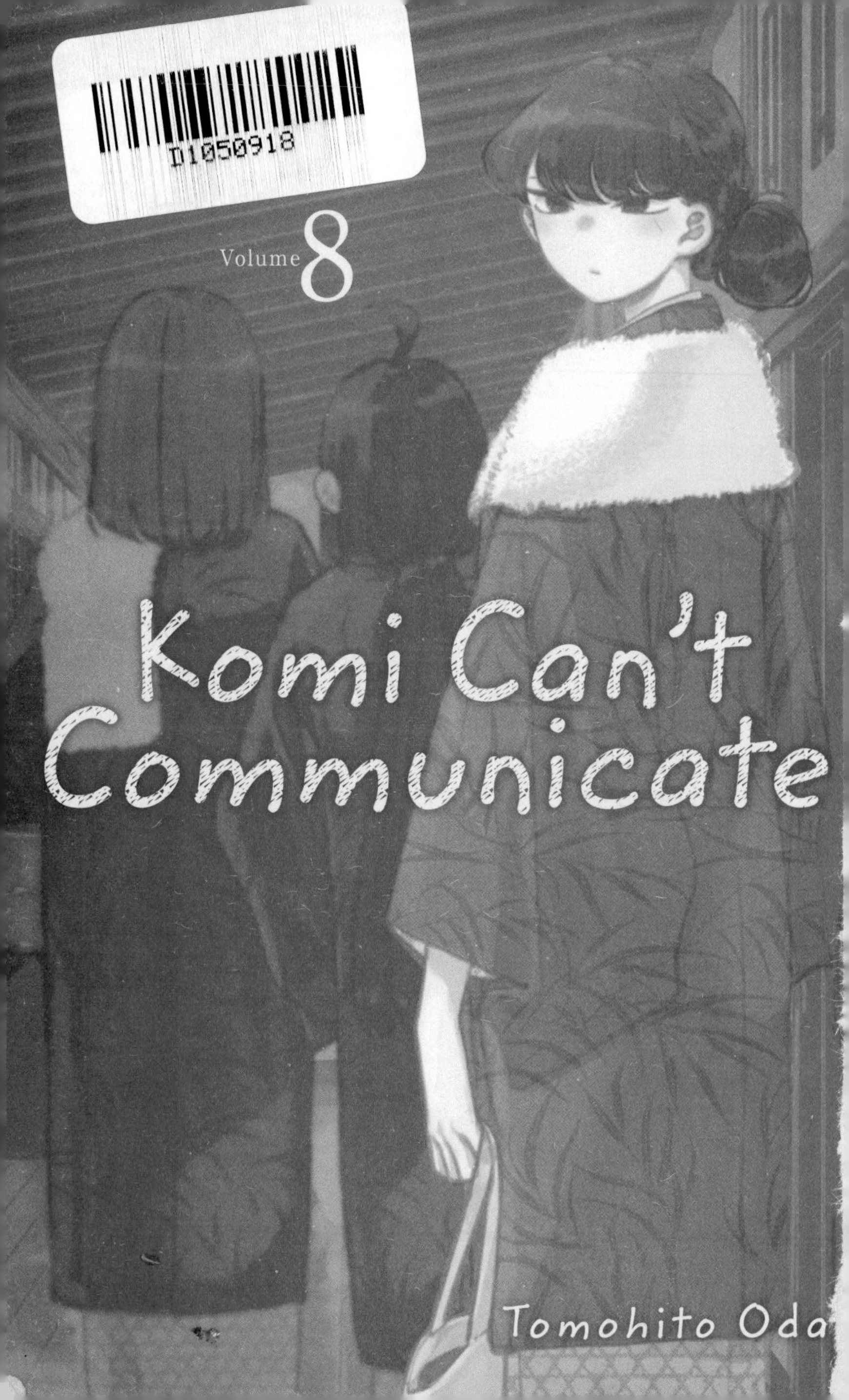
Volume 8
Komi Can't Communicate
Tomohito Oda

Contents

Komi Can't Communicate

Life with a communication disorder

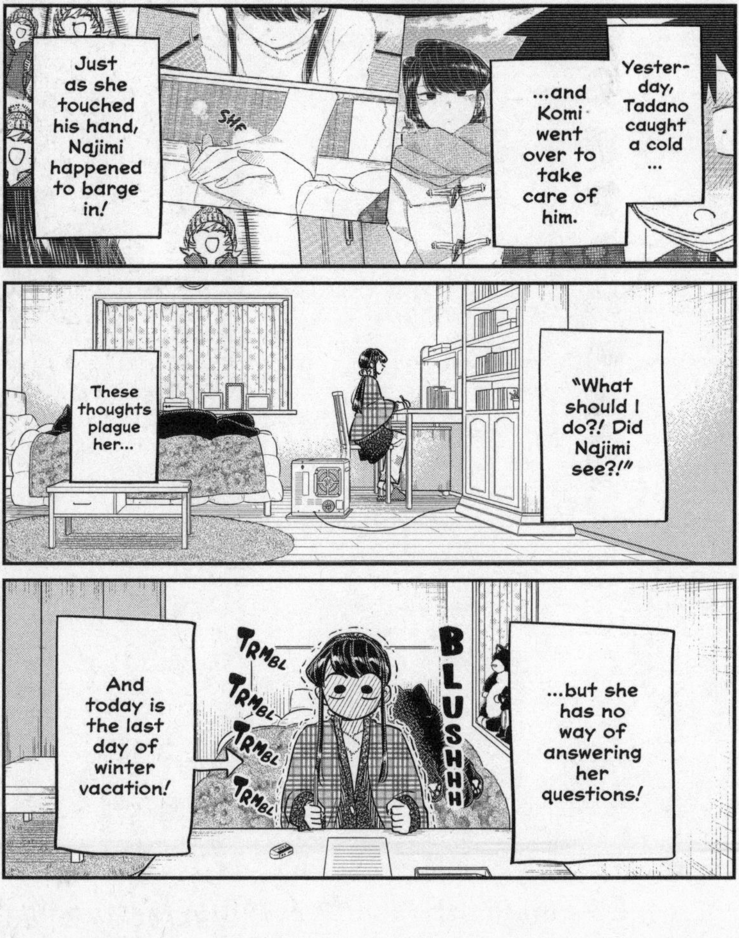
Yesterday, Tadano caught a cold...
...and Komi went over to take care of him.
SHF
Just as she touched his hand, Najimi happened to barge in!
"What should I do?! Did Najimi see?!"
These thoughts plague her...
...but she has no way of answering her questions!
BLUSHHH
TRMBL
TRMBL
TRMBL
TRMBL
And today is the last day of winter vacation!

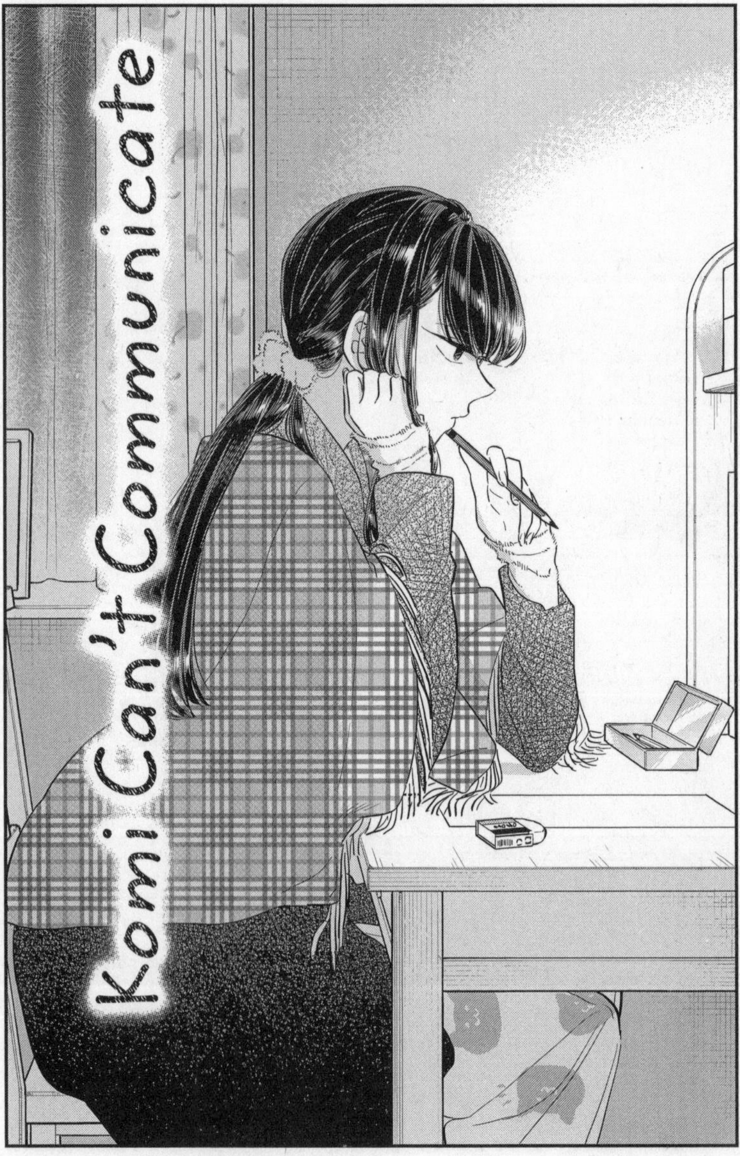
Komi Can't Communicate

Communication 100: A Misunderstanding

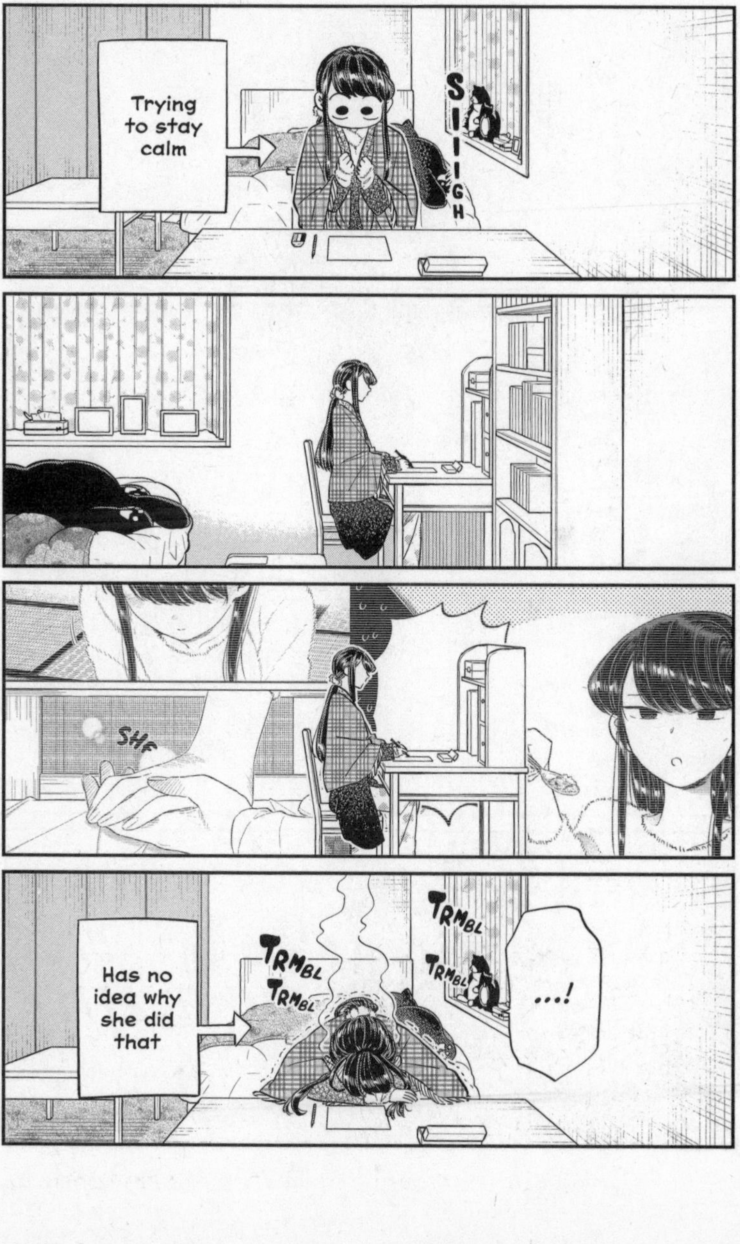
SIIIGH
Trying to stay calm
SHF
TRMBL
TRMBL
...!
TRMBL
TRMBL
Has no idea why she did that

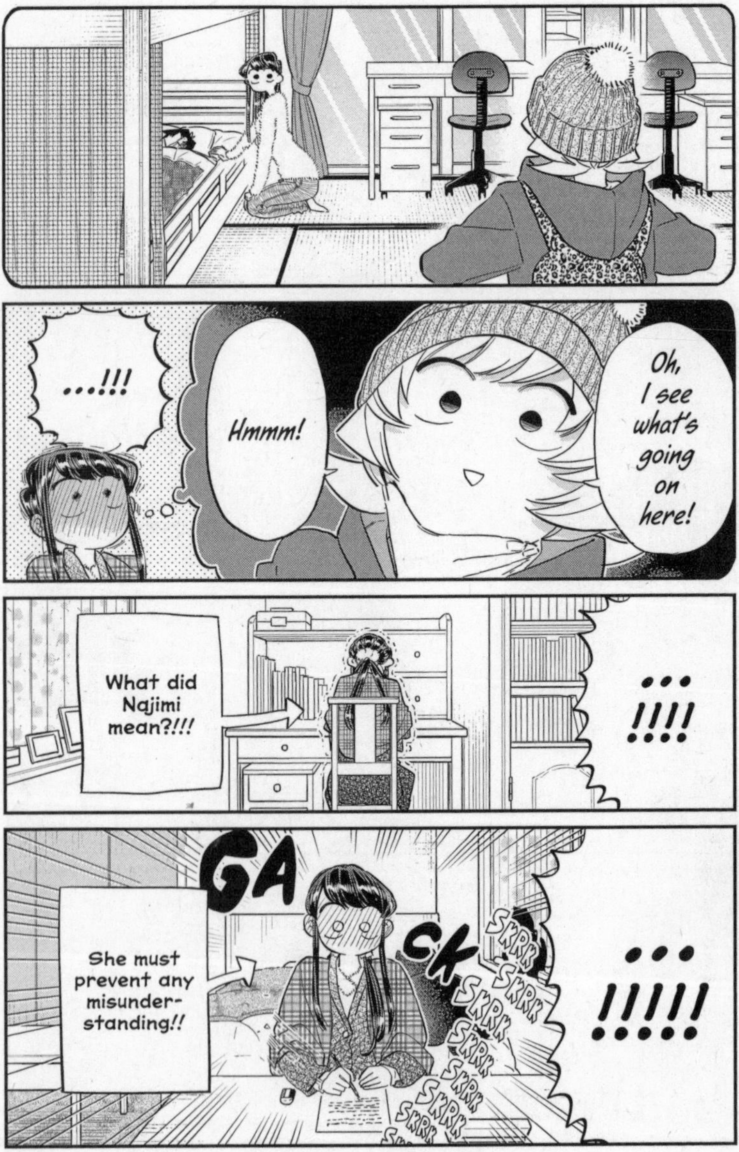
Oh, I see what's going on here!
Hmmm!
...!!!
...!!!!
What did Najimi mean?!!!
GACK
SKRK SKRK SKRK SKRK SKRK SKRK SKRK SKRK
...!!!!!
She must prevent any misunder-standing!!

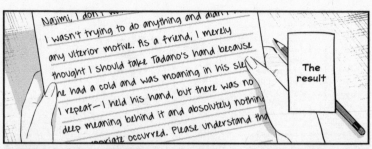

Najimi, I don't wa... I wasn't trying to do anything and didn't... any ulterior motive. As a friend, I merely thought I should take Tadano's hand because he had a cold and was moaning in his sle... I repeat—I held his hand, but there was no deep meaning behind it and absolutely nothing ...opriate occurred. Please understand tha...

The result

It totally sounds like something inappropriate occurred.

RRIP
RRIP
RRIP
RRIP

· · ·
!!!

She isn't certain that Najimi noticed, so if she gives Najimi a letter like that...

· · ·!

· · ·
!!!!

Hmmm!

Oh, I see what's going on here!

SHAKESHAK

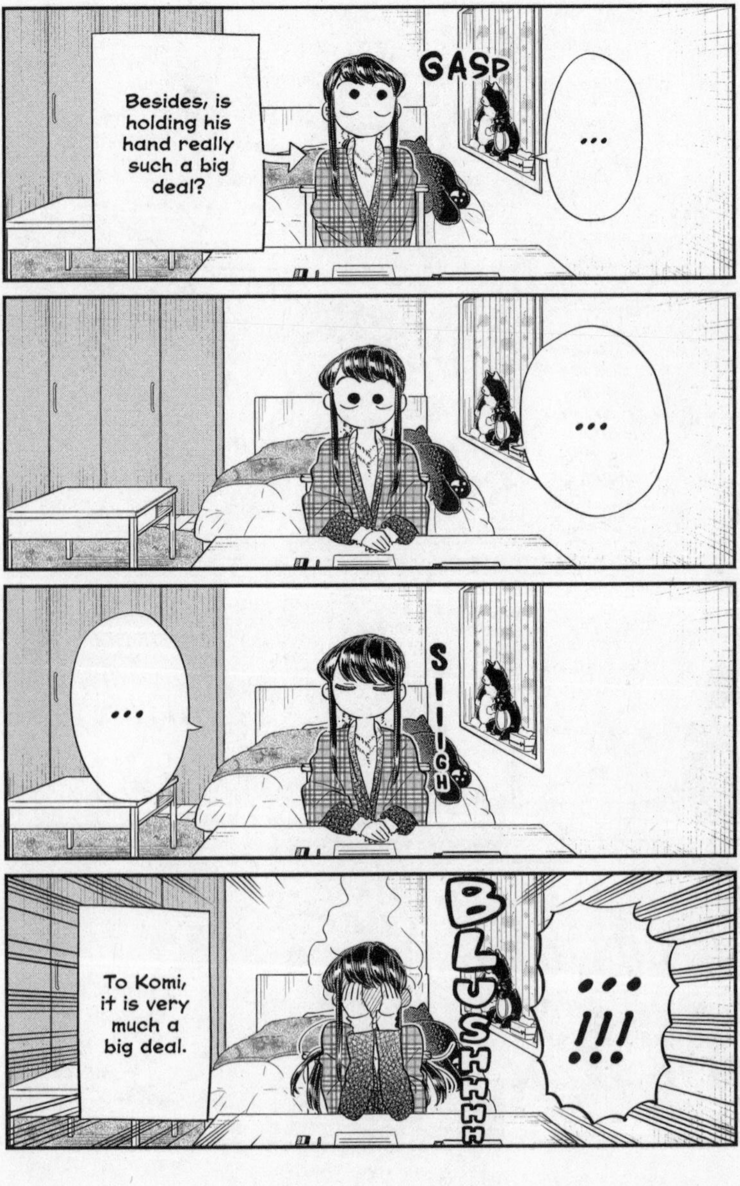
...
GASP
Besides, is holding his hand really such a big deal?
...
SIIIGH
...
...!!!
BLUSHHHHH
To Komi, it is very much a big deal.

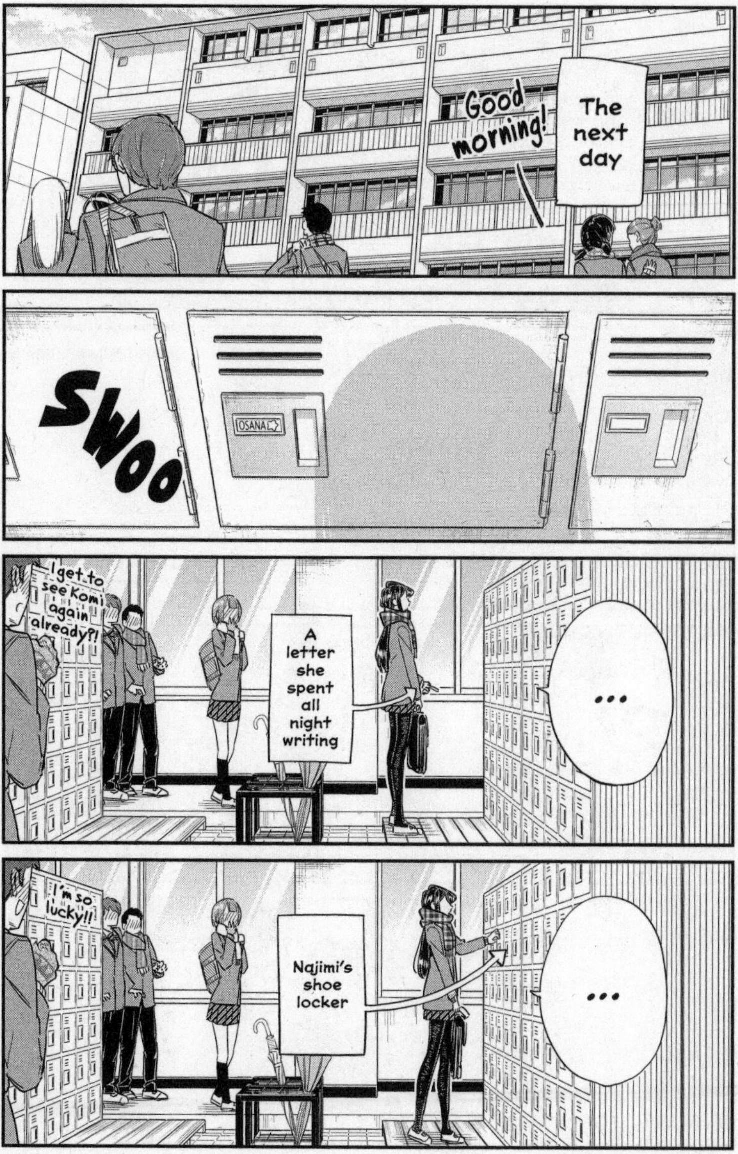
The next day
Good morning!
SWOO
OSANA
...
A letter she spent all night writing
I get to see Komi again already?!
...
Najimi's shoe locker
I'm so lucky!!

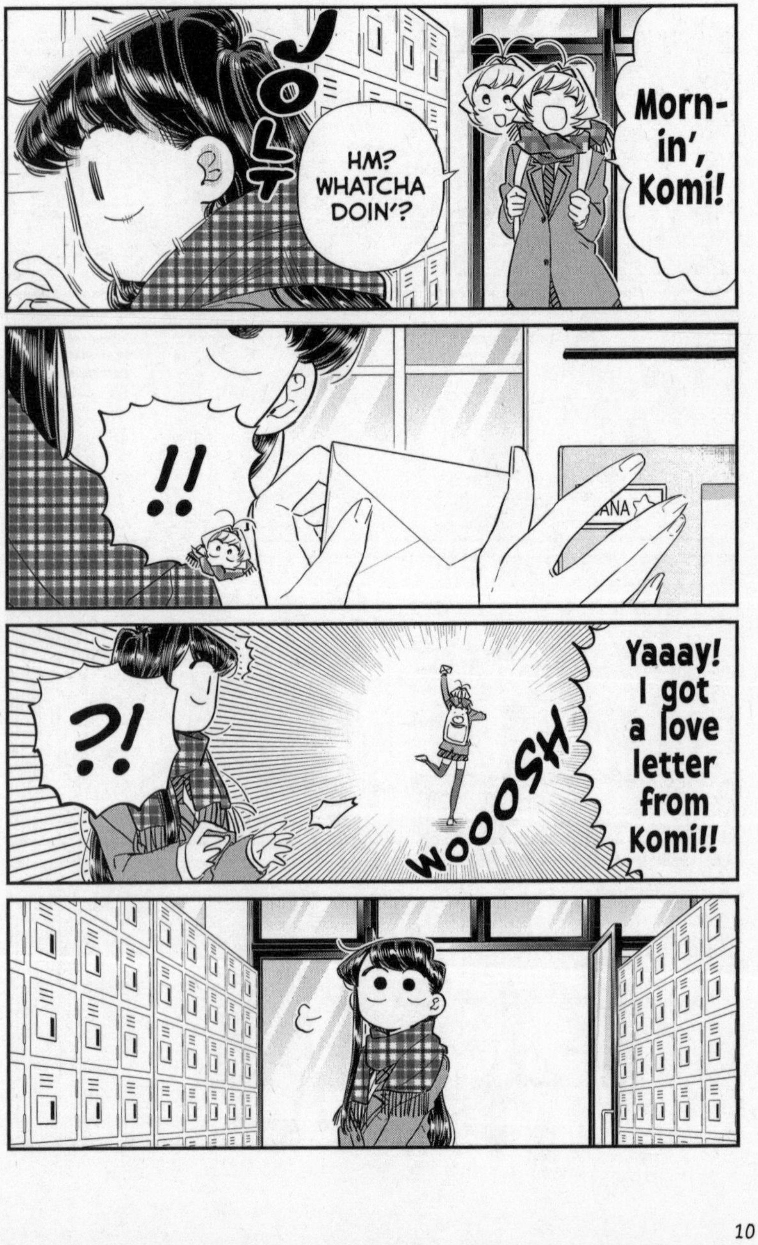
Morn-in', Komi!
JOLT
HM? WHATCHA DOIN'?
!!
Yaaay! I got a love letter from Komi!!
WOOOSH
?!

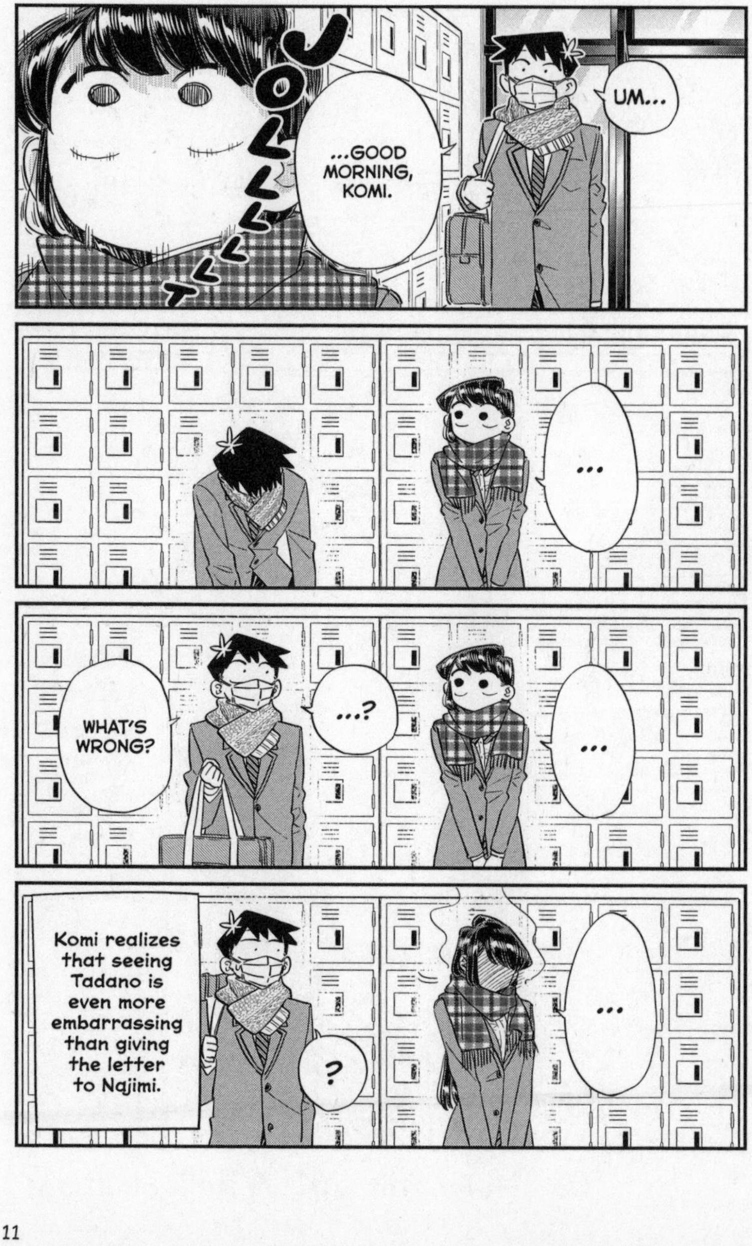
UM...
...GOOD MORNING, KOMI.
JOLLLLLT
...
...
...?
WHAT'S WRONG?
...
?
Komi realizes that seeing Tadano is even more embarrassing than giving the letter to Najimi.

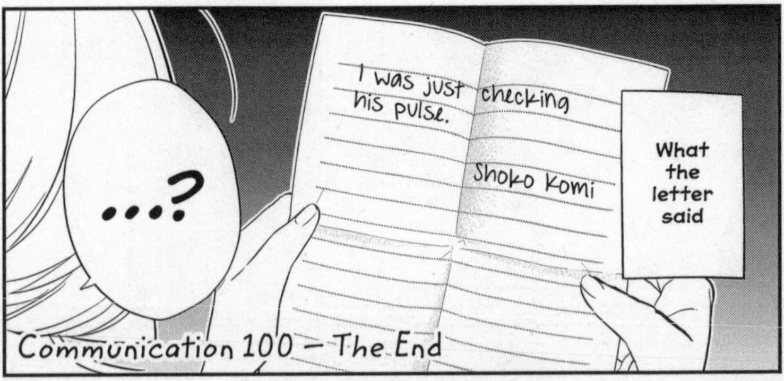
What the letter said
I was just checking his pulse.
Shoko Komi
...?
Communication 100 — The End

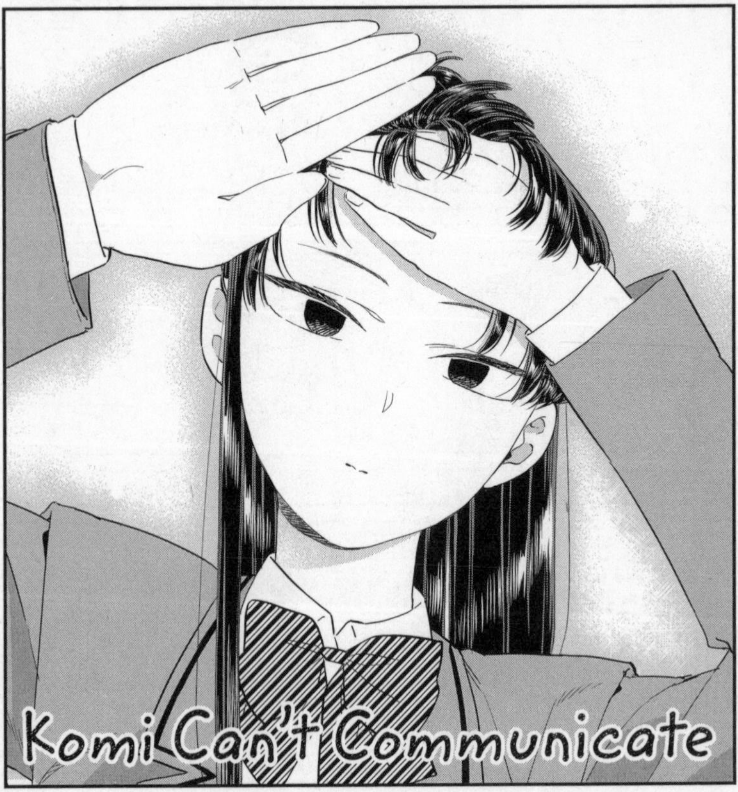
Komi Can't Communicate

Communication 101: A Hallucination?

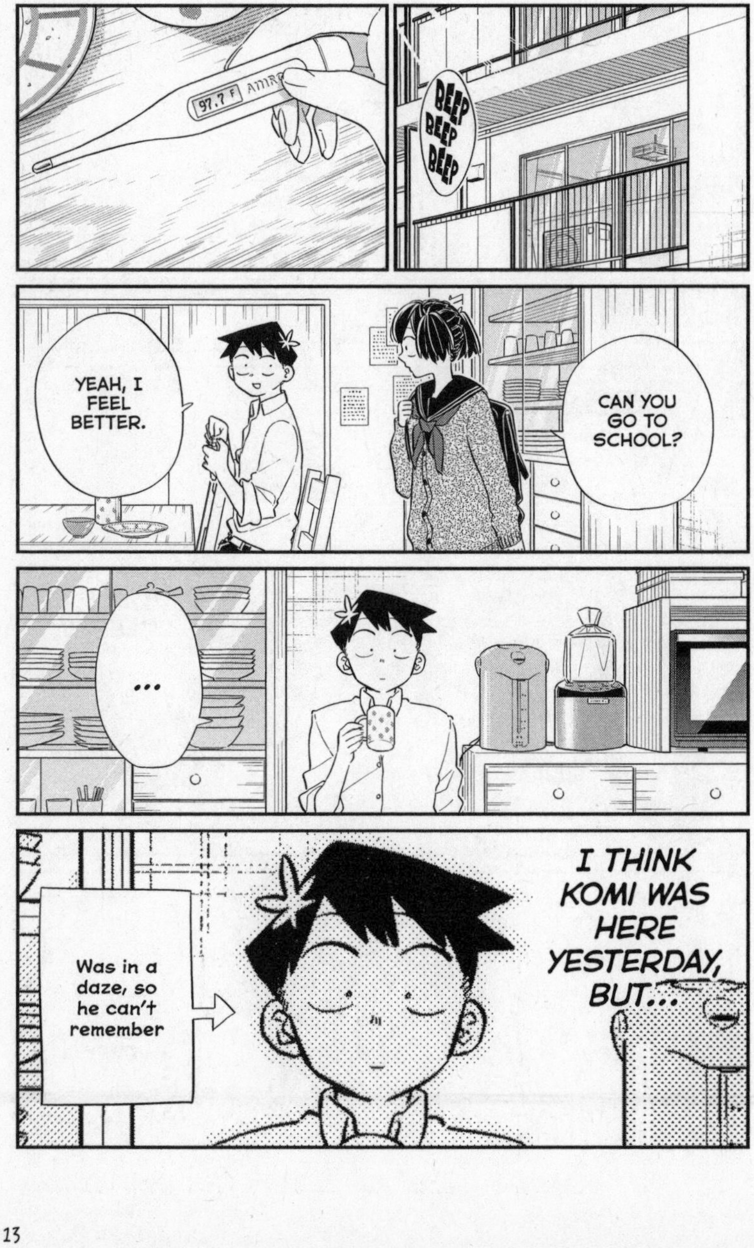
BEEP BEEP BEEP
CAN YOU GO TO SCHOOL?
YEAH, I FEEL BETTER.
...
I THINK KOMI WAS HERE YESTERDAY, BUT...
Was in a daze, so he can't remember

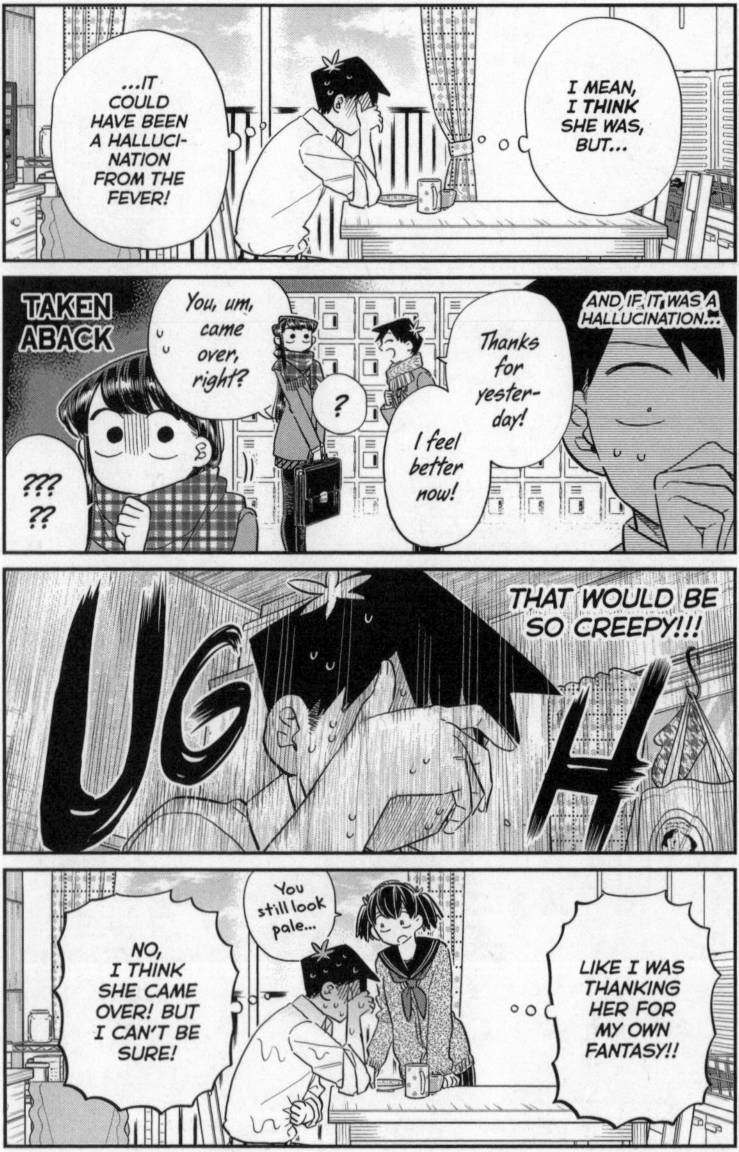
I MEAN, I THINK SHE WAS, BUT...
...IT COULD HAVE BEEN A HALLUCINATION FROM THE FEVER!
AND IF IT WAS A HALLUCINATION...
Thanks for yesterday!
I feel better now!
?
You, um, came over, right?
TAKEN ABACK
??? ??
THAT WOULD BE SO CREEPY!!!
UGH
LIKE I WAS THANKING HER FOR MY OWN FANTASY!!
You still look pale...
NO, I THINK SHE CAME OVER! BUT I CAN'T BE SURE!

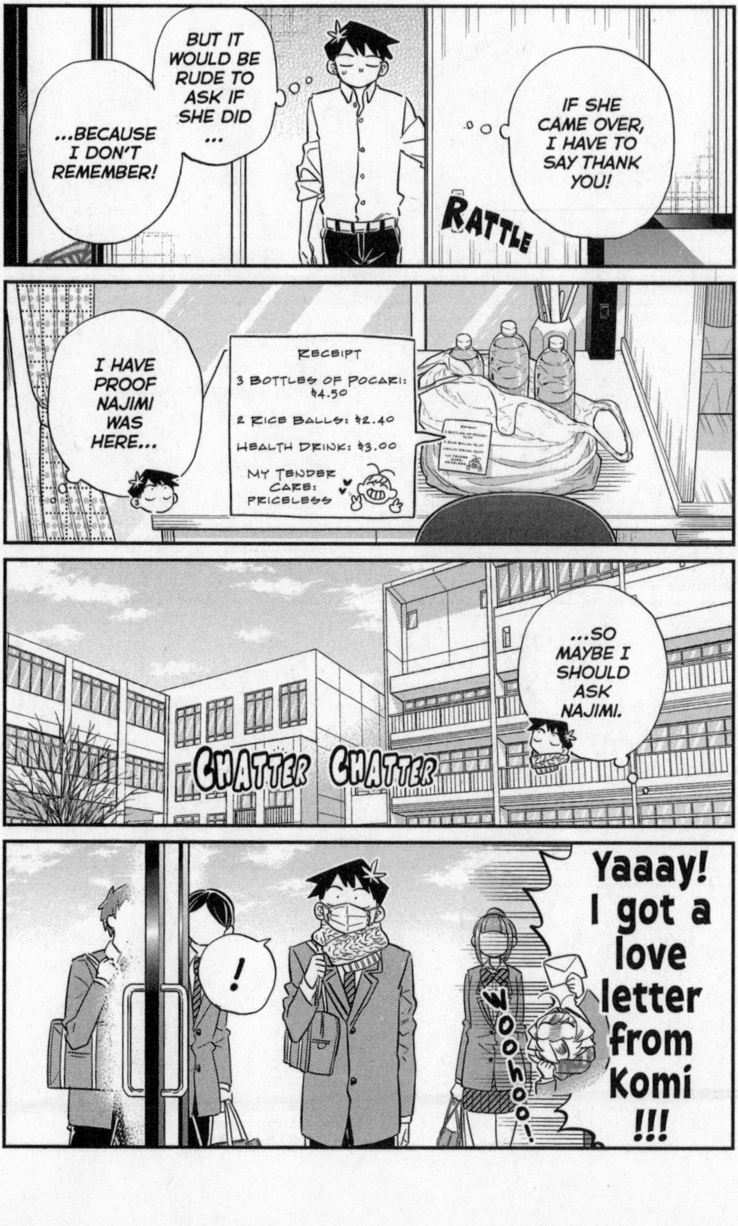
IF SHE CAME OVER, I HAVE TO SAY THANK YOU!
RATTLE
BUT IT WOULD BE RUDE TO ASK IF SHE DID ...
...BECAUSE I DON'T REMEMBER!
I HAVE PROOF NAJIMI WAS HERE...
RECEIPT
3 BOTTLES OF POCARI: $4.50
2 RICE BALLS: $2.40
HEALTH DRINK: $3.00
MY TENDER CARE: PRICELESS
...SO MAYBE I SHOULD ASK NAJIMI.
CHATTER CHATTER
Yaaay! I got a love letter from Komi !!!
WOOHOO!
!

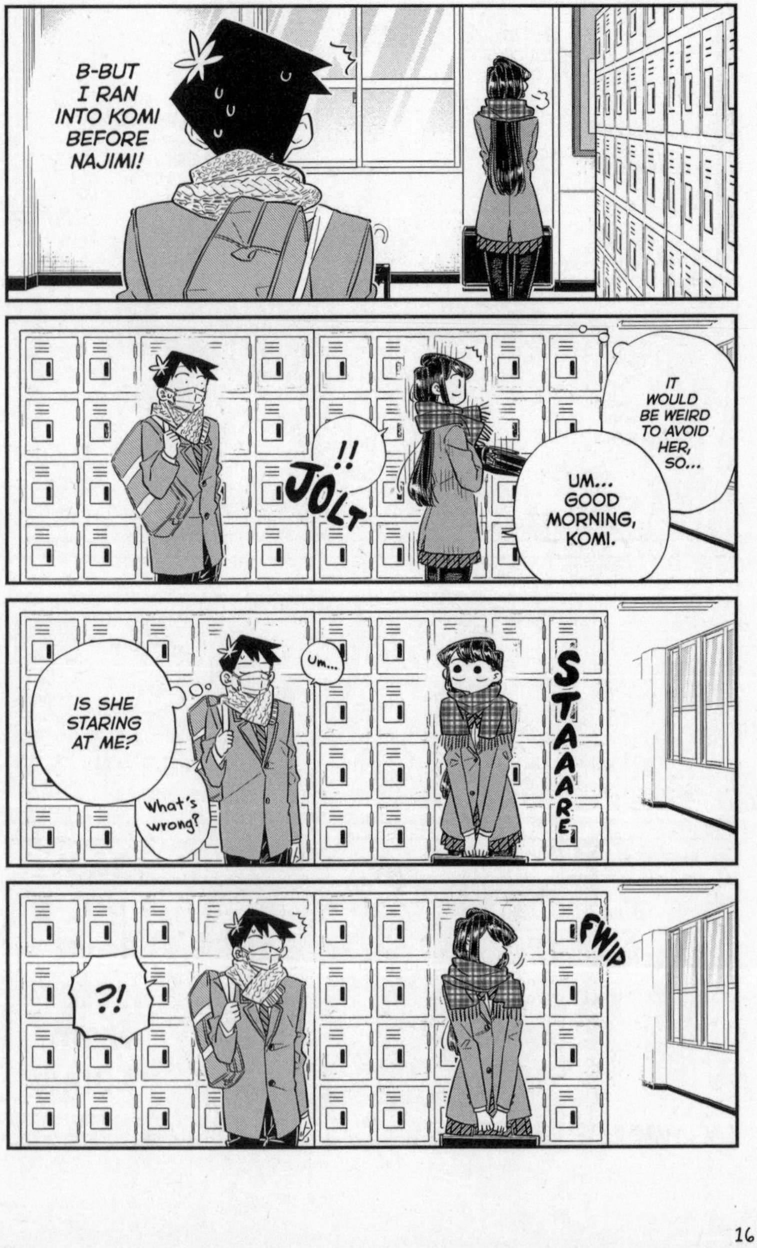
B-BUT I RAN INTO KOMI BEFORE NAJIMI!
IT WOULD BE WEIRD TO AVOID HER, SO...
UM... GOOD MORNING, KOMI.
!!
JOLT
STAAARE
Um...
IS SHE STARING AT ME?
What's wrong?
FWIP
?!

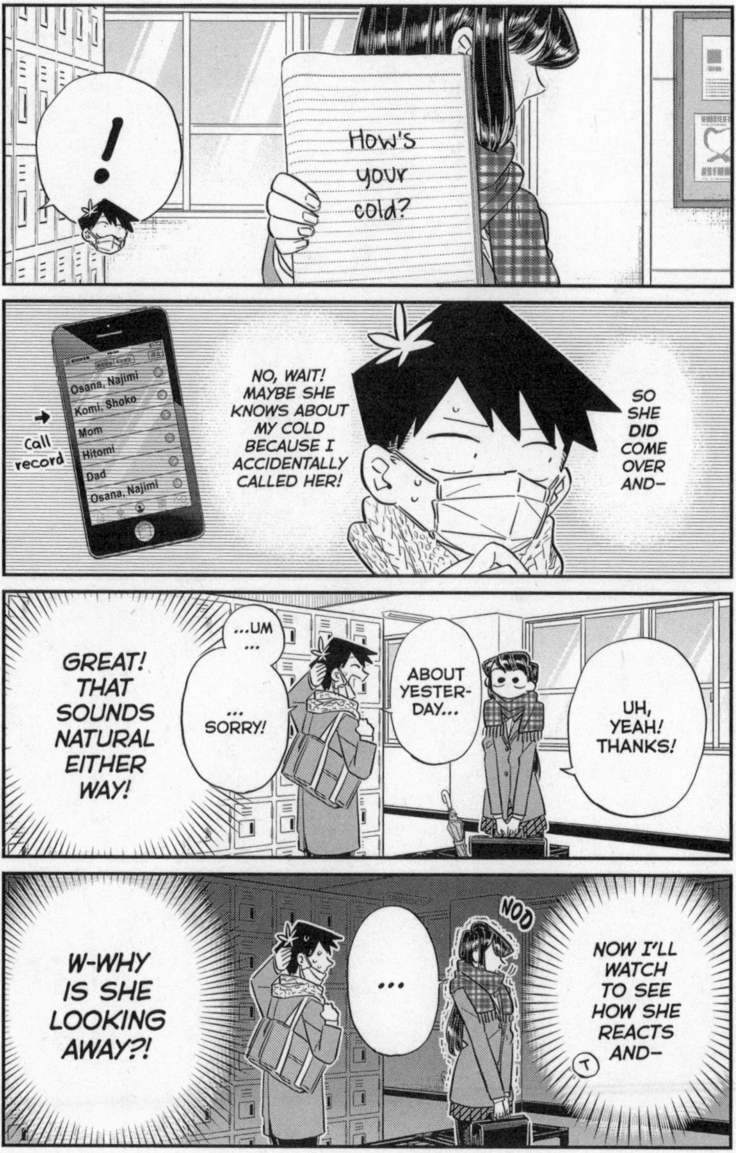
How's your cold?
!
SO SHE DID COME OVER AND–
NO, WAIT! MAYBE SHE KNOWS ABOUT MY COLD BECAUSE I ACCIDENTALLY CALLED HER!
Osana, Najimi
Komi, Shoko
Mom
Hitomi
Dad
Osana, Najimi
Call record
UH, YEAH! THANKS!
ABOUT YESTER-DAY...
...UM ...
... SORRY!
GREAT! THAT SOUNDS NATURAL EITHER WAY!
NOD
NOW I'LL WATCH TO SEE HOW SHE REACTS AND–
...
W-WHY IS SHE LOOKING AWAY?!

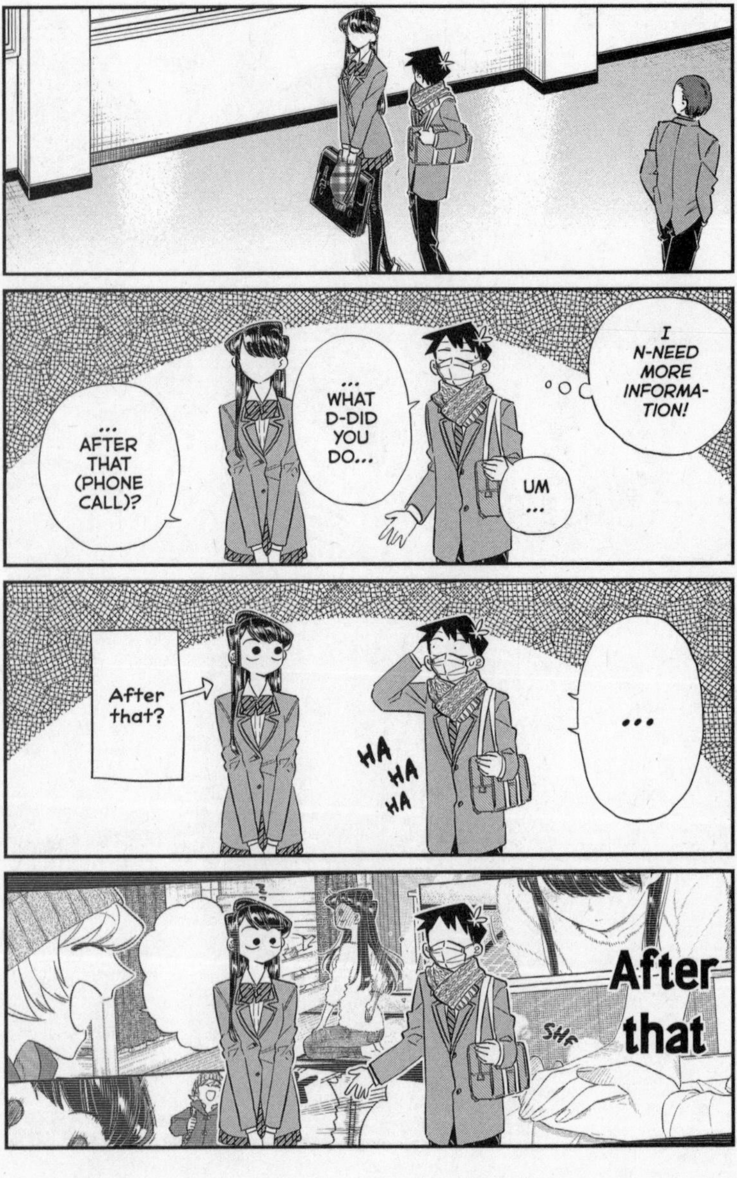
I N-NEED MORE INFORMATION!
UM ...
... WHAT D-DID YOU DO...
... AFTER THAT (PHONE CALL)?
...
HA HA HA
After that?
After that
SHF

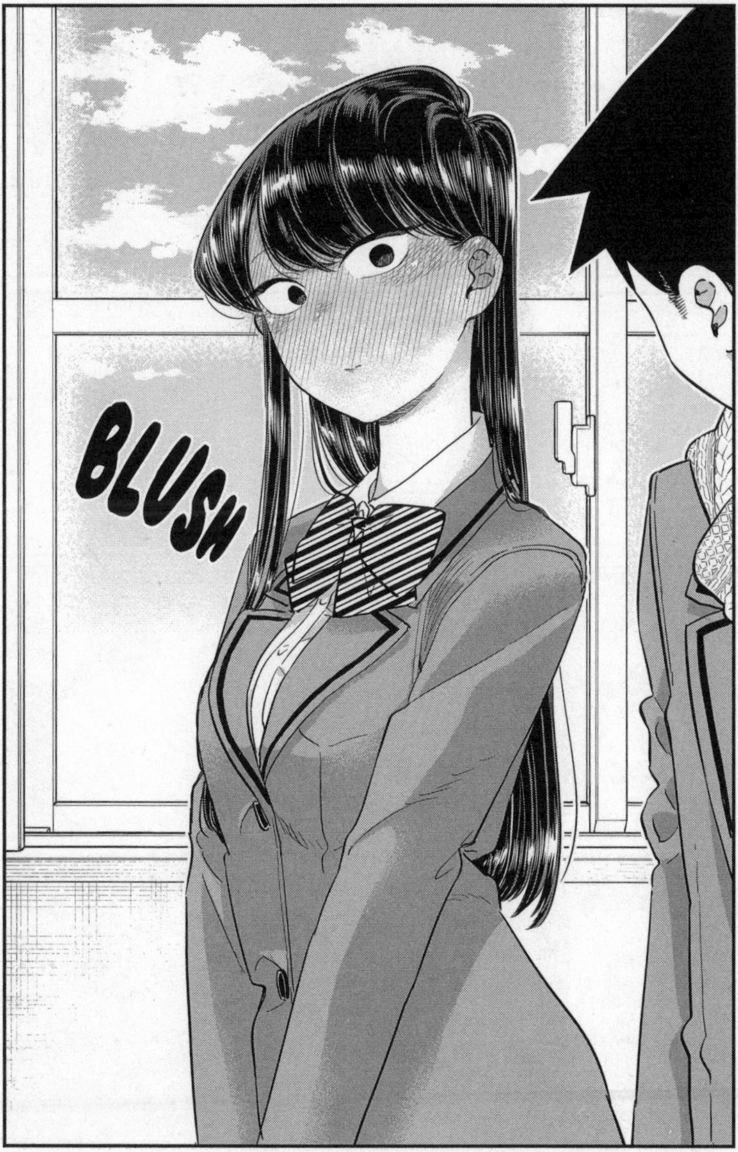
BLUSH

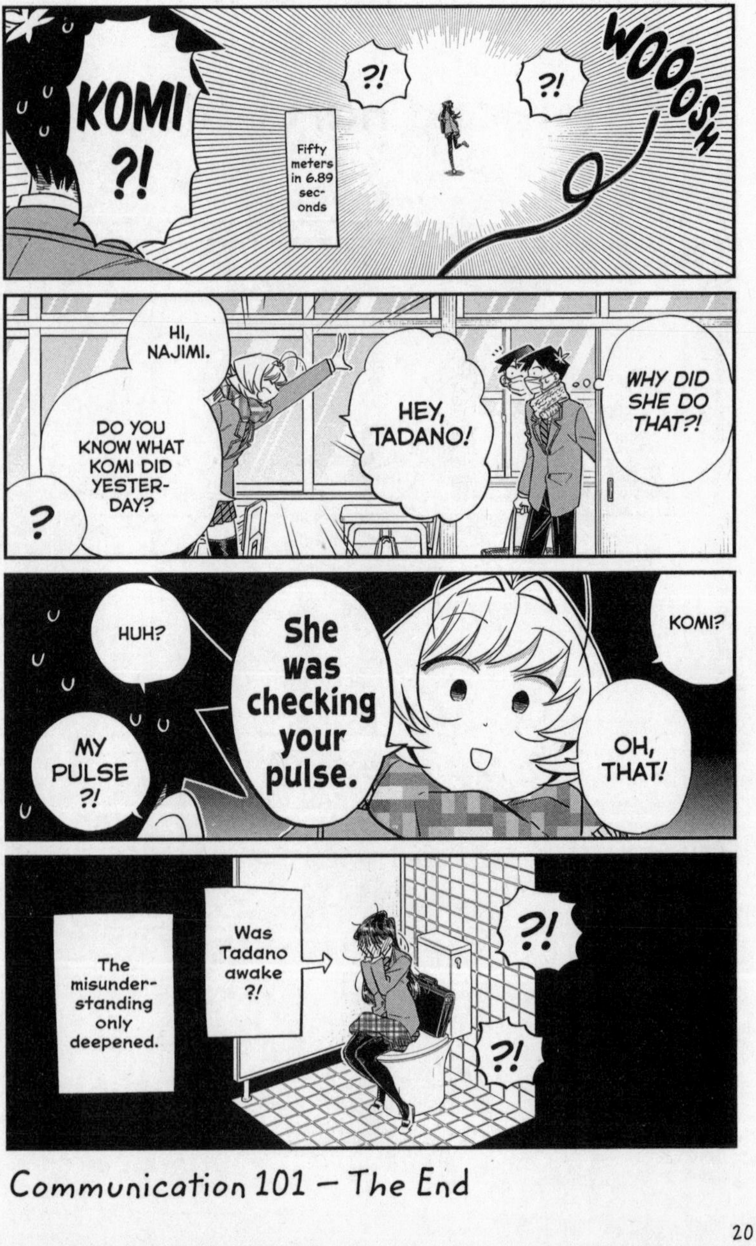
WOOOSH
?!
?!
Fifty meters in 6.89 seconds
KOMI ?!
WHY DID SHE DO THAT?!
HEY, TADANO!
HI, NAJIMI.
DO YOU KNOW WHAT KOMI DID YESTERDAY?
?
KOMI?
OH, THAT!
She was checking your pulse.
HUH?
MY PULSE ?!
?!
?!
Was Tadano awake ?!
The misunderstanding only deepened.

Communication 101 – The End

Komi Can't Communicate

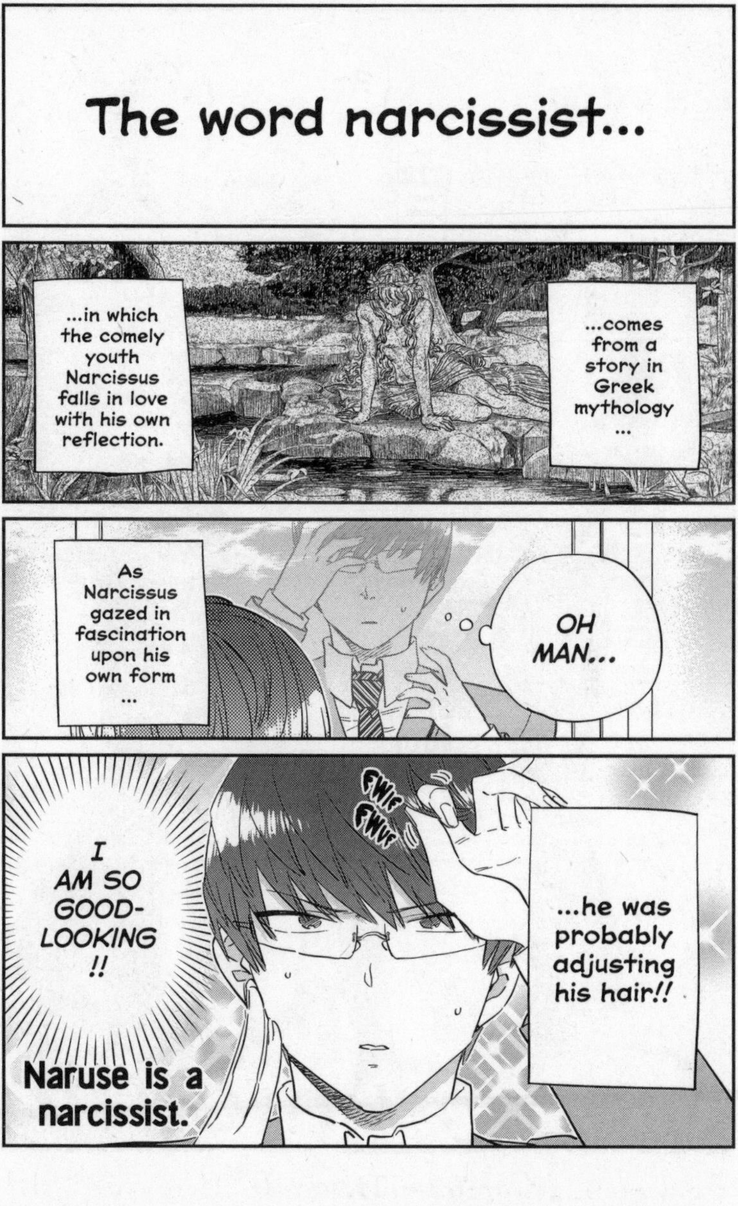

The word narcissist...
...comes from a story in Greek mythology...
...in which the comely youth Narcissus falls in love with his own reflection.
OH MAN...
As Narcissus gazed in fascination upon his own form...
...he was probably adjusting his hair!!
I AM SO GOOD-LOOKING!!
Naruse is a narcissist.

Komi Can't Communicate

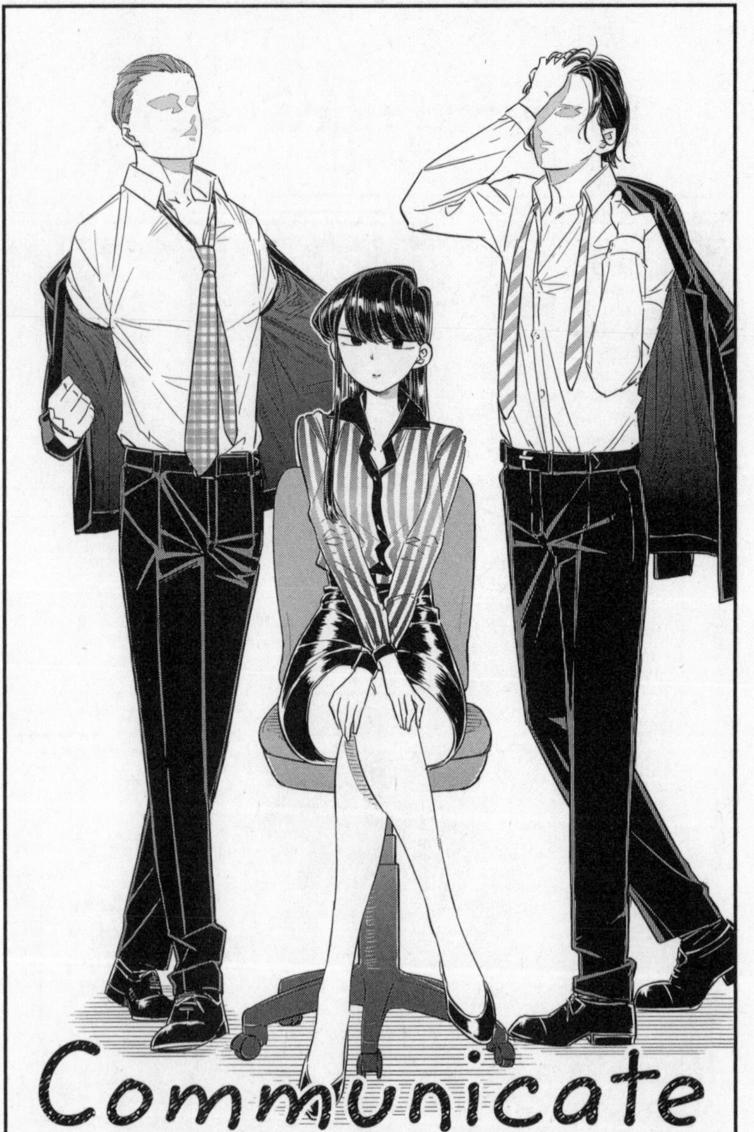

Communication 102: The Narcissist

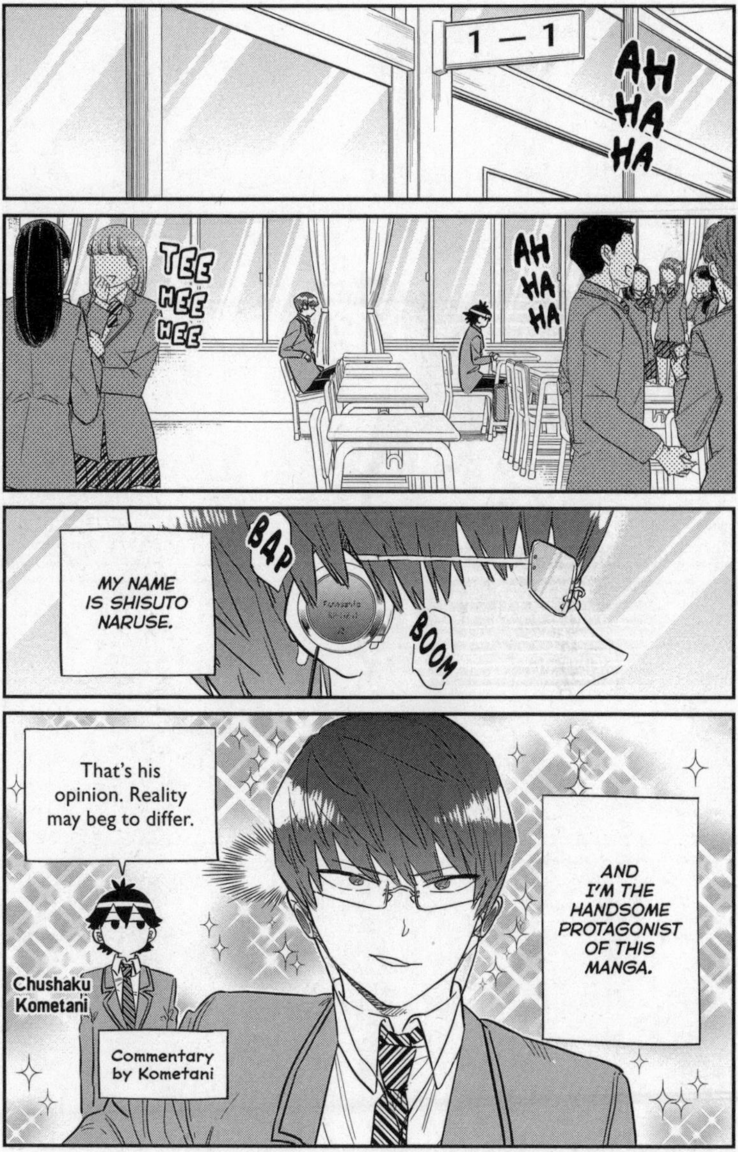
1 — 1
AH HA HA
AH HA HA
TEE HEE HEE
BAP
BOOM
MY NAME IS SHISUTO NARUSE.
AND I'M THE HANDSOME PROTAGONIST OF THIS MANGA.
That's his opinion. Reality may beg to differ.
Chushaku Kometani
Commentary by Kometani

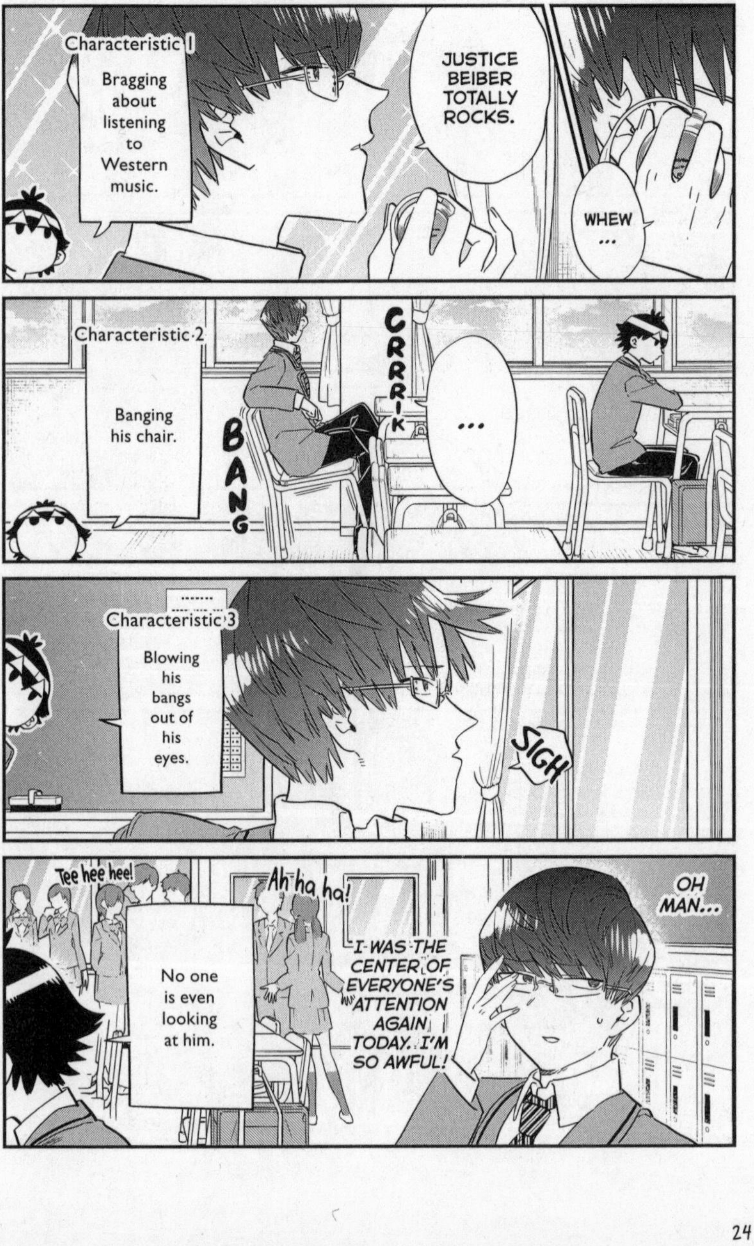
WHEW ...
JUSTICE BEIBER TOTALLY ROCKS.
Characteristic 1
Bragging about listening to Western music.
CRRRIK
...
Characteristic 2
Banging his chair.
BANG
SIGH
Characteristic 3
Blowing his bangs out of his eyes.
OH MAN...
I WAS THE CENTER OF EVERYONE'S ATTENTION AGAIN TODAY. I'M SO AWFUL!
Ah ha ha!
No one is even looking at him.
Tee hee hee!

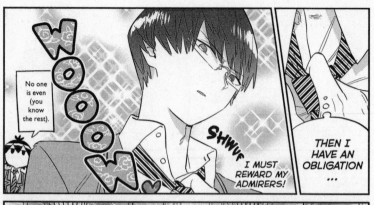

THEN I HAVE AN OBLIGATION ...
SHWUF
I MUST REWARD MY ADMIRERS!
WOOOOW
No one is even (you know the rest).
YOU MAY GAZE UPON ME FROM A DISTANCE ...
HWUP
...OR WE CAN CHAT A BIT IF YOU WANT!
He's completely alone.
WHY DOES HE ALWAYS DO THAT?

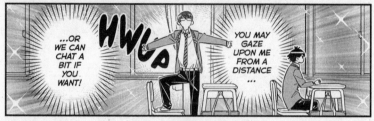

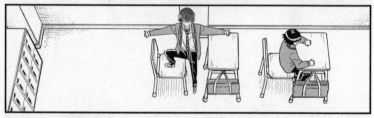

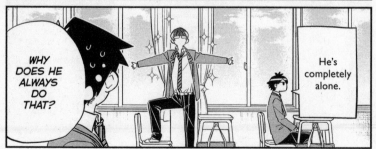

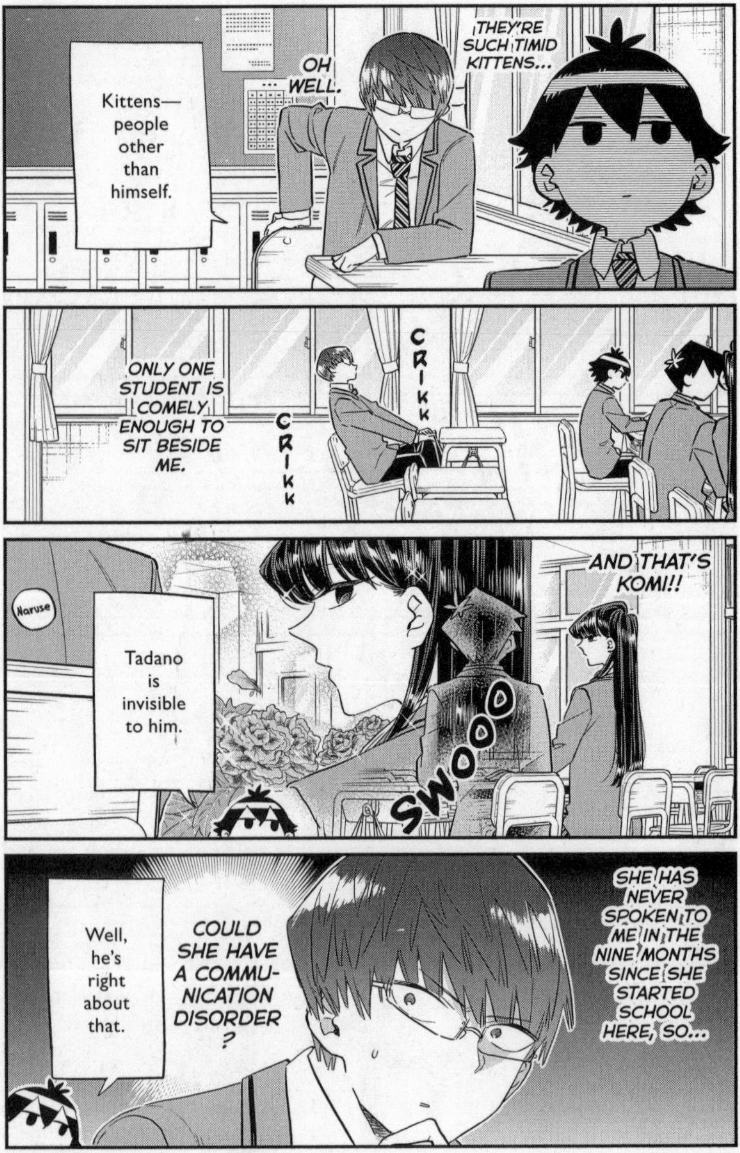
THEY'RE SUCH TIMID KITTENS...
OH WELL.
Kittens— people other than himself.
CRIKK
ONLY ONE STUDENT IS COMELY ENOUGH TO SIT BESIDE ME.
CRIKK
AND THAT'S KOMI!!
SWOOO
Naruse
Tadano is invisible to him.
SHE HAS NEVER SPOKEN TO ME IN THE NINE MONTHS SINCE SHE STARTED SCHOOL HERE, SO...
COULD SHE HAVE A COMMU-NICATION DISORDER?
Well, he's right about that.

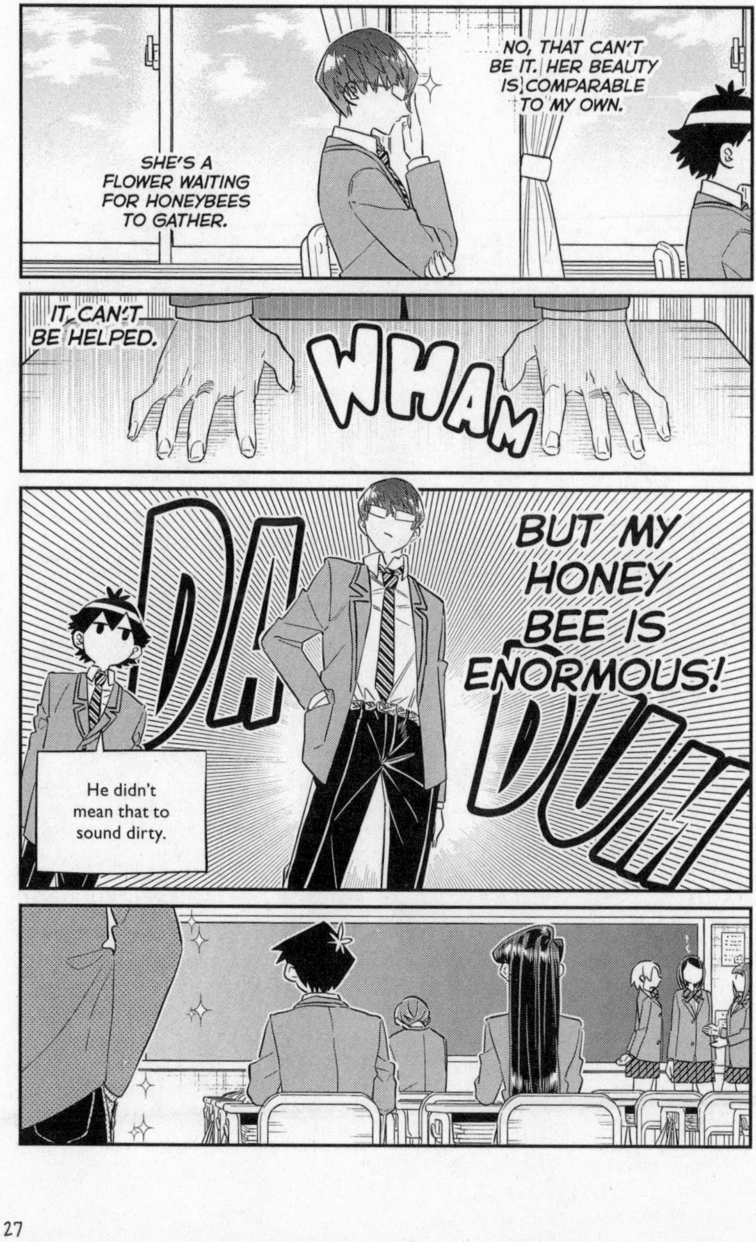
NO, THAT CAN'T BE IT. HER BEAUTY IS COMPARABLE TO MY OWN.
SHE'S A FLOWER WAITING FOR HONEYBEES TO GATHER.
IT CAN'T BE HELPED.
WHAM
BUT MY HONEY BEE IS ENORMOUS!
DA
DUM
He didn't mean that to sound dirty.

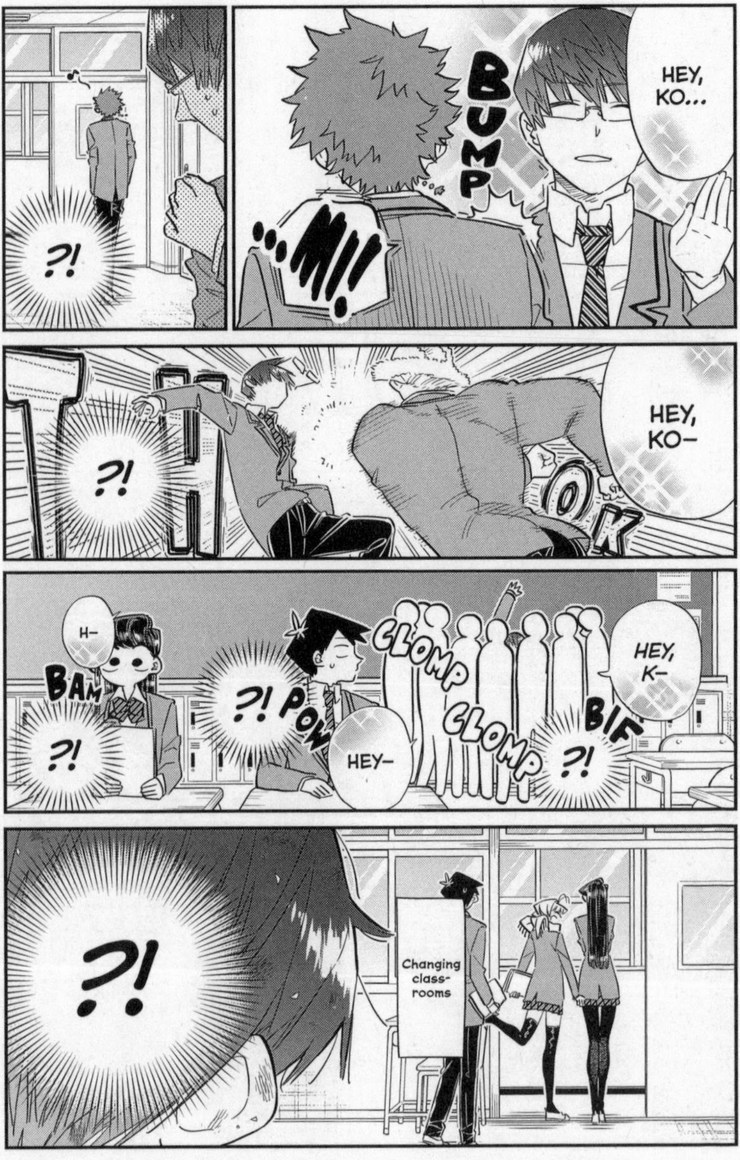
HEY, KO...
BUMP
...M!!
?!
HEY, KO–
?!
HEY, K–
BIF
?!
CLOMP
CLOMP
HEY–
POW
?!
H–
BAM
?!
Changing class-rooms
?!

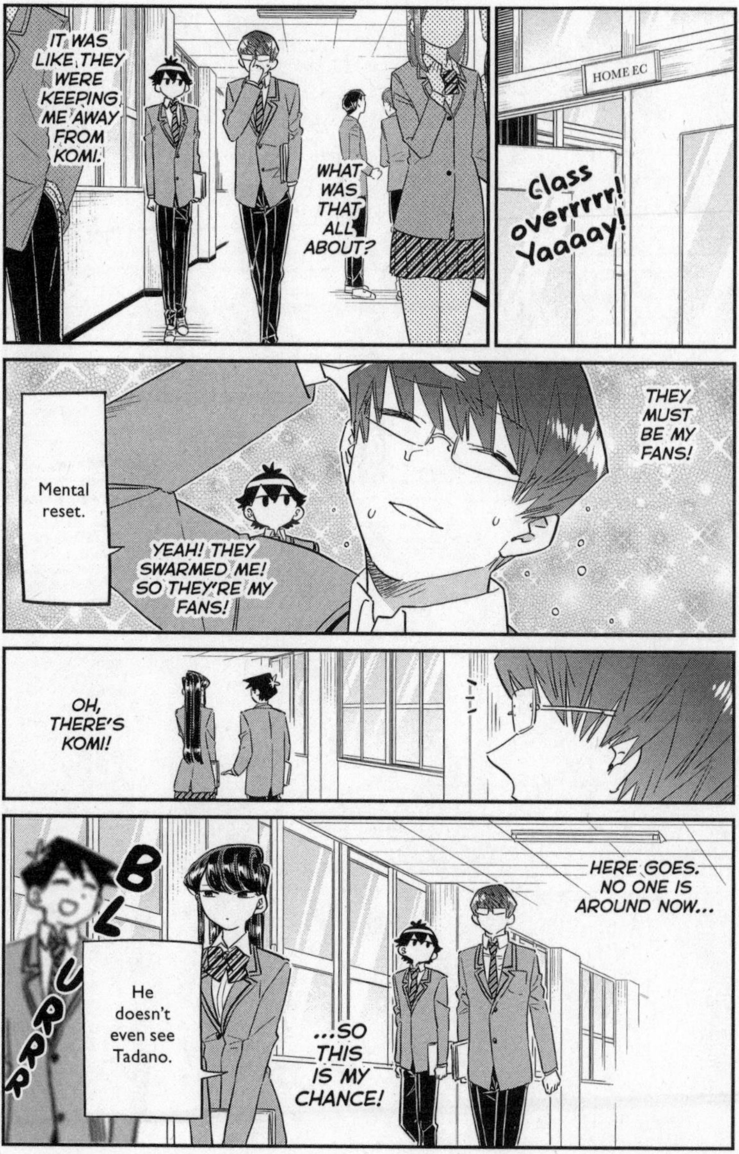
HOME EC
Class overrrrr! Yaaaay!
WHAT WAS THAT ALL ABOUT?
IT WAS LIKE THEY WERE KEEPING ME AWAY FROM KOMI.
THEY MUST BE MY FANS!
YEAH! THEY SWARMED ME! SO THEY'RE MY FANS!
Mental reset.
OH, THERE'S KOMI!
HERE GOES. NO ONE IS AROUND NOW...
...SO THIS IS MY CHANCE!
BLURRRR
He doesn't even see Tadano.

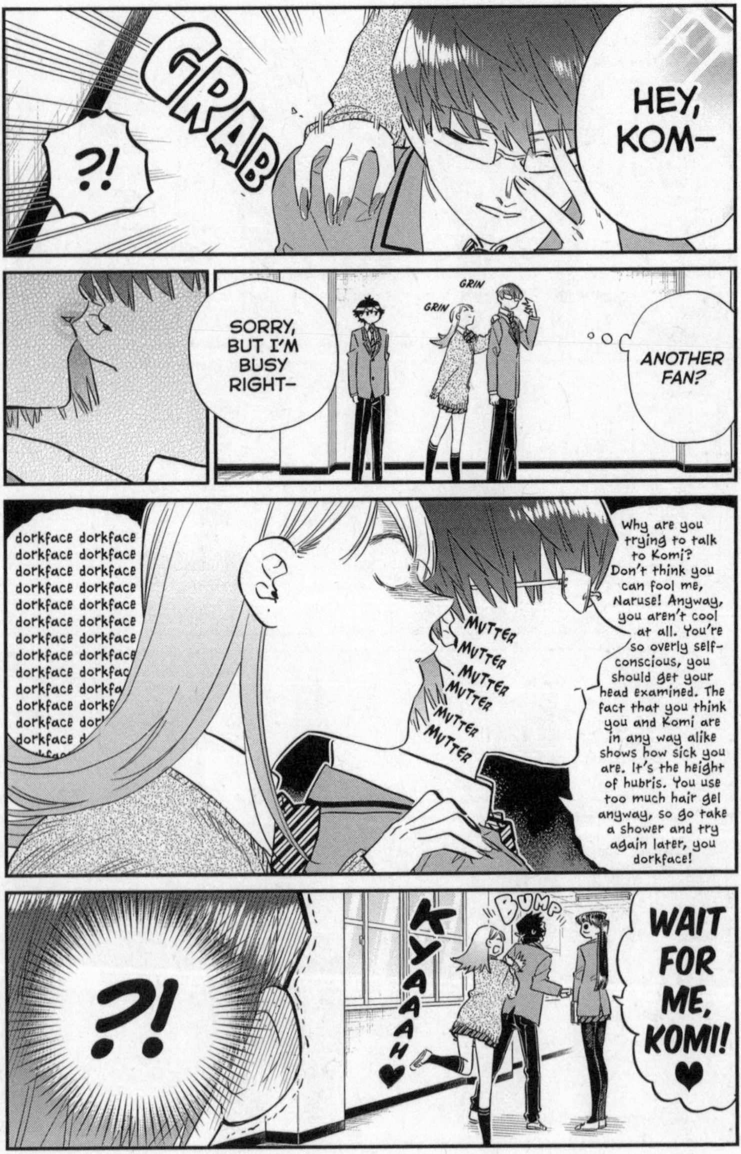
HEY, KOM–
GRAB
?!
ANOTHER FAN?
GRIN
GRIN
SORRY, BUT I'M BUSY RIGHT–
Why are you trying to talk to Komi? Don't think you can fool me, Naruse! Anyway, you aren't cool at all. You're so overly self-conscious, you should get your head examined. The fact that you think you and Komi are in any way alike shows how sick you are. It's the height of hubris. You use too much hair gel anyway, so go take a shower and try again later, you dorkface!
MUTTER MUTTER MUTTER MUTTER MUTTER MUTTER
dorkface dorkface
WAIT FOR ME, KOMI! ♥
BUMP
KYAAAAH ♥
?!

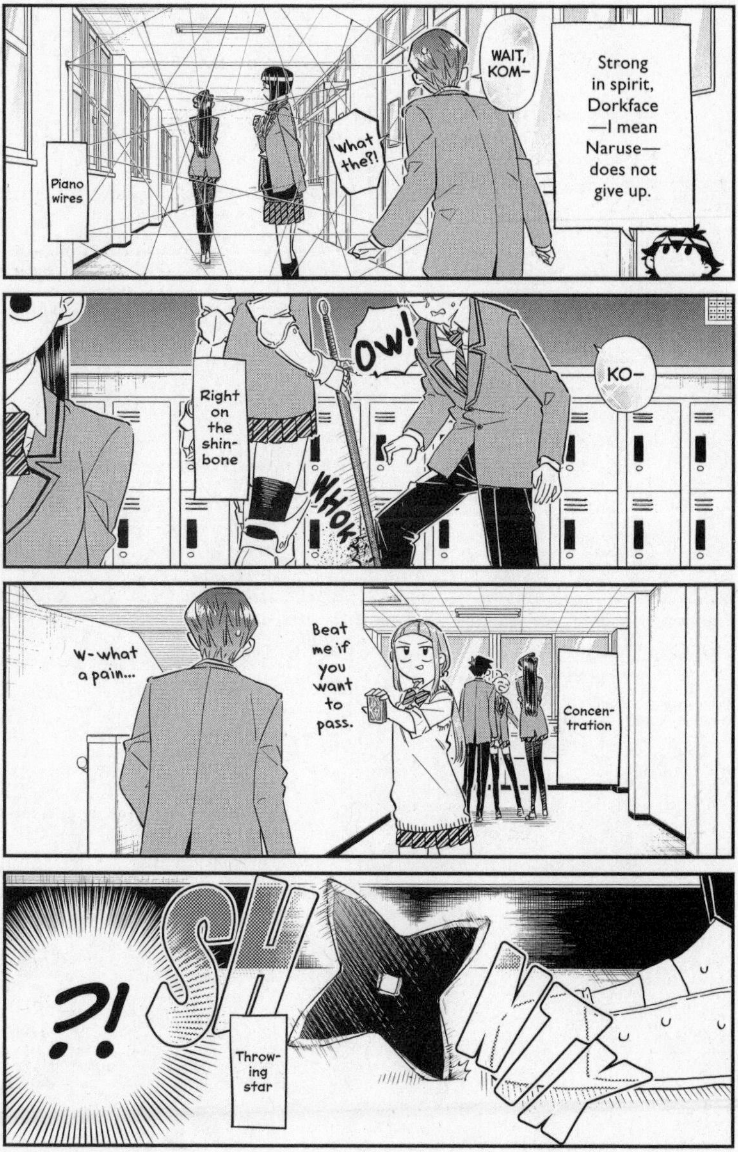
Strong in spirit, Dorkface—I mean Naruse—does not give up.
WAIT, KOM–
What the?!
Piano wires
KO–
OW!
Right on the shin-bone
WHOK
Concen-tration
Beat me if you want to pass.
W-what a pain...
SHNKK
Throw-ing star
?!

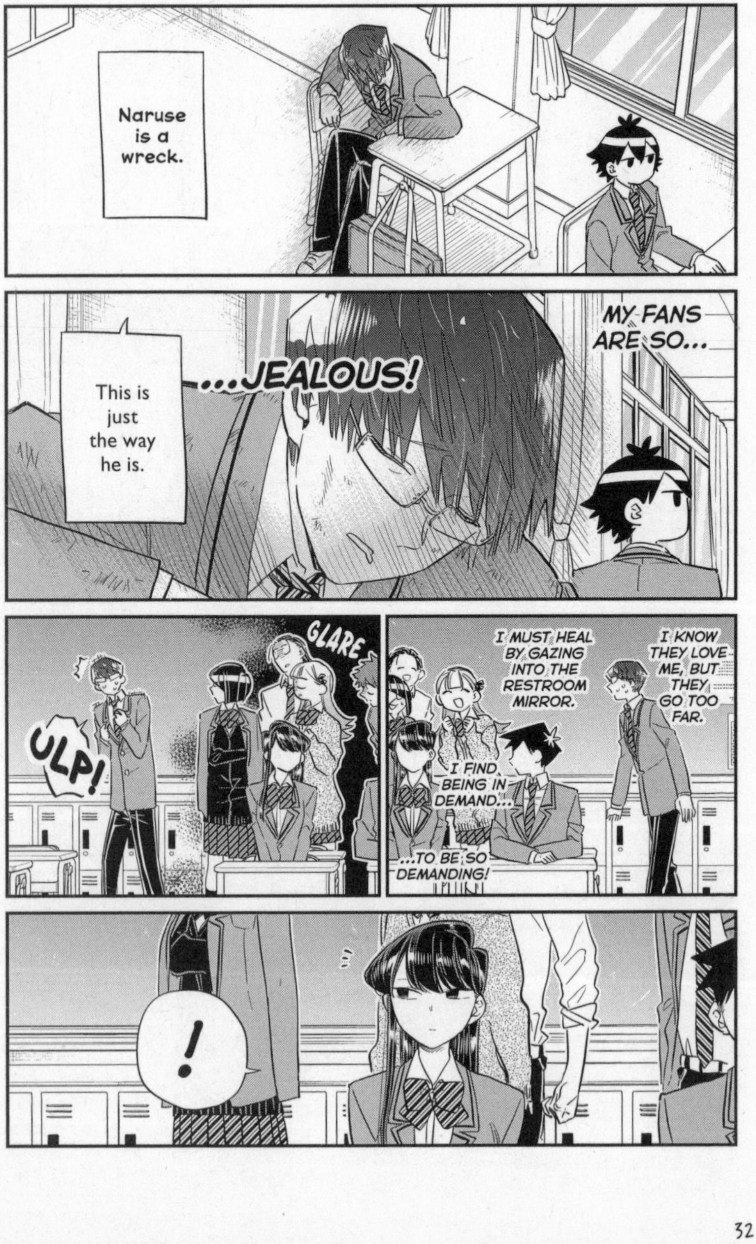
Naruse is a wreck.
MY FANS ARE SO...
...JEALOUS!
This is just the way he is.
I KNOW THEY LOVE ME, BUT THEY GO TOO FAR.
I MUST HEAL BY GAZING INTO THE RESTROOM MIRROR.
I FIND BEING IN DEMAND...
...TO BE SO DEMANDING!
GLARE
ULP!
!

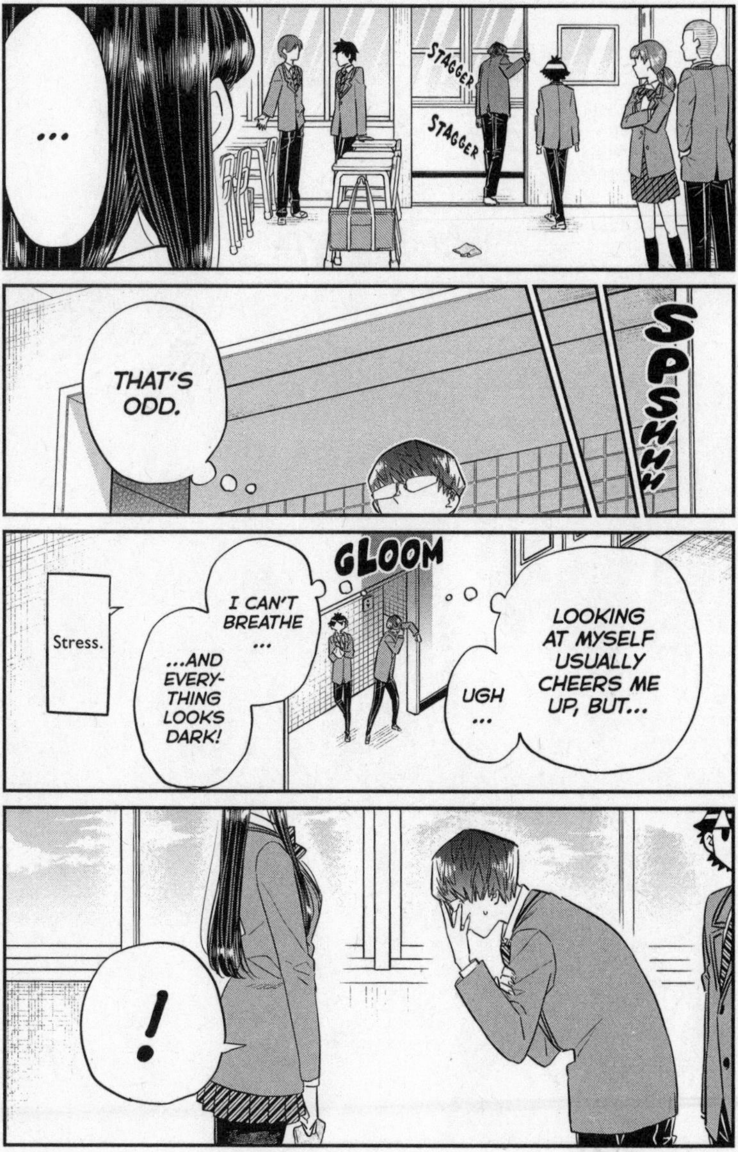
STAGGER
STAGGER
...
SPSHHH
THAT'S ODD.
LOOKING AT MYSELF USUALLY CHEERS ME UP, BUT...
UGH...
GLOOM
I CAN'T BREATHE... ...AND EVERYTHING LOOKS DARK!
Stress.
!

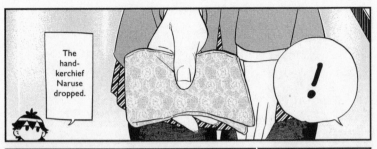

The hand-kerchief Naruse dropped.

!

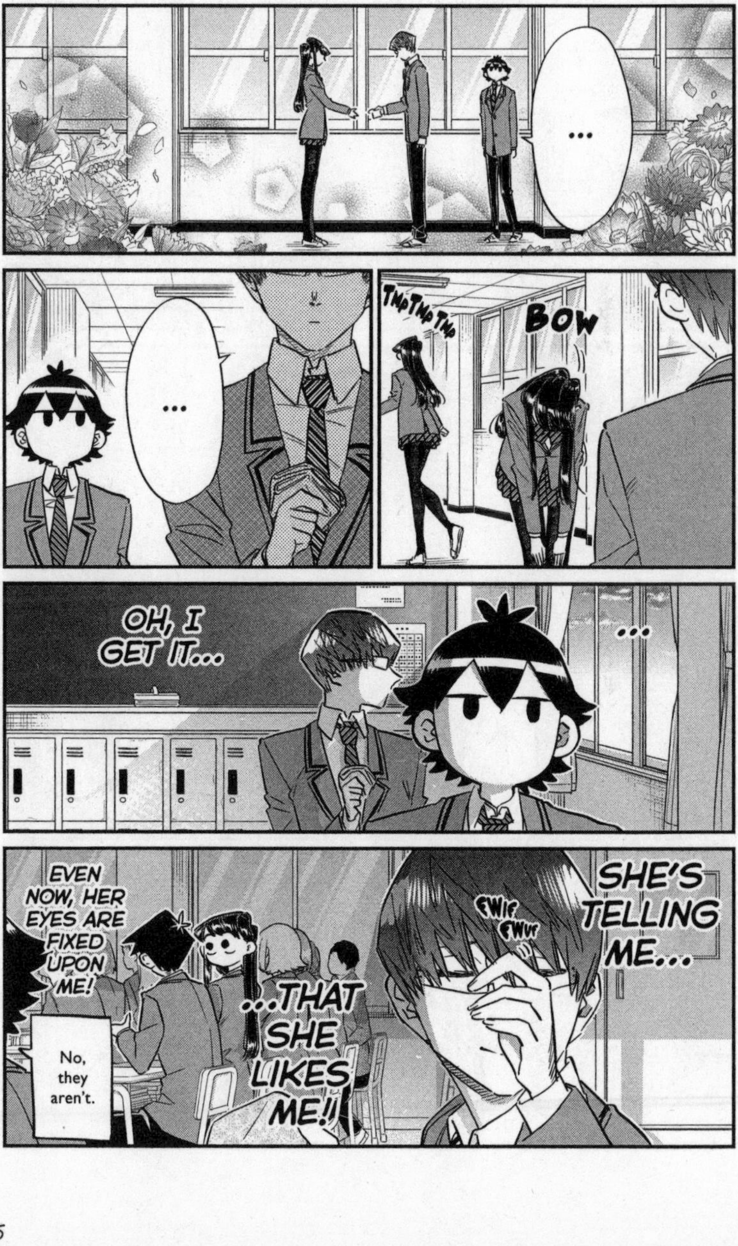
...
TMP TMP TMP TMP
BOW
...
...
OH, I GET IT...
SHE'S TELLING ME...
...THAT SHE LIKES ME!!
EVEN NOW, HER EYES ARE FIXED UPON ME!
No, they aren't.

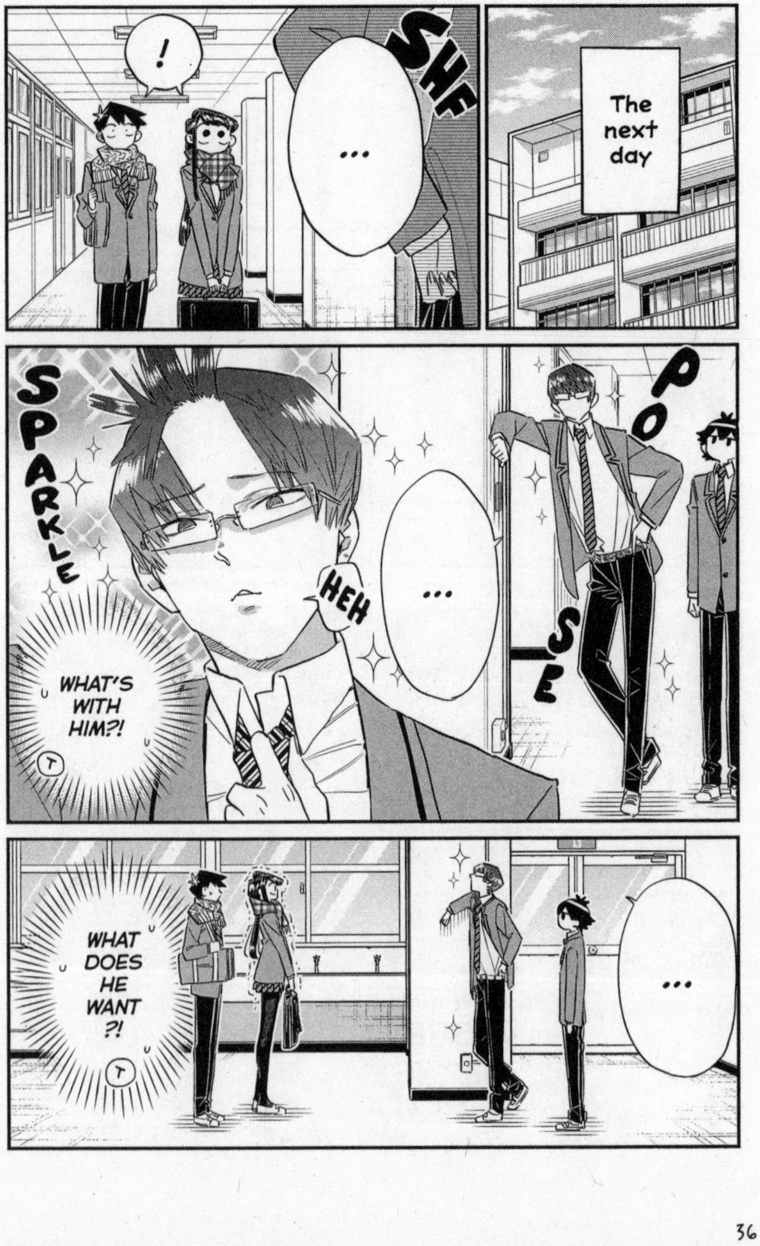
The next day
SHF
...
!
POSE
...
HEH
SPARKLE
WHAT'S WITH HIM?!
...
WHAT DOES HE WANT ?!

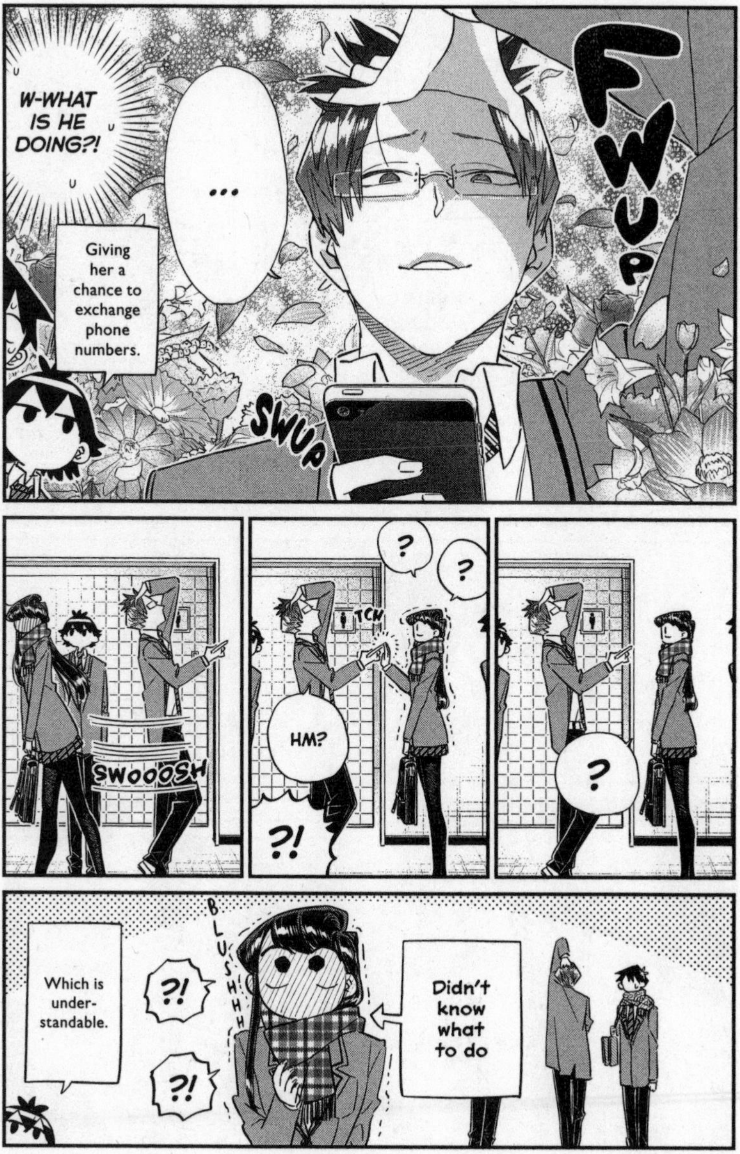
FWUP
...
W-WHAT IS HE DOING?!
Giving her a chance to exchange phone numbers.
SWUP
?
?
?
TCH
HM?
?!
SWOOOSH
Didn't know what to do
BLUSHHH
?!
?!
Which is under-standable.

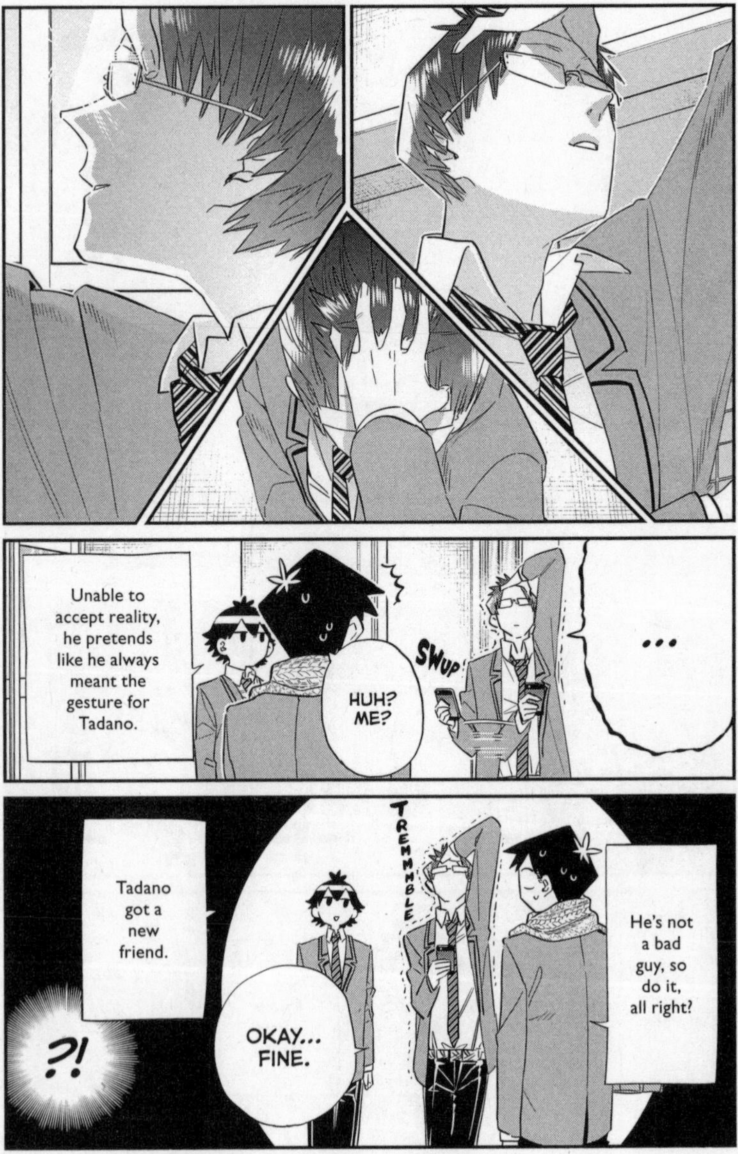
...
SWUP
HUH? ME?
Unable to accept reality, he pretends like he always meant the gesture for Tadano.
He's not a bad guy, so do it, all right?
TREMMMBLE
Tadano got a new friend.
OKAY... FINE.
?!

Communication 102 — The End

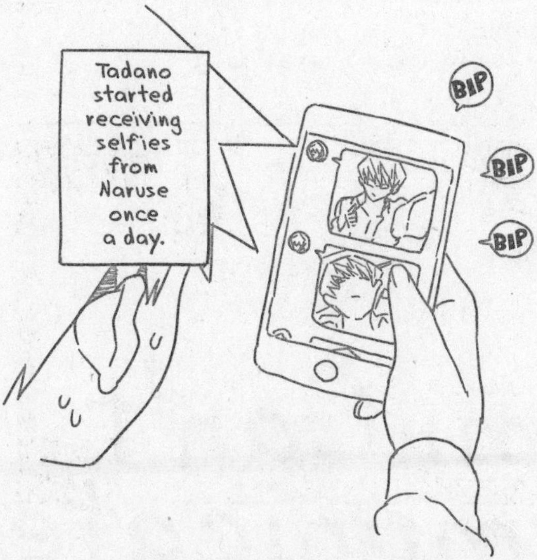
Tadano started receiving selfies from Naruse once a day.
BIP
BIP
BIP

Komi Can't Communicate

Komi Can't Communicate

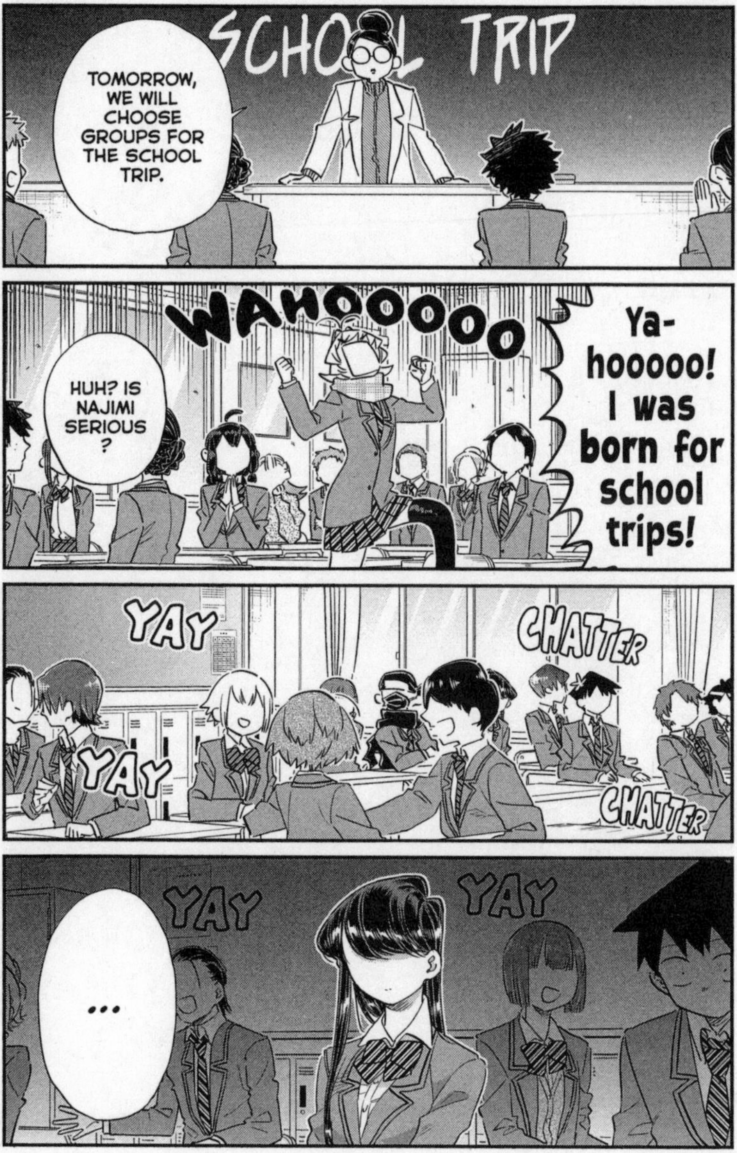
SCHOOL TRIP
TOMORROW, WE WILL CHOOSE GROUPS FOR THE SCHOOL TRIP.
Ya-hooooo! I was born for school trips!
WAHOOOOOO
HUH? IS NAJIMI SERIOUS?
CHATTER
YAY
YAY
CHATTER
YAY
YAY
...

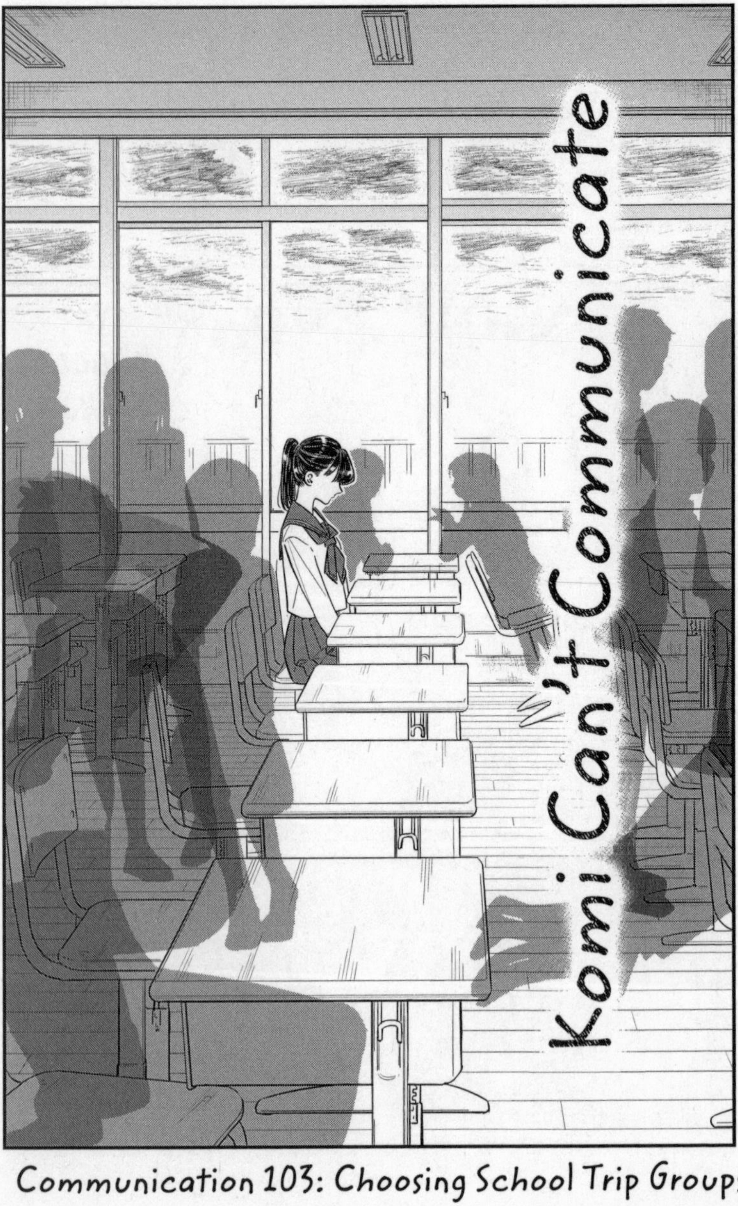
Komi Can't Communicate

Communication 103: Choosing School Trip Groups

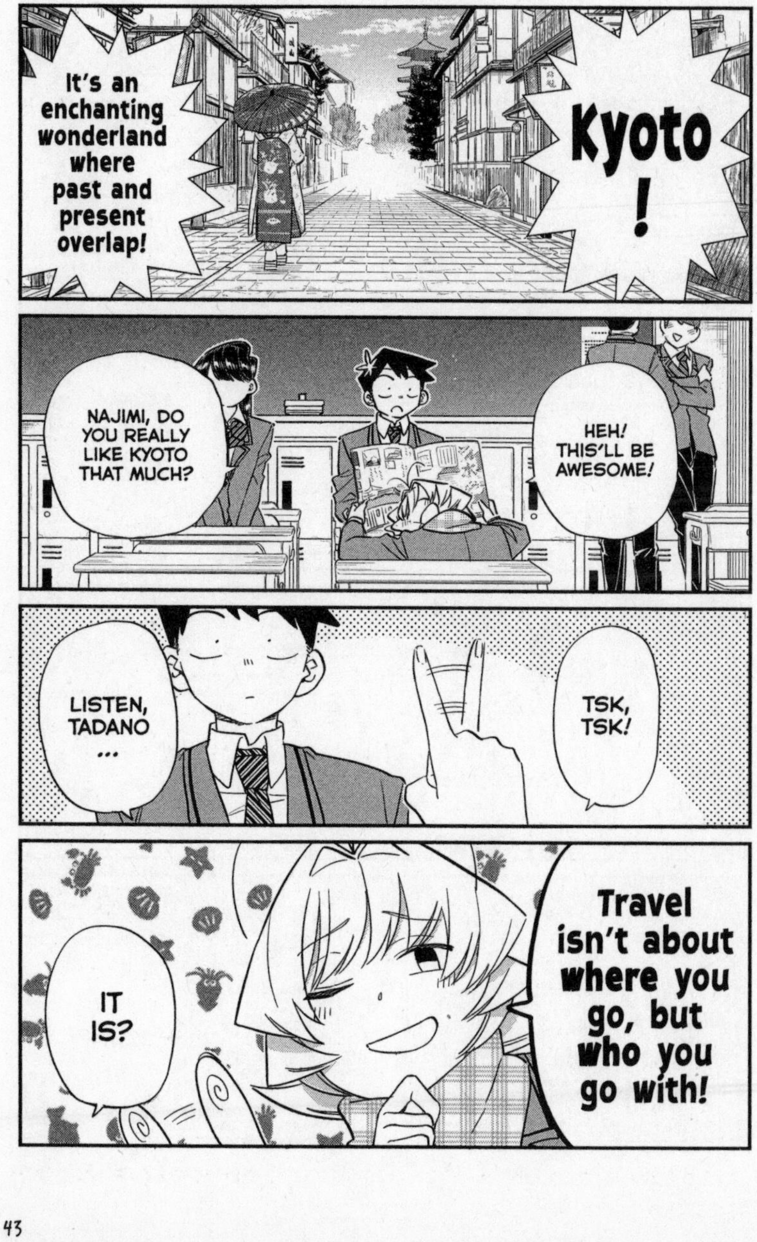
Kyoto!
It's an enchanting wonderland where past and present overlap!
HEH! THIS'LL BE AWESOME!
NAJIMI, DO YOU REALLY LIKE KYOTO THAT MUCH?
TSK, TSK!
LISTEN, TADANO ...
Travel isn't about where you go, but who you go with!
IT IS?

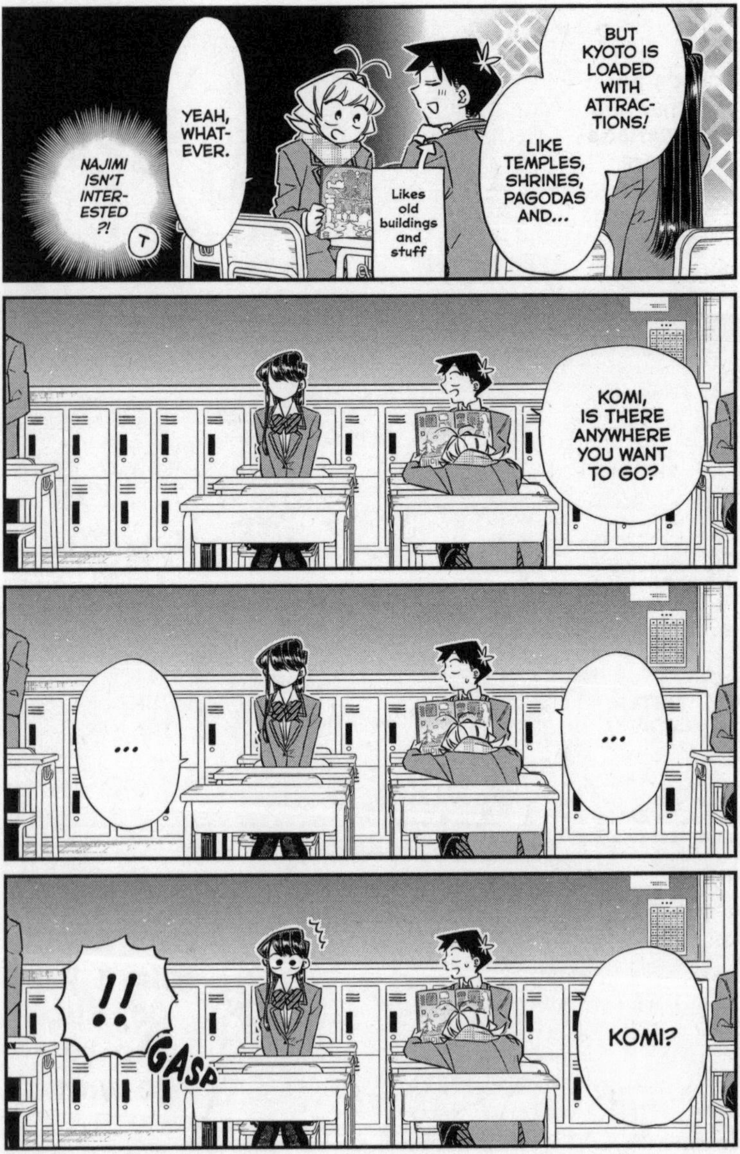
BUT KYOTO IS LOADED WITH ATTRACTIONS!
LIKE TEMPLES, SHRINES, PAGODAS AND...
Likes old buildings and stuff
YEAH, WHATEVER.
NAJIMI ISN'T INTERESTED ?!
T
KOMI, IS THERE ANYWHERE YOU WANT TO GO?
...
...
KOMI?
!!
GASP

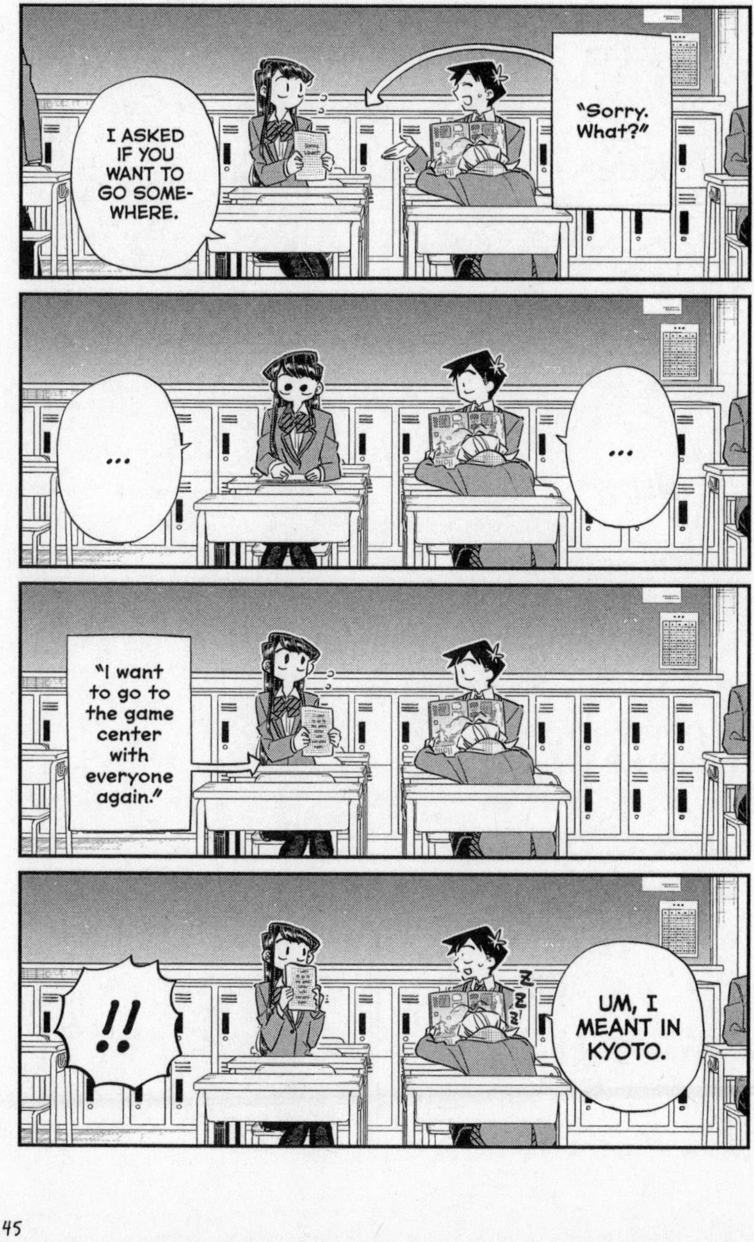
"Sorry. What?"
I ASKED IF YOU WANT TO GO SOME-WHERE.
...
...
"I want to go to the game center with everyone again."
UM, I MEANT IN KYOTO.
ZZZ
!!

I want to see the Ginkaku-ji.
OH, NICE!
GOOD IDEA! THE KINKAKU-JI IS NICE TOO.
WHEN VIEWED WITH THE SURROUNDING GARDEN, THE OVERALL BALANCE IS–
WHAT-EVER, OLD MAN.
HUH?
"Pardon me a second."
OH, OKAY.
POTTY BREAK?
?

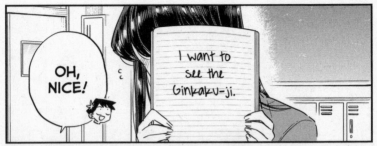

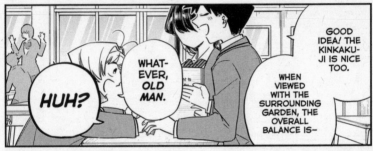

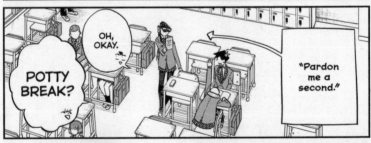

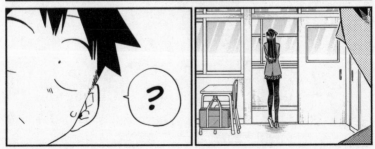

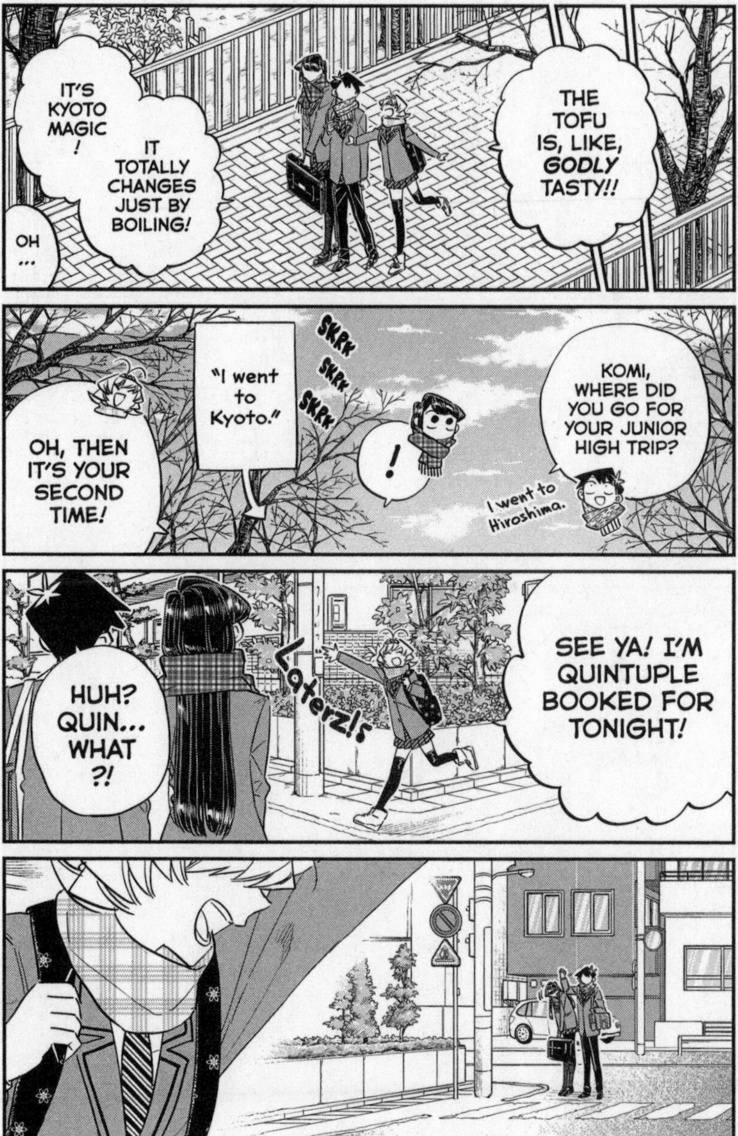
THE TOFU IS, LIKE, GODLY TASTY!!
IT'S KYOTO MAGIC!
IT TOTALLY CHANGES JUST BY BOILING!
OH ...
KOMI, WHERE DID YOU GO FOR YOUR JUNIOR HIGH TRIP?
I went to Hiroshima.
SKRK SKRK SKRK
!
"I went to Kyoto."
OH, THEN IT'S YOUR SECOND TIME!
SEE YA! I'M QUINTUPLE BOOKED FOR TONIGHT!
Laterz!s
HUH? QUIN... WHAT?!

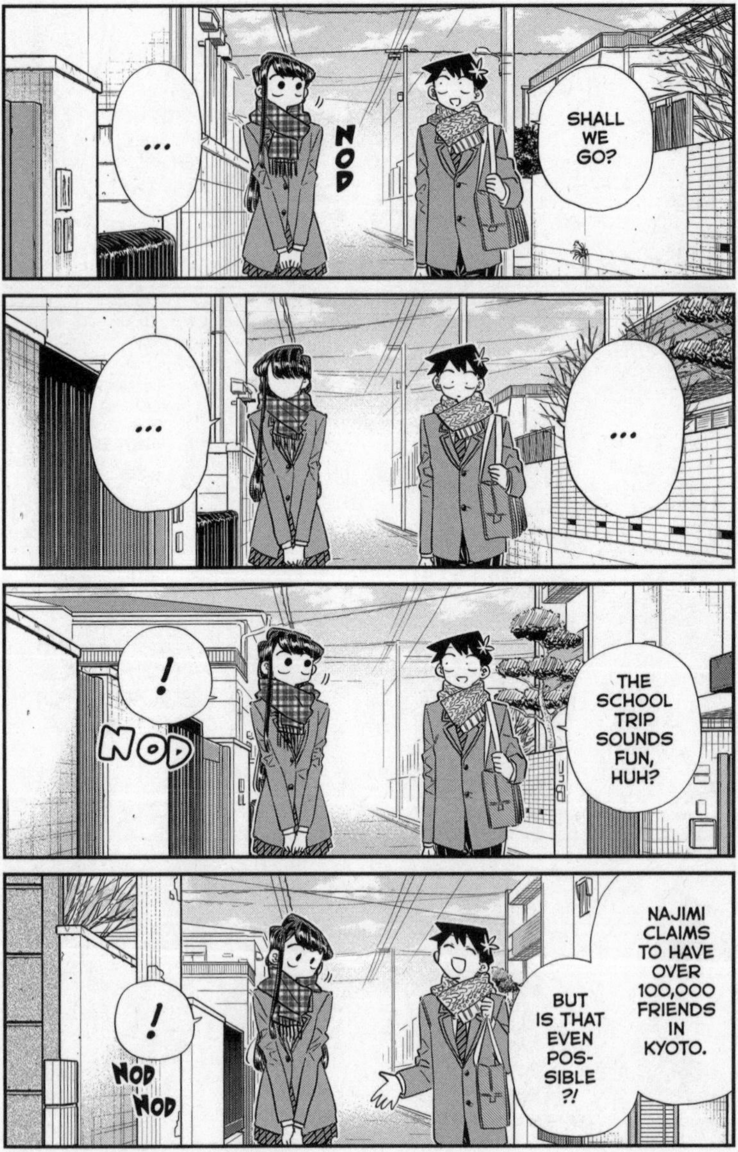
SHALL WE GO?
NOD
...
...
...
THE SCHOOL TRIP SOUNDS FUN, HUH?
!
NOD
NAJIMI CLAIMS TO HAVE OVER 100,000 FRIENDS IN KYOTO.
BUT IS THAT EVEN POS-SIBLE?!
!
NOD NOD

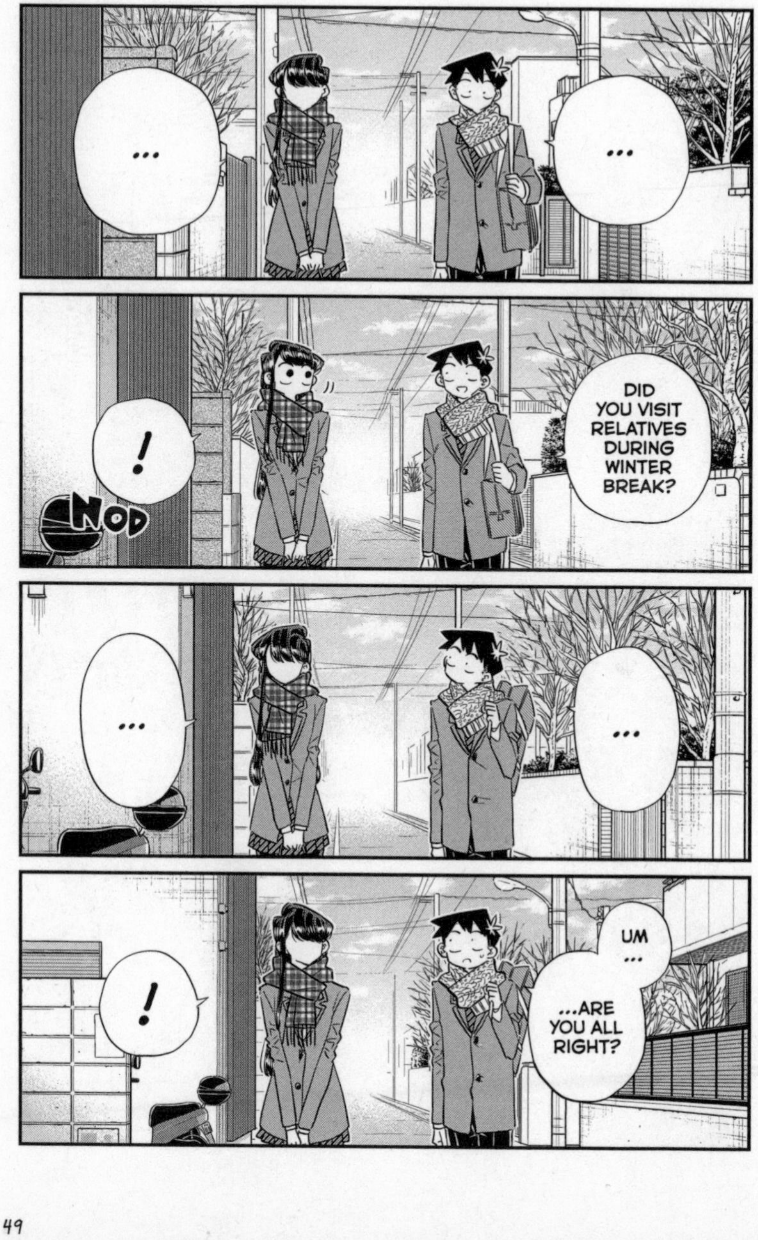
...
...
DID YOU VISIT RELATIVES DURING WINTER BREAK?
!
NOD
...
...
UM ...
...ARE YOU ALL RIGHT?
!

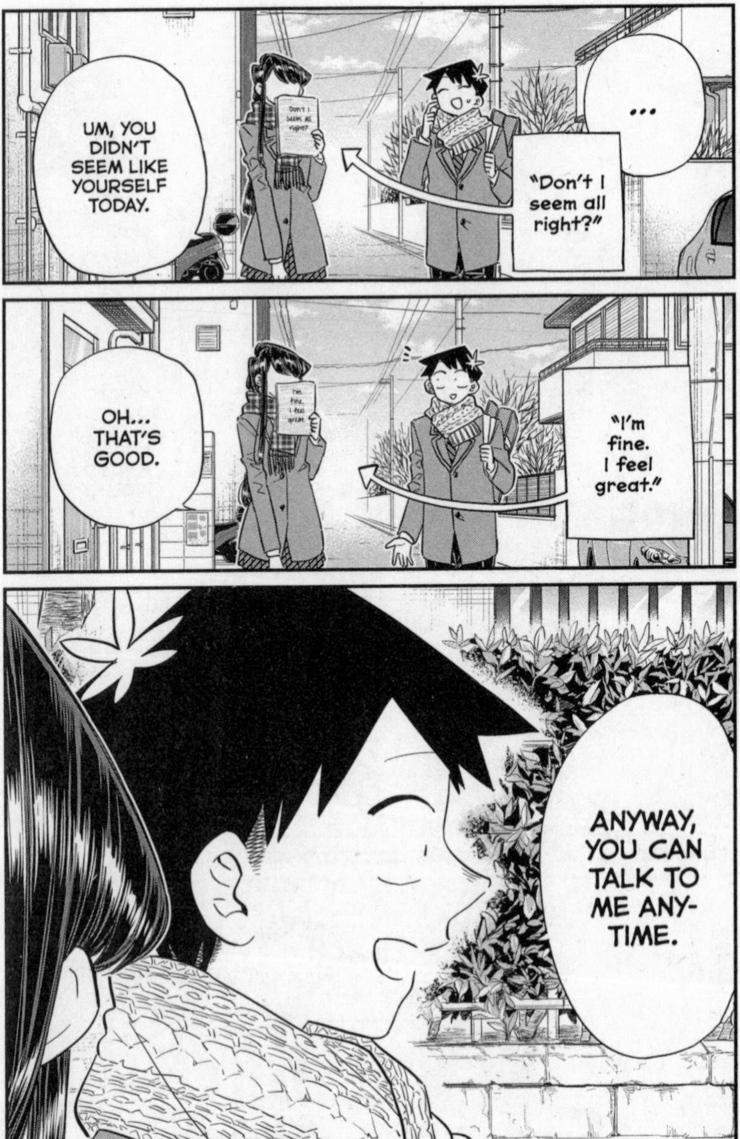
...
"Don't I seem all right?"
UM, YOU DIDN'T SEEM LIKE YOURSELF TODAY.
"I'm fine. I feel great."
OH... THAT'S GOOD.
ANYWAY, YOU CAN TALK TO ME ANY-TIME.

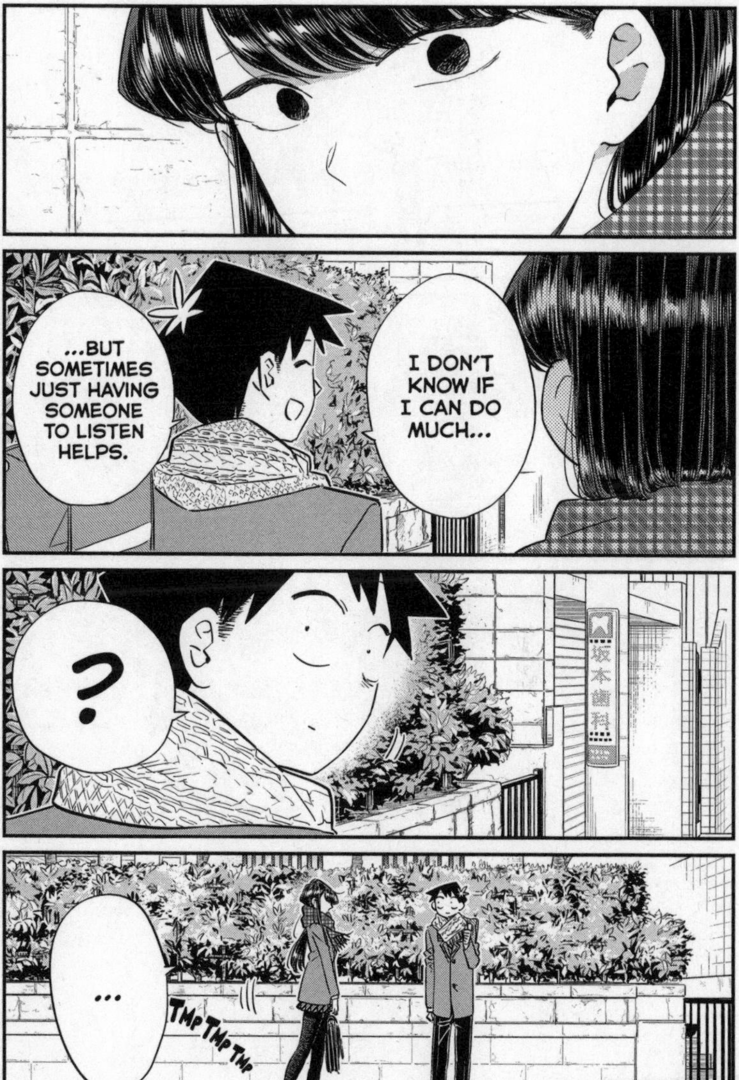

I DON'T KNOW IF I CAN DO MUCH...
...BUT SOMETIMES JUST HAVING SOMEONE TO LISTEN HELPS.
坂本歯科
?
TMP TMP TMP TMP
...

THIS IS WHERE WE PART WAYS.
TAKE CARE ON THE WAY HOME.
...!
BOW
VVVVVVT
JOLT
AGH!
Komi, Shoko
KOMI?

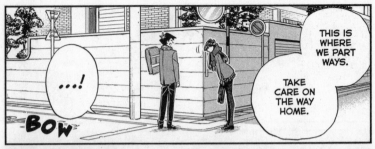

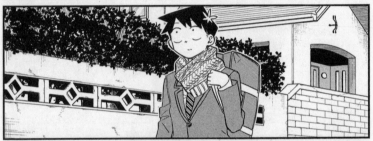

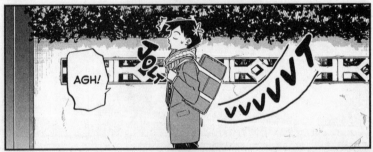

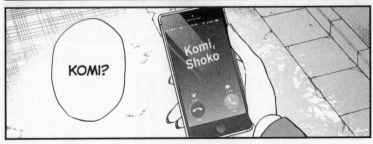

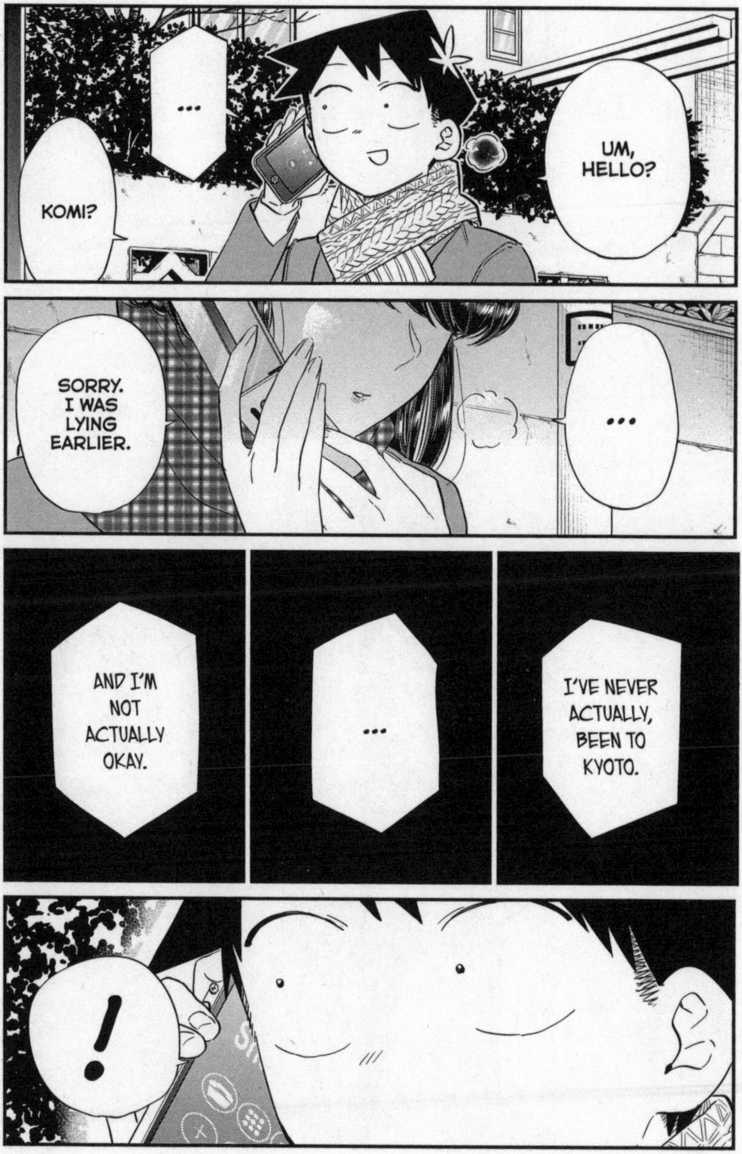
UM, HELLO?
...
KOMI?
...
SORRY. I WAS LYING EARLIER.
I'VE NEVER ACTUALLY, BEEN TO KYOTO.
...
AND I'M NOT ACTUALLY OKAY.
!

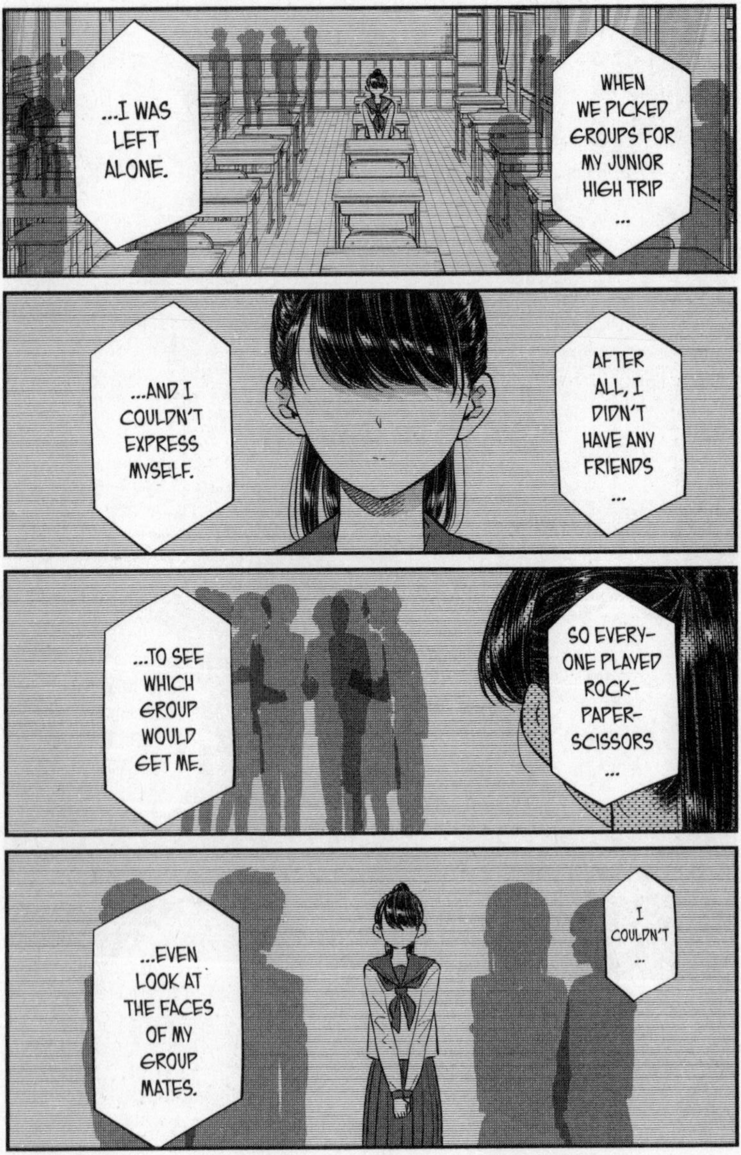
WHEN WE PICKED GROUPS FOR MY JUNIOR HIGH TRIP ...
...I WAS LEFT ALONE.
AFTER ALL, I DIDN'T HAVE ANY FRIENDS ...
...AND I COULDN'T EXPRESS MYSELF.
SO EVERY-ONE PLAYED ROCK-PAPER-SCISSORS ...
...TO SEE WHICH GROUP WOULD GET ME.
I COULDN'T ...
...EVEN LOOK AT THE FACES OF MY GROUP MATES.

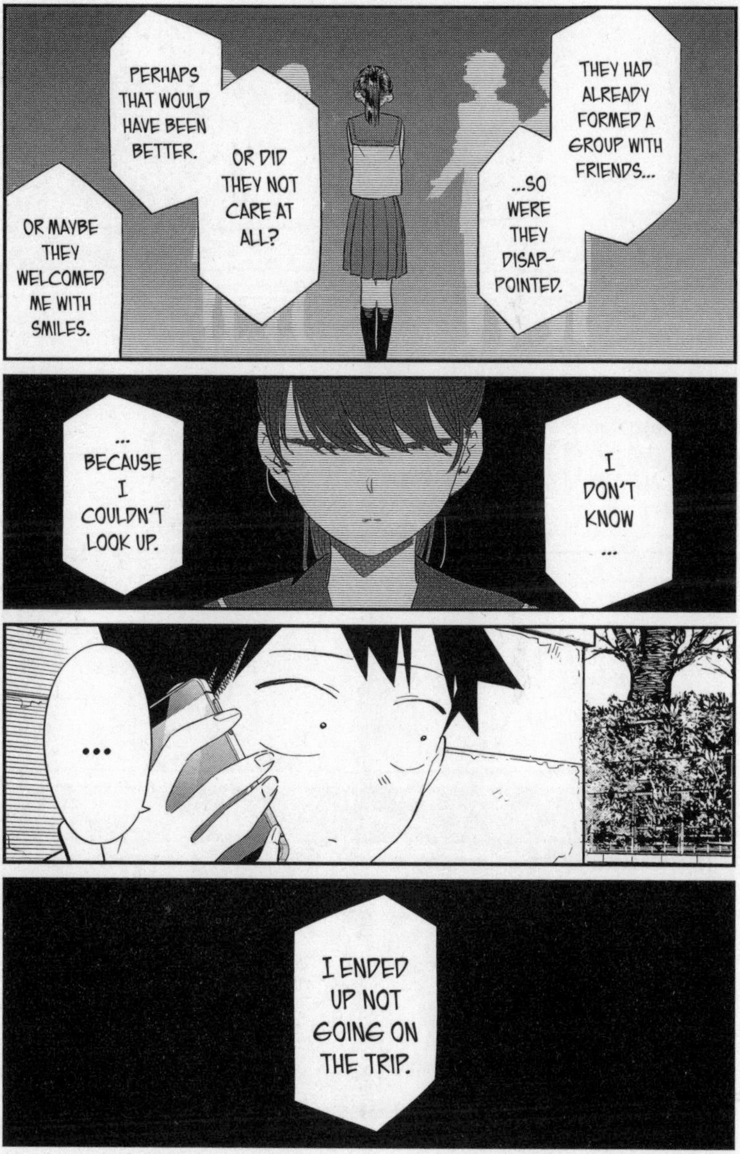
THEY HAD ALREADY FORMED A GROUP WITH FRIENDS...
...SO WERE THEY DISAPPOINTED.
OR DID THEY NOT CARE AT ALL?
PERHAPS THAT WOULD HAVE BEEN BETTER.
OR MAYBE THEY WELCOMED ME WITH SMILES.
I DON'T KNOW...
...BECAUSE I COULDN'T LOOK UP.
...
I ENDED UP NOT GOING ON THE TRIP.

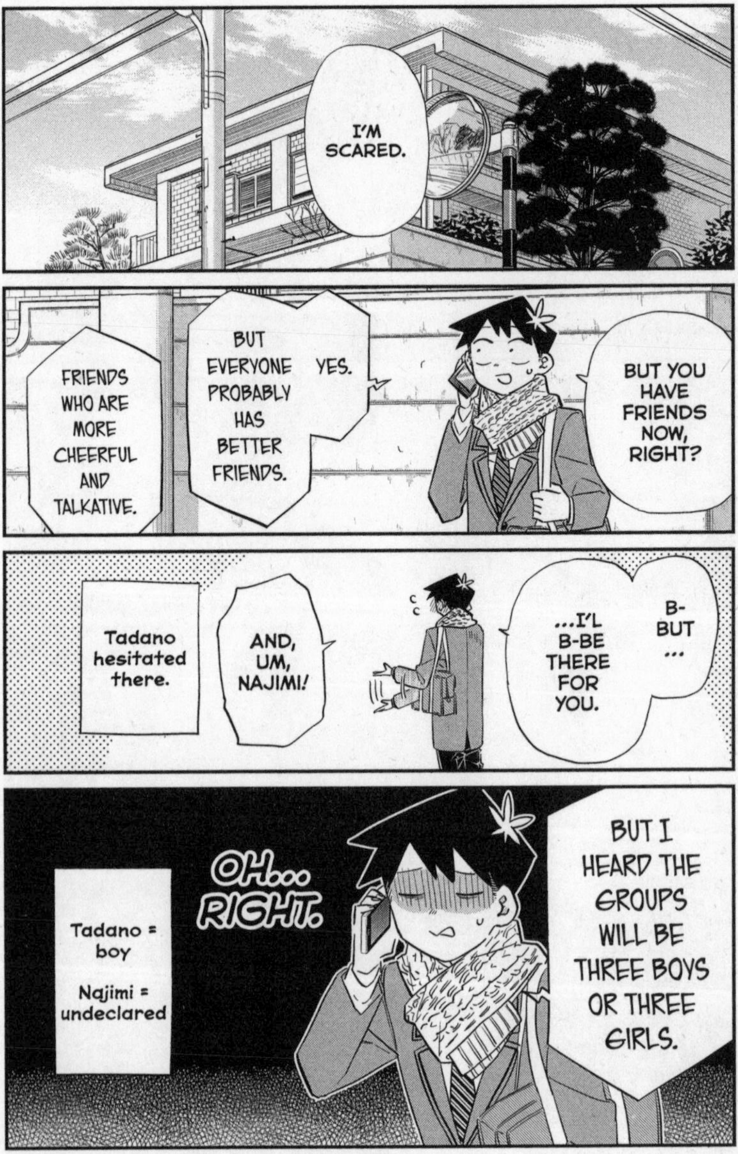
I'M SCARED.
BUT YOU HAVE FRIENDS NOW, RIGHT?
YES.
BUT EVERYONE PROBABLY HAS BETTER FRIENDS.
FRIENDS WHO ARE MORE CHEERFUL AND TALKATIVE.
B-BUT...
...I'L B-BE THERE FOR YOU.
AND, UM, NAJIMI!
Tadano hesitated there.
BUT I HEARD THE GROUPS WILL BE THREE BOYS OR THREE GIRLS.
OH... RIGHT.
Tadano = boy
Najimi = undeclared

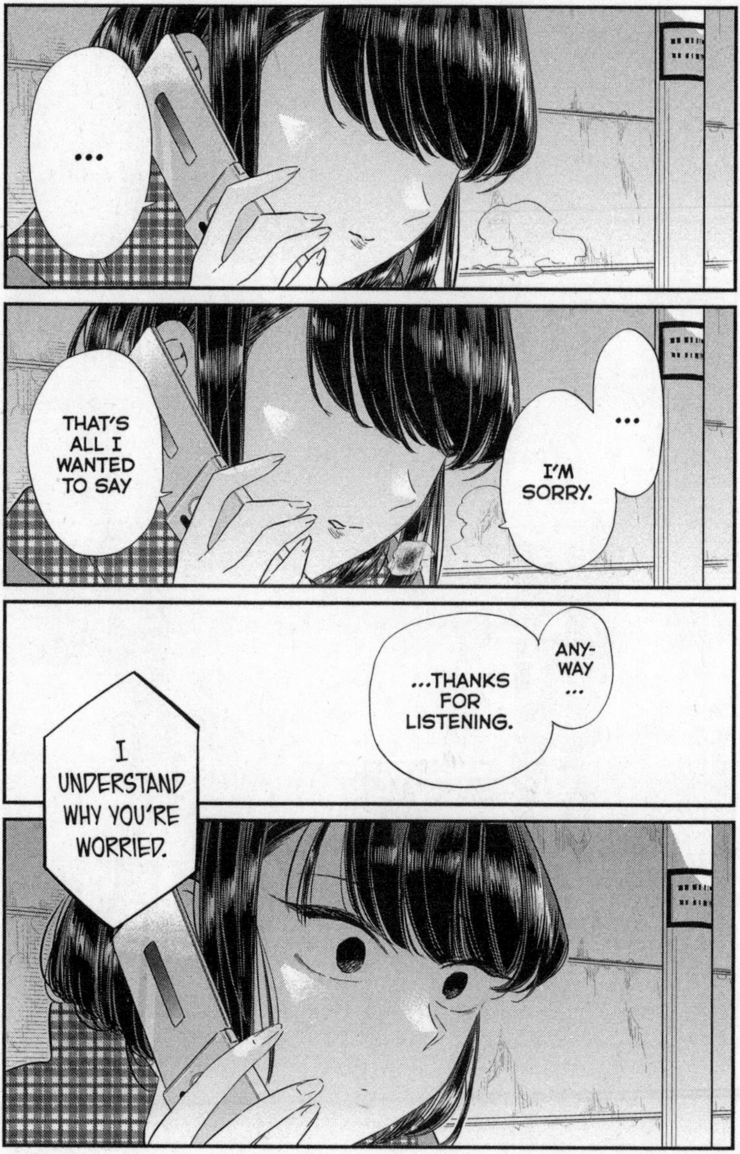
...
... I'M SORRY.
THAT'S ALL I WANTED TO SAY
ANY-WAY ...
...THANKS FOR LISTENING.
I UNDERSTAND WHY YOU'RE WORRIED.

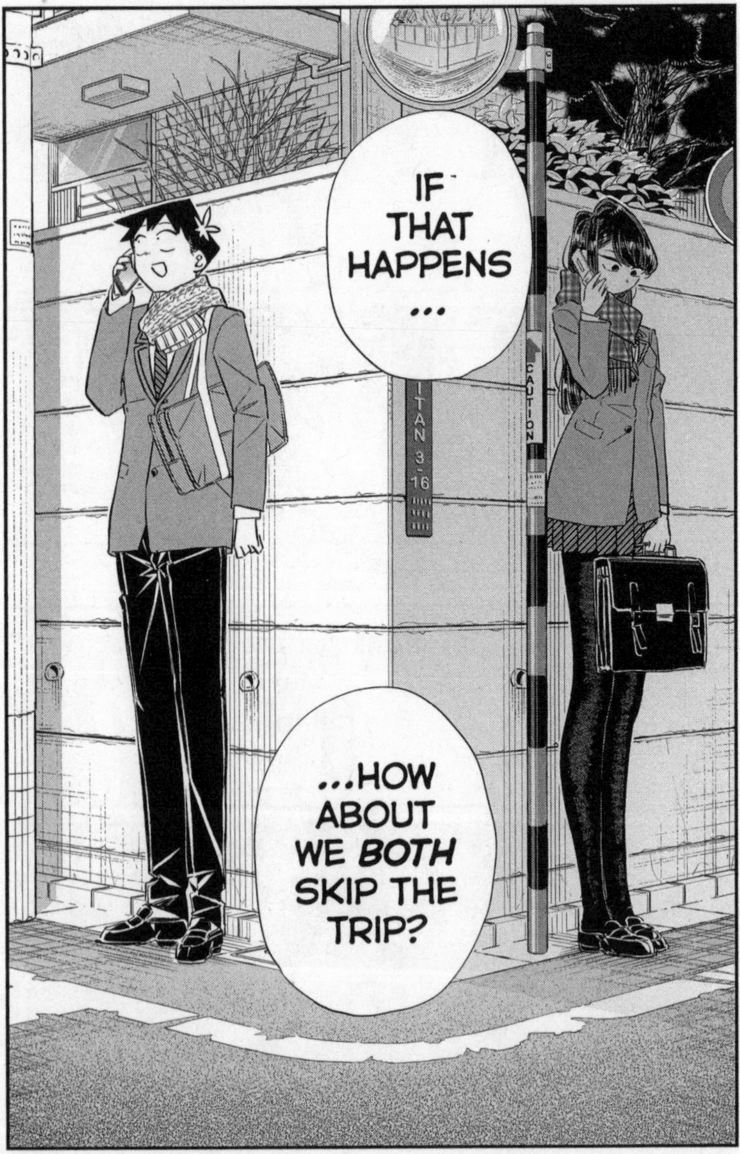
IF THAT HAPPENS...
...HOW ABOUT WE *BOTH* SKIP THE TRIP?
CAUTION
ITAN 3-16

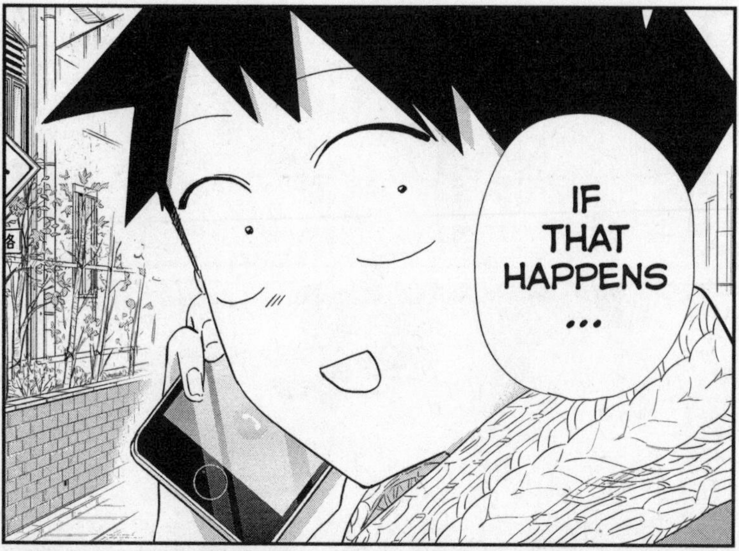
IF THAT HAPPENS ...

Komi Can't Communicate

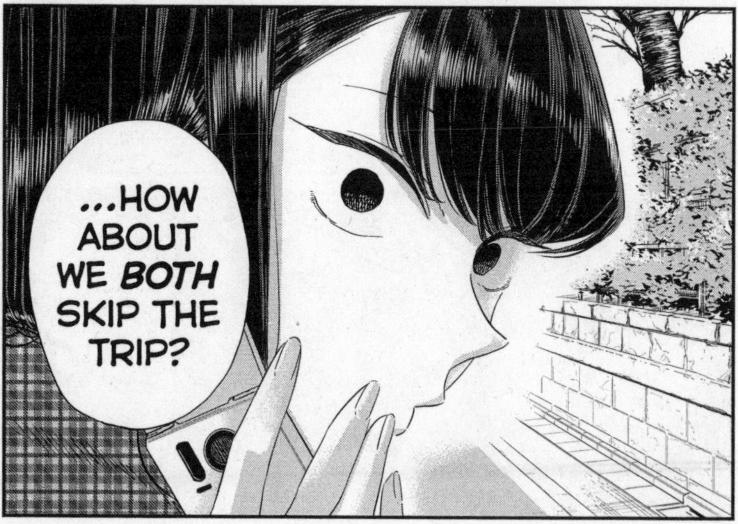
...HOW ABOUT WE *BOTH* SKIP THE TRIP?

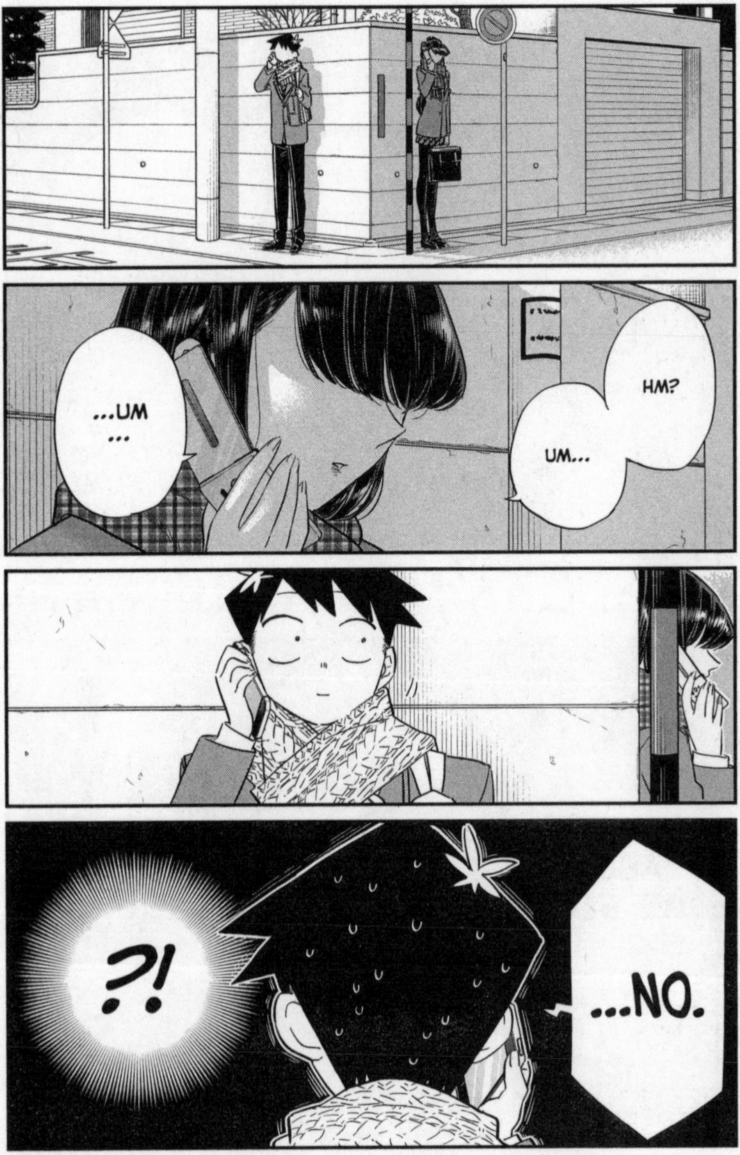
HM?
UM...
...UM ...
...NO.
?!

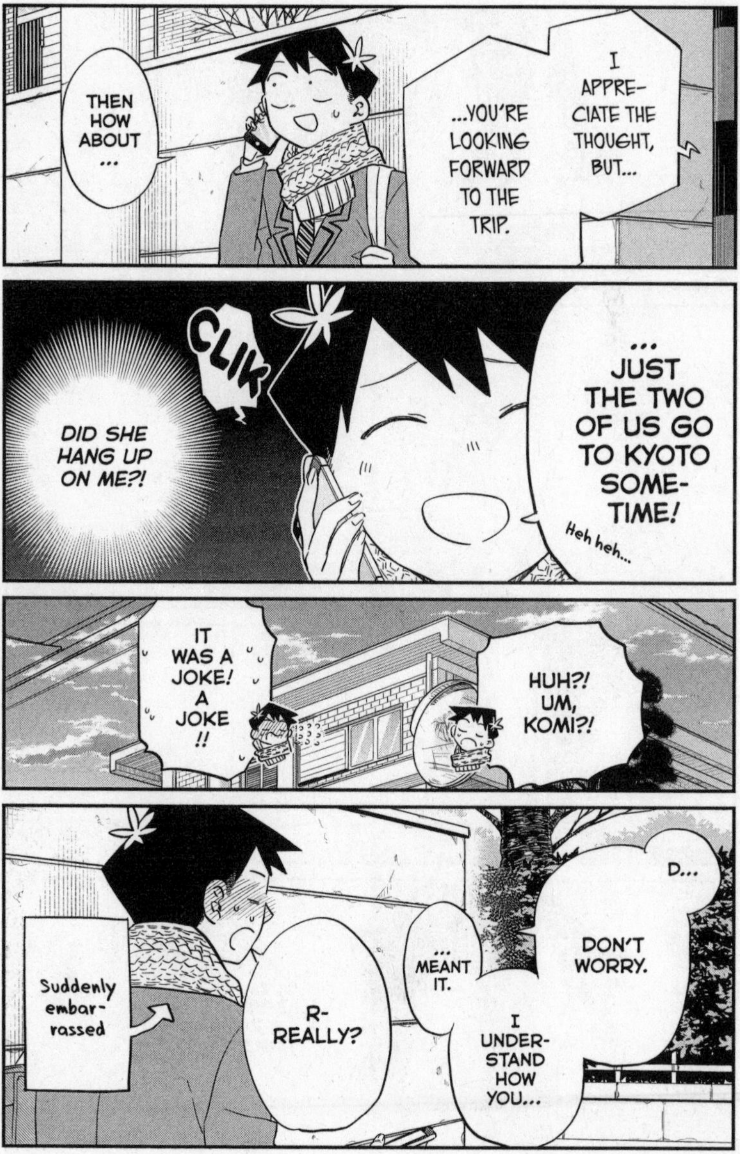
I APPRECIATE THE THOUGHT, BUT...
...YOU'RE LOOKING FORWARD TO THE TRIP.
THEN HOW ABOUT ...
... JUST THE TWO OF US GO TO KYOTO SOMETIME!
Heh heh...
CLIK
DID SHE HANG UP ON ME?!
HUH?! UM, KOMI?!
IT WAS A JOKE! A JOKE !!
D...
DON'T WORRY.
I UNDERSTAND HOW YOU...
... MEANT IT.
R-REALLY?
Suddenly embarrassed

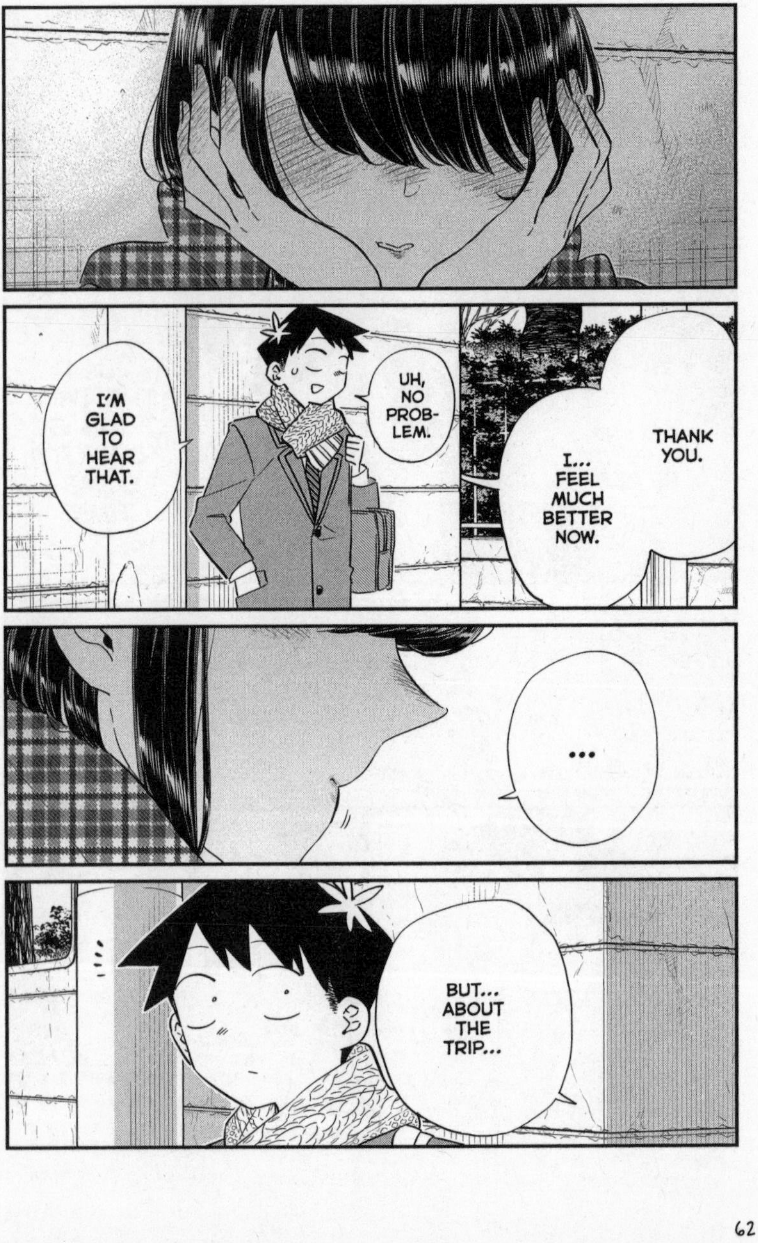
THANK YOU.
I... FEEL MUCH BETTER NOW.
UH, NO PROB-LEM.
I'M GLAD TO HEAR THAT.
...
BUT... ABOUT THE TRIP...

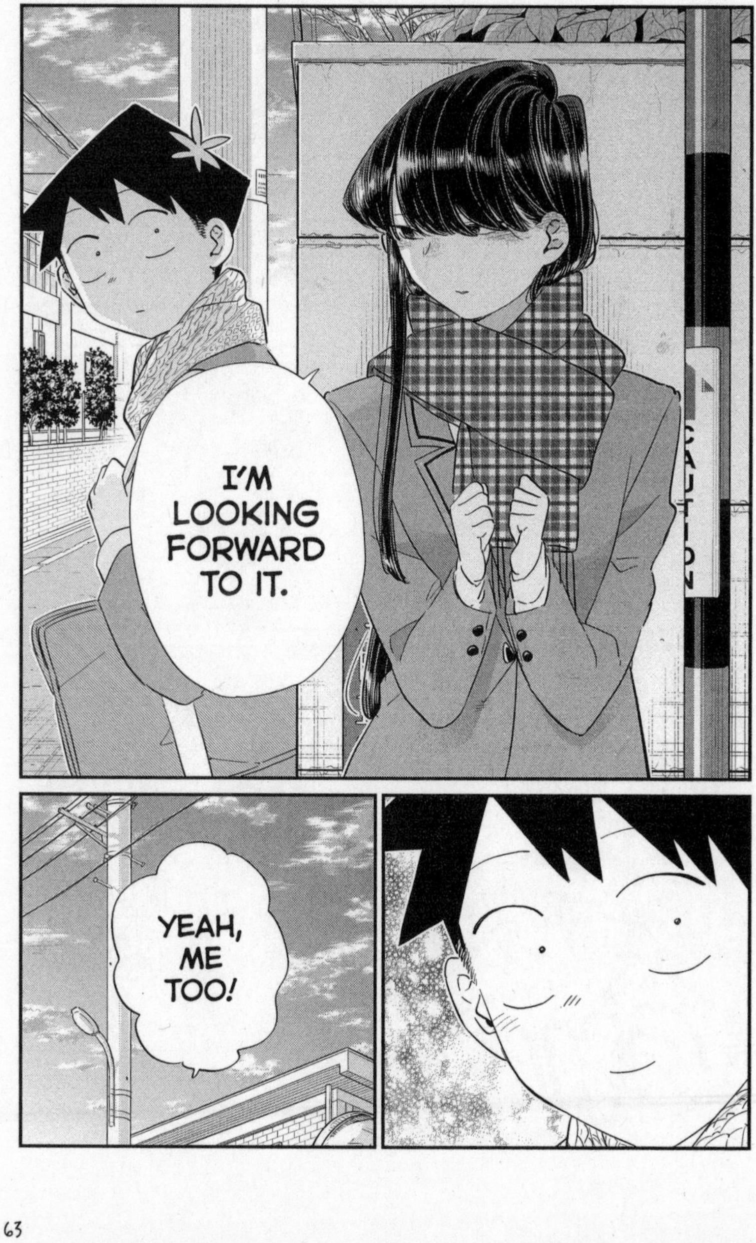
CAUTION
I'M LOOKING FORWARD TO IT.
YEAH, ME TOO!

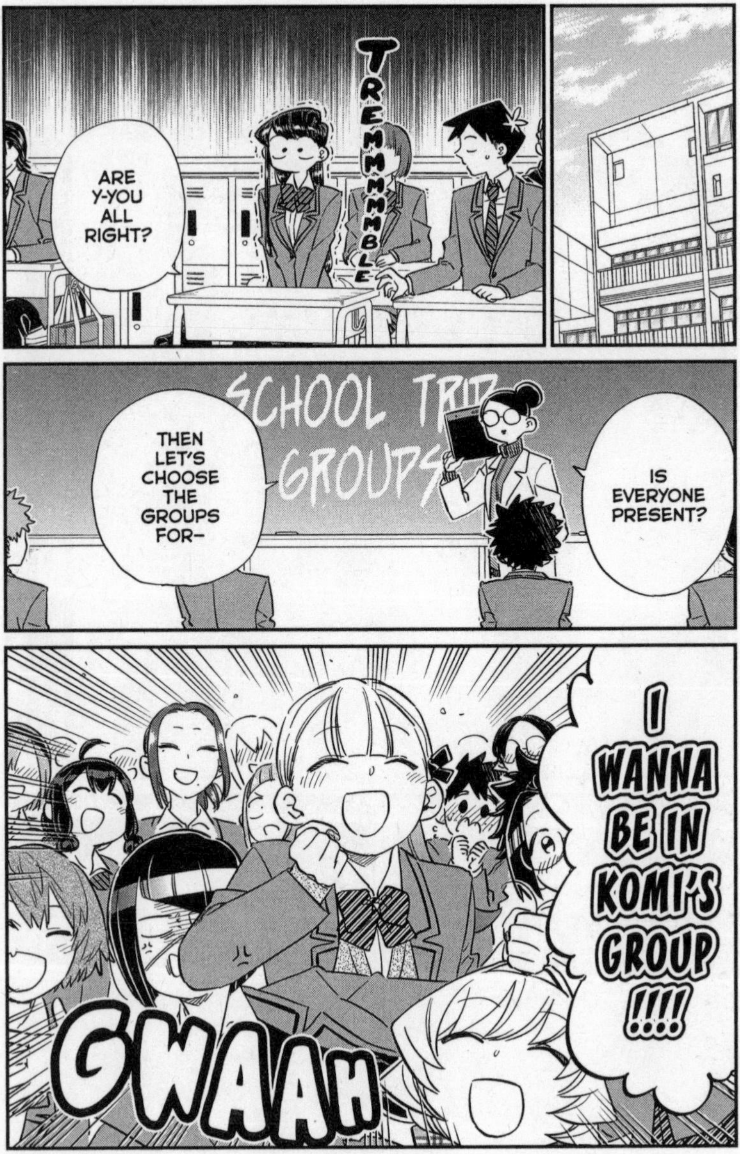
TREMMMMBLE
ARE Y-YOU ALL RIGHT?
IS EVERYONE PRESENT?
SCHOOL TRIP GROUPS
THEN LET'S CHOOSE THE GROUPS FOR–
I WANNA BE IN KOMI'S GROUP!!!!
GWAAH

!
CHATTER
CHATTER
I EX-PECTED THIS. WE'LL DRAW LOTS.
No arguing!
LOTS
?!
What will Komi's group be like?!

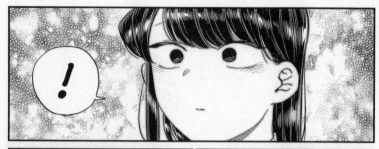

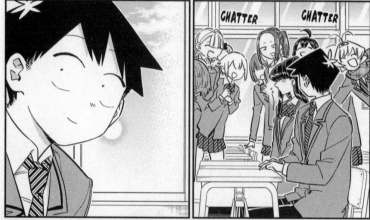

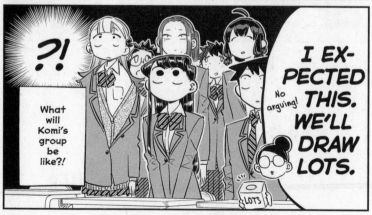

Communication 103 — The End

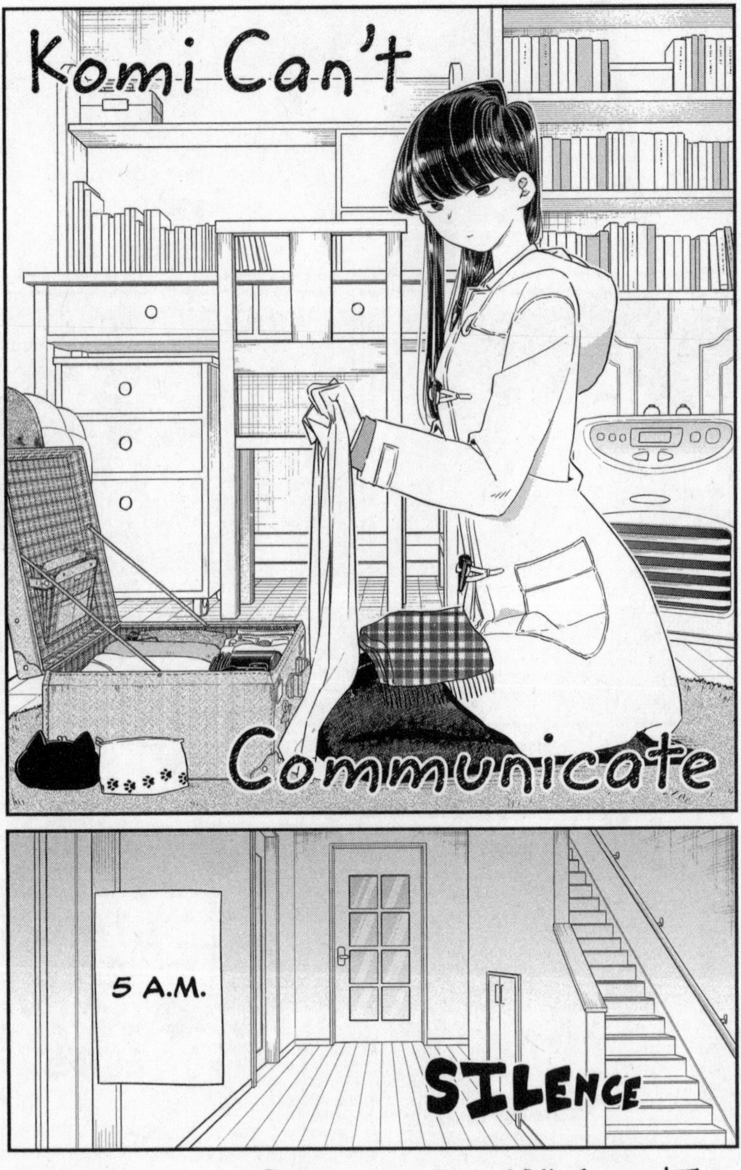
Komi Can't
Communicate
5 A.M.
SILENCE

Communication 104: School Trip

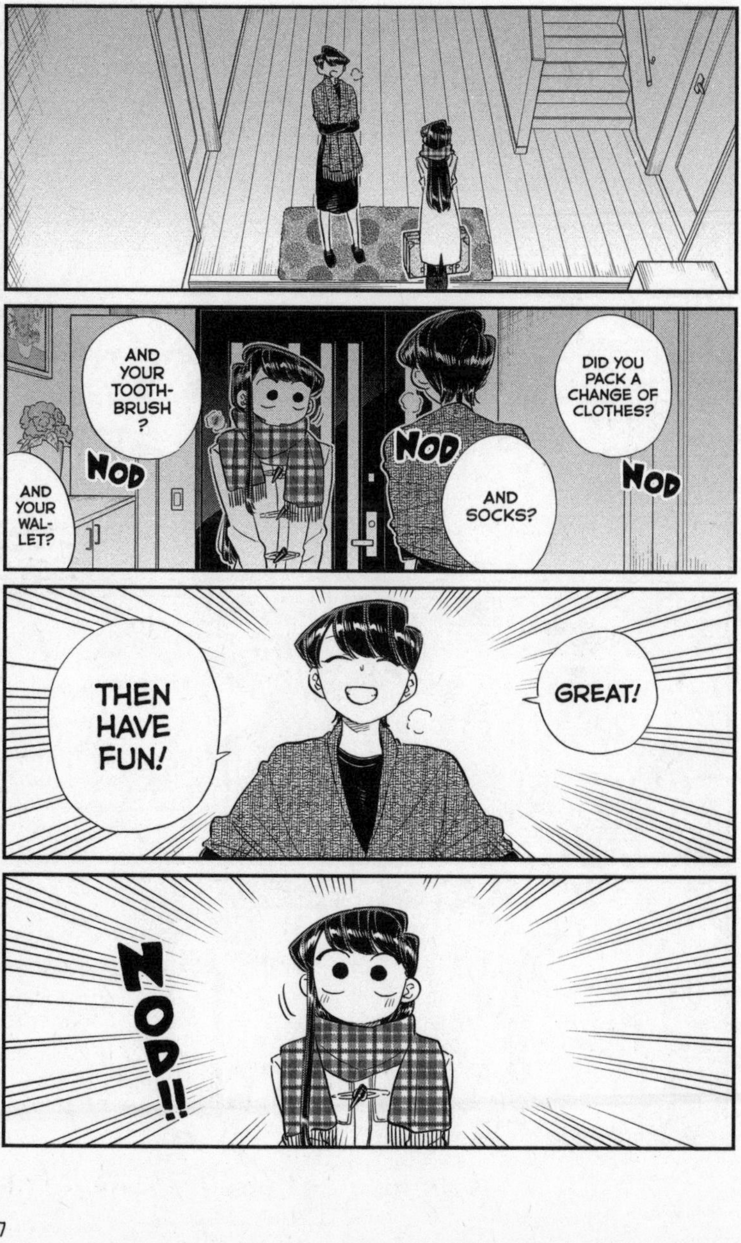

DID YOU PACK A CHANGE OF CLOTHES?
NOD
AND SOCKS?
NOD
AND YOUR TOOTH-BRUSH?
NOD
AND YOUR WAL-LET?
GREAT!
THEN HAVE FUN!
NOD!!

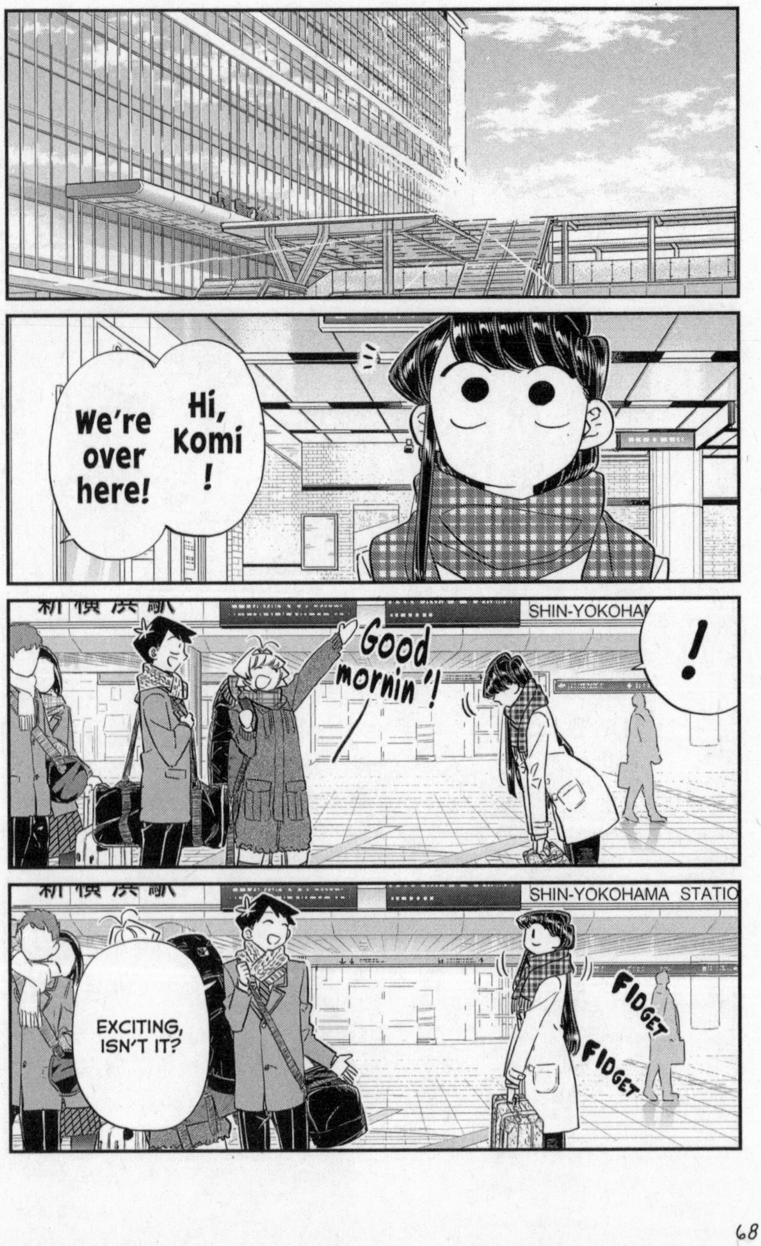
Hi, Komi!
We're over here!
!
Good mornin'!
新横浜駅
SHIN-YOKOHAMA STATIO
新横浜駅
FIDGET FIDGET
EXCITING, ISN'T IT?

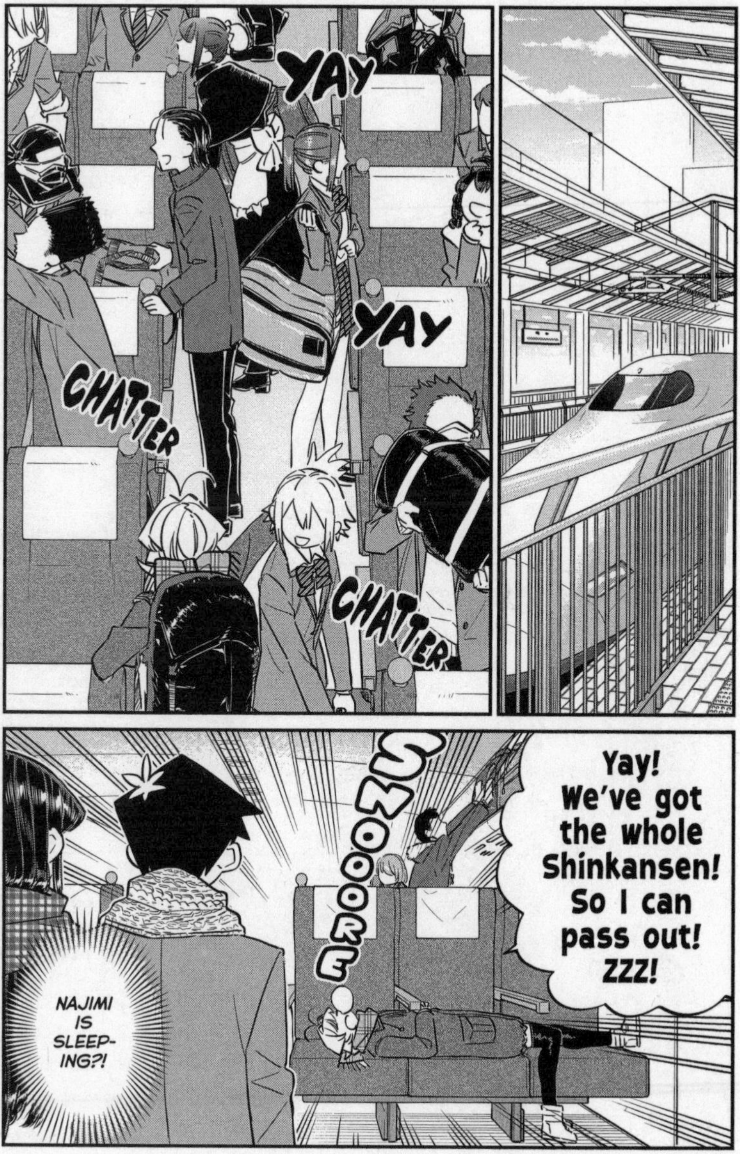
YAY
YAY
CHATTER
CHATTER
Yay! We've got the whole Shinkansen! So I can pass out! ZZZ!
SNOOOORE
NAJIMI IS SLEEPING?!

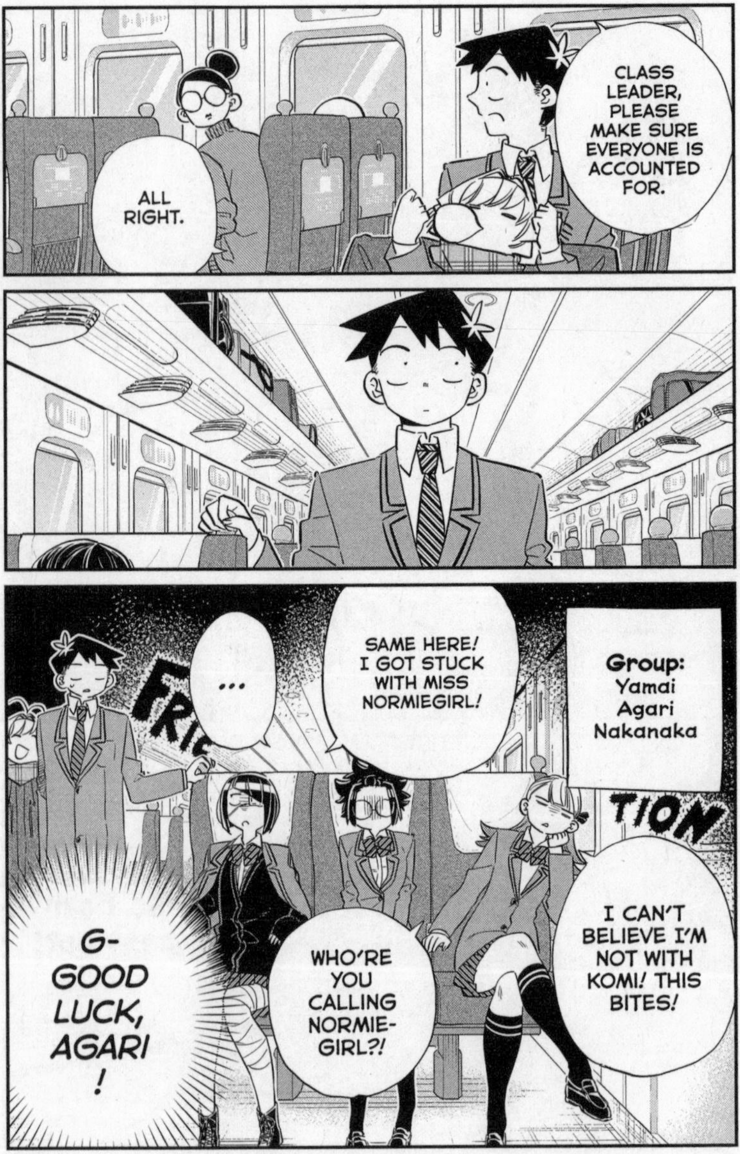
CLASS LEADER, PLEASE MAKE SURE EVERYONE IS ACCOUNTED FOR.
ALL RIGHT.
Group: Yamai Agari Nakanaka
FRICTION
I CAN'T BELIEVE I'M NOT WITH KOMI! THIS BITES!
SAME HERE! I GOT STUCK WITH MISS NORMIEGIRL!
...
WHO'RE YOU CALLING NORMIE-GIRL?!
G-GOOD LUCK, AGARI!

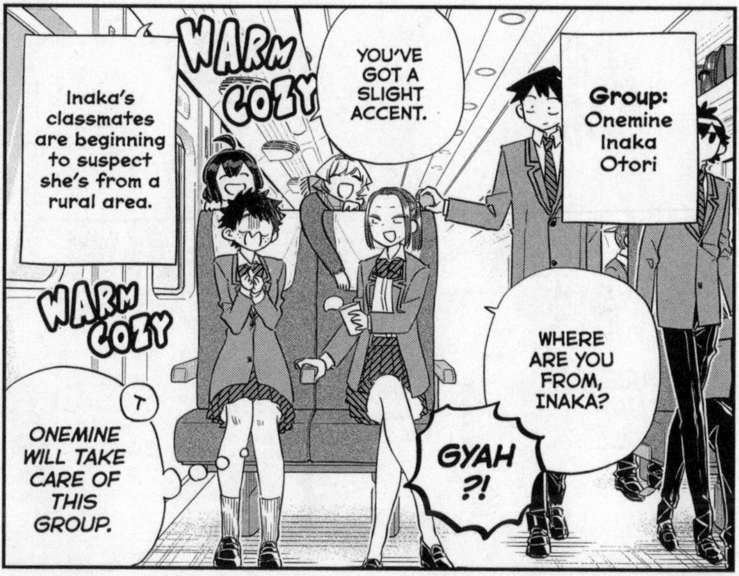
Group: Onemine Inaka Otori
YOU'VE GOT A SLIGHT ACCENT.
WARM COZY
Inaka's classmates are beginning to suspect she's from a rural area.
WHERE ARE YOU FROM, INAKA?
GYAH ?!
WARM COZY
T
ONEMINE WILL TAKE CARE OF THIS GROUP.
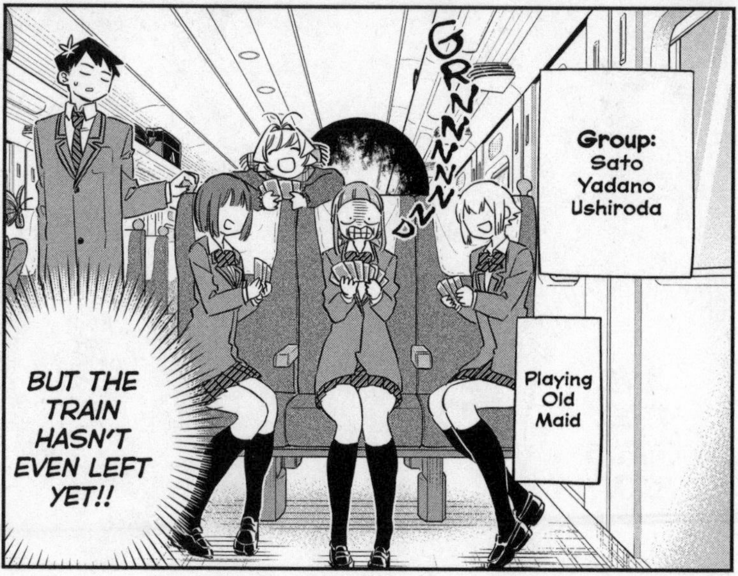
GRNNNNN
Group: Sato Yadano Ushiroda
Playing Old Maid
BUT THE TRAIN HASN'T EVEN LEFT YET!!

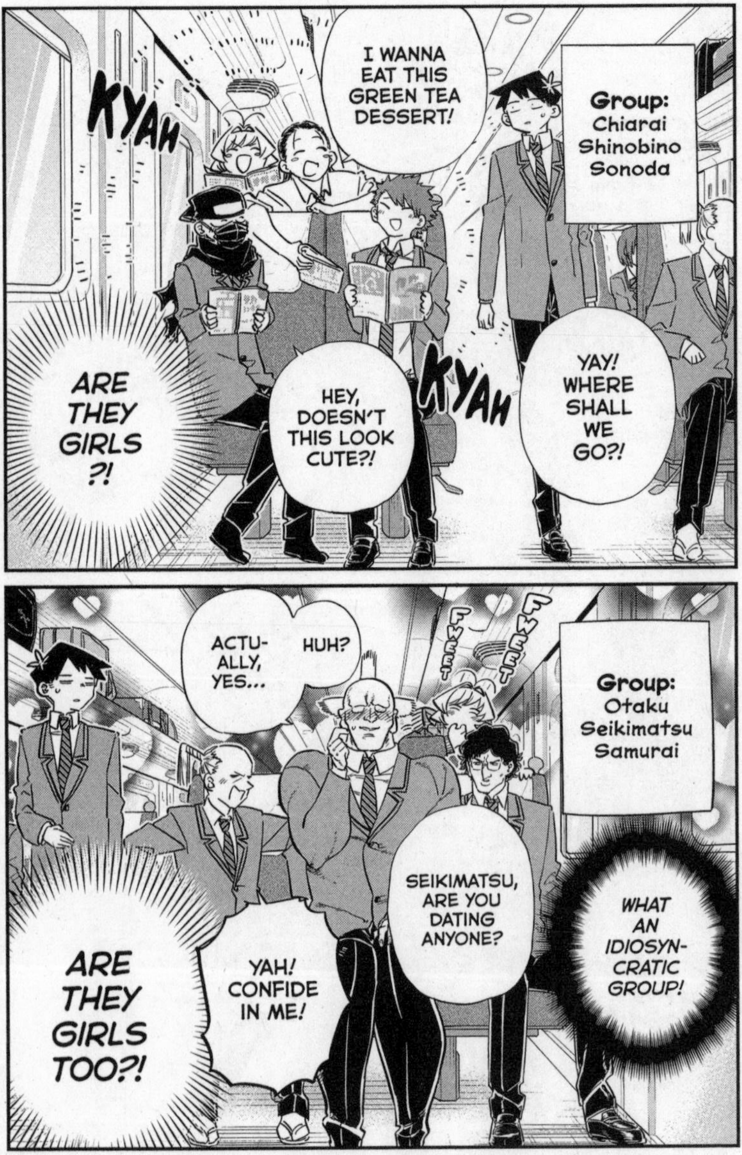
Group:
Chiarai
Shinobino
Sonoda
I WANNA EAT THIS GREEN TEA DESSERT!
KYAH
YAY! WHERE SHALL WE GO?!
KYAH
HEY, DOESN'T THIS LOOK CUTE?!
ARE THEY GIRLS ?!
Group:
Otaku
Seikimatsu
Samurai
FWEET
FWEET
HUH?
ACTU- ALLY, YES...
WHAT AN IDIOSYN- CRATIC GROUP!
SEIKIMATSU, ARE YOU DATING ANYONE?
YAH! CONFIDE IN ME!
ARE THEY GIRLS TOO?!

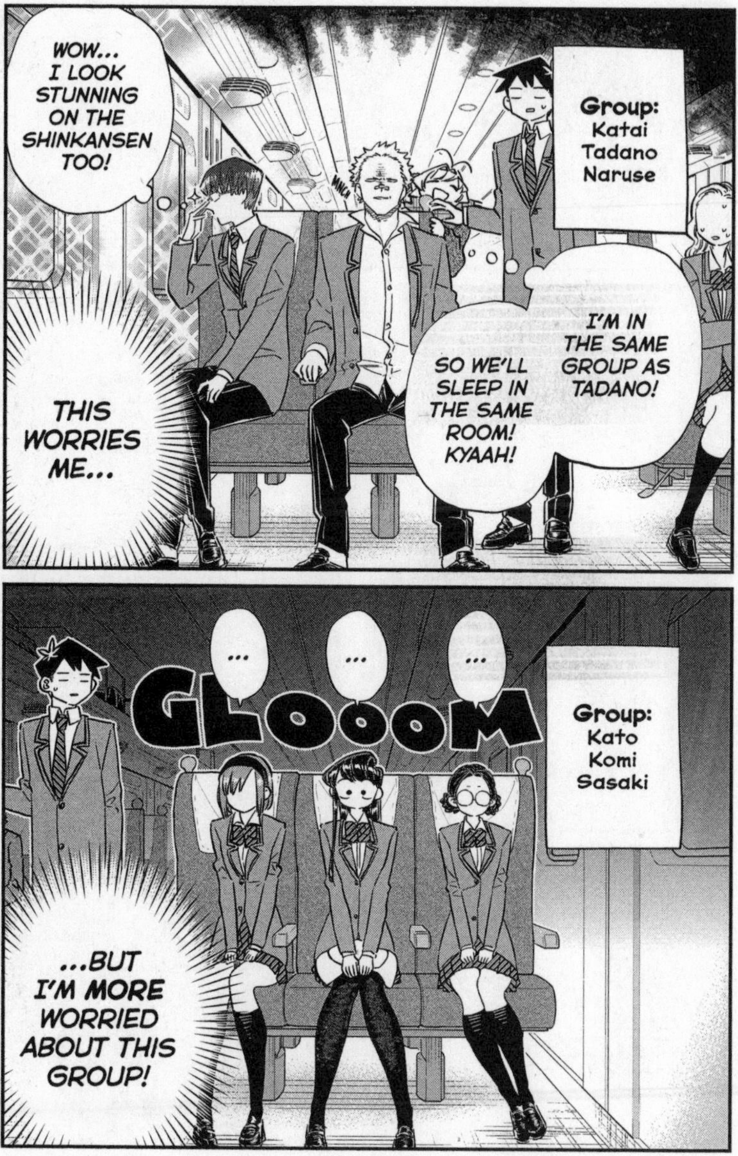
Group: Katai Tadano Naruse
WOW... I LOOK STUNNING ON THE SHINKANSEN TOO!
I'M IN THE SAME GROUP AS TADANO!
SO WE'LL SLEEP IN THE SAME ROOM! KYAAH!
THIS WORRIES ME...
Group: Kato Komi Sasaki
...
...
...
GLOOOM
...BUT I'M MORE WORRIED ABOUT THIS GROUP!

Mikuni
Kato

...

Shoko
Komi

...

Ayami
Sasaki

...

THEY LOOK UNCOMFORTABLE!

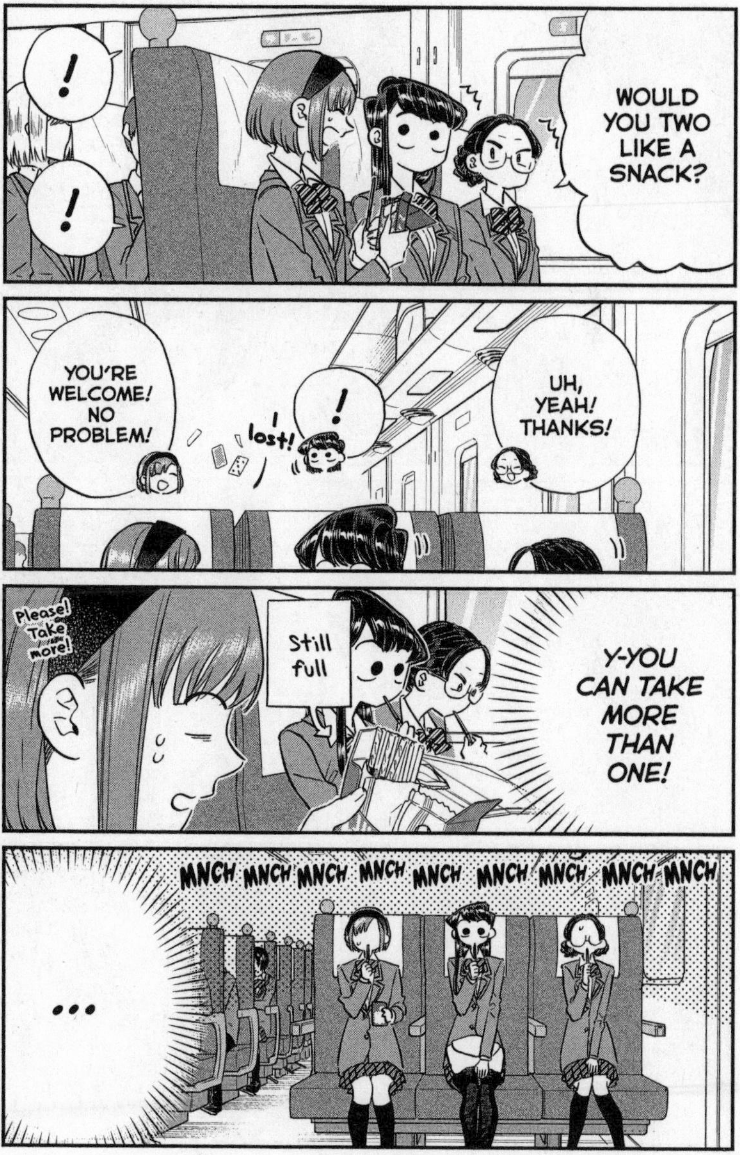

WOULD YOU TWO LIKE A SNACK?
!
!
UH, YEAH! THANKS!
!
I lost!
YOU'RE WELCOME! NO PROBLEM!
Y-YOU CAN TAKE MORE THAN ONE!
Still full
Please! Take more!
MNCH MNCH MNCH MNCH MNCH MNCH MNCH MNCH MNCH
...

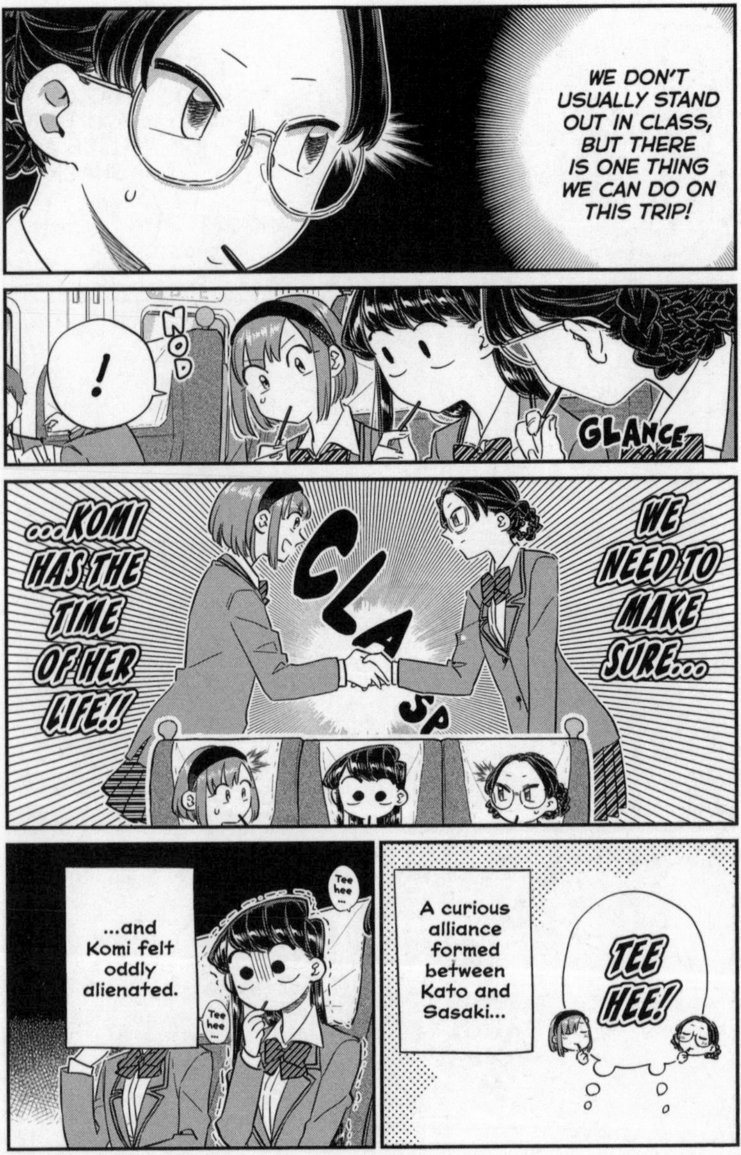
WE DON'T USUALLY STAND OUT IN CLASS, BUT THERE IS ONE THING WE CAN DO ON THIS TRIP!
GLANCE
NOD
!
WE NEED TO MAKE SURE...
CLASP
...KOMI HAS THE TIME OF HER LIFE!!
A curious alliance formed between Kato and Sasaki...
TEE HEE!
Tee hee...
...and Komi felt oddly alienated.
Tee hee...

Communication 104 – The End

Komi Can't Communicate

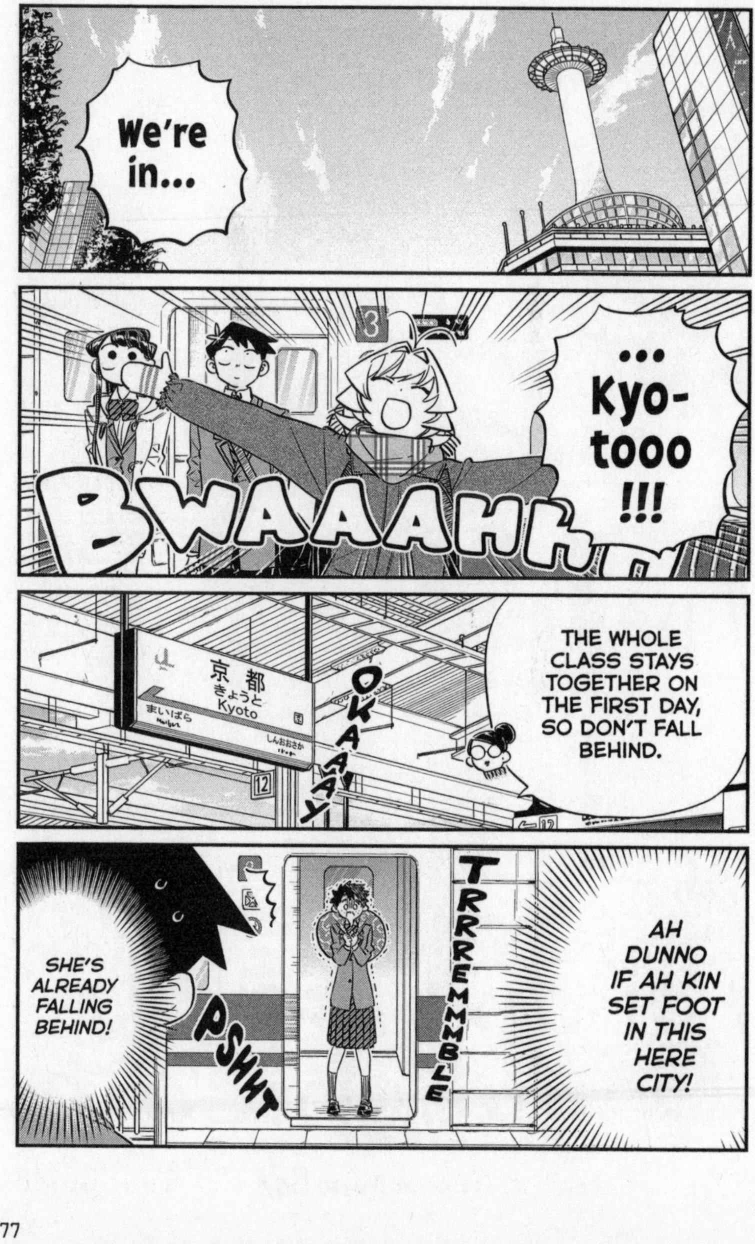
We're in...
...Kyo-tooo!!!
BWAAAHH
THE WHOLE CLASS STAYS TOGETHER ON THE FIRST DAY, SO DON'T FALL BEHIND.
OKAAAY
京都
きょうと
Kyoto
まいばら
しんおおさか
AH DUNNO IF AH KIN SET FOOT IN THIS HERE CITY!
TRRREMMMBLE
PSHHT
SHE'S ALREADY FALLING BEHIND!

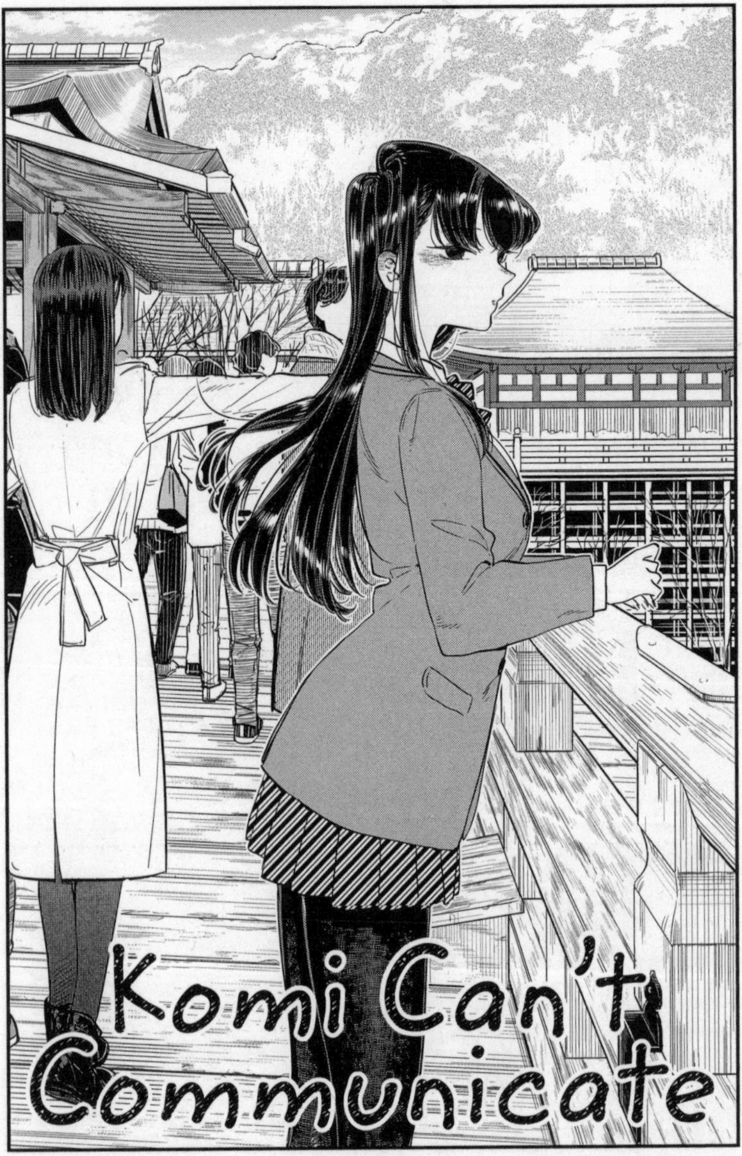
Komi Can't Communicate

Communication 105: Tour Guide

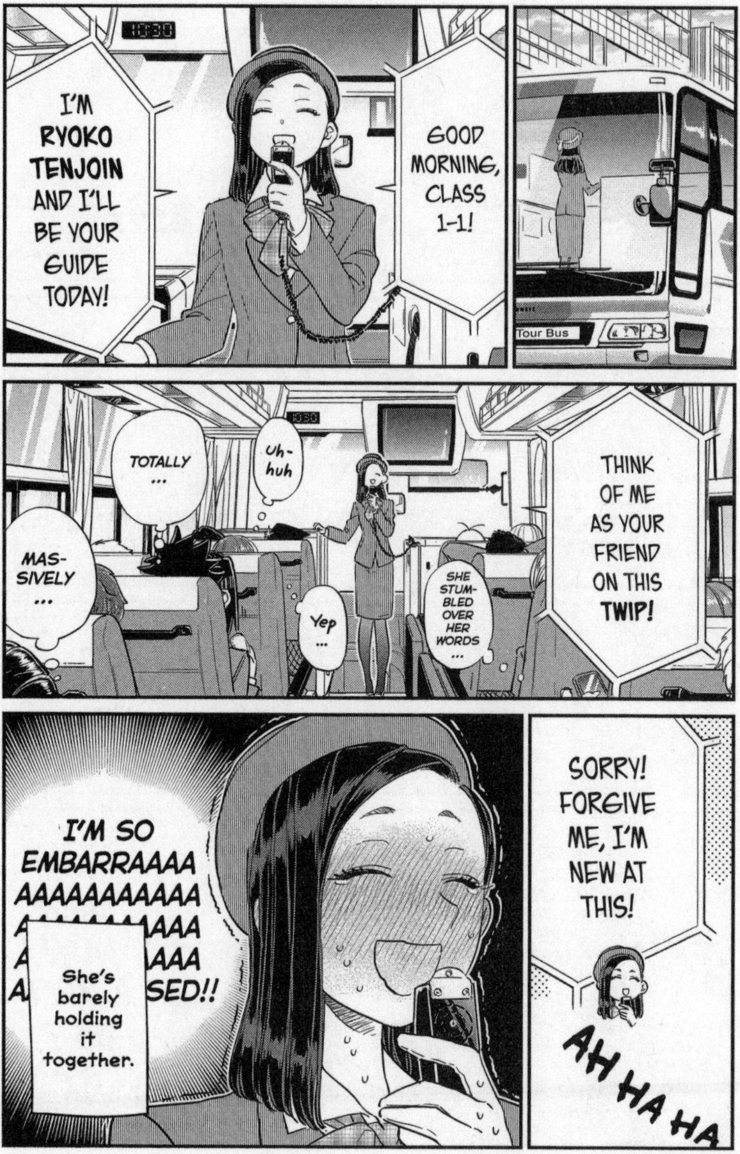
GOOD MORNING, CLASS 1-1!
I'M RYOKO TENJOIN AND I'LL BE YOUR GUIDE TODAY!
Tour Bus
THINK OF ME AS YOUR FRIEND ON THIS TWIP!
SHE STUMBLED OVER HER WORDS ...
Uh-huh
Yep ...
TOTALLY ...
MASSIVELY ...
SORRY! FORGIVE ME, I'M NEW AT THIS!
AH HA HA
I'M SO EMBARRAAAA AAAAAAAAAAA
SED!!
She's barely holding it together.

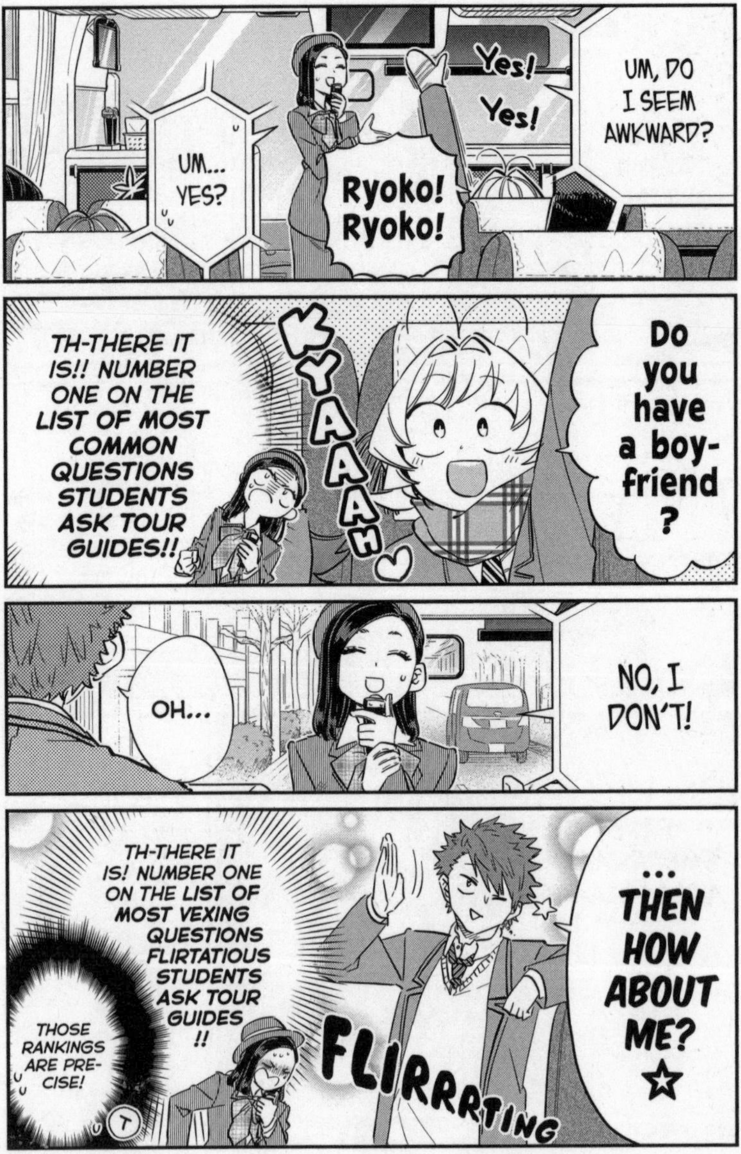
UM, DO I SEEM AWKWARD?
Yes!
Yes!
Ryoko! Ryoko!
UM... YES?
Do you have a boy-friend?
KYAAAAH
TH-THERE IT IS!! NUMBER ONE ON THE LIST OF MOST COMMON QUESTIONS STUDENTS ASK TOUR GUIDES!!
NO, I DON'T!
OH...
...THEN HOW ABOUT ME? ☆
FLIRRRTING
TH-THERE IT IS! NUMBER ONE ON THE LIST OF MOST VEXING QUESTIONS FLIRTATIOUS STUDENTS ASK TOUR GUIDES!!
THOSE RANKINGS ARE PRE-CISE!

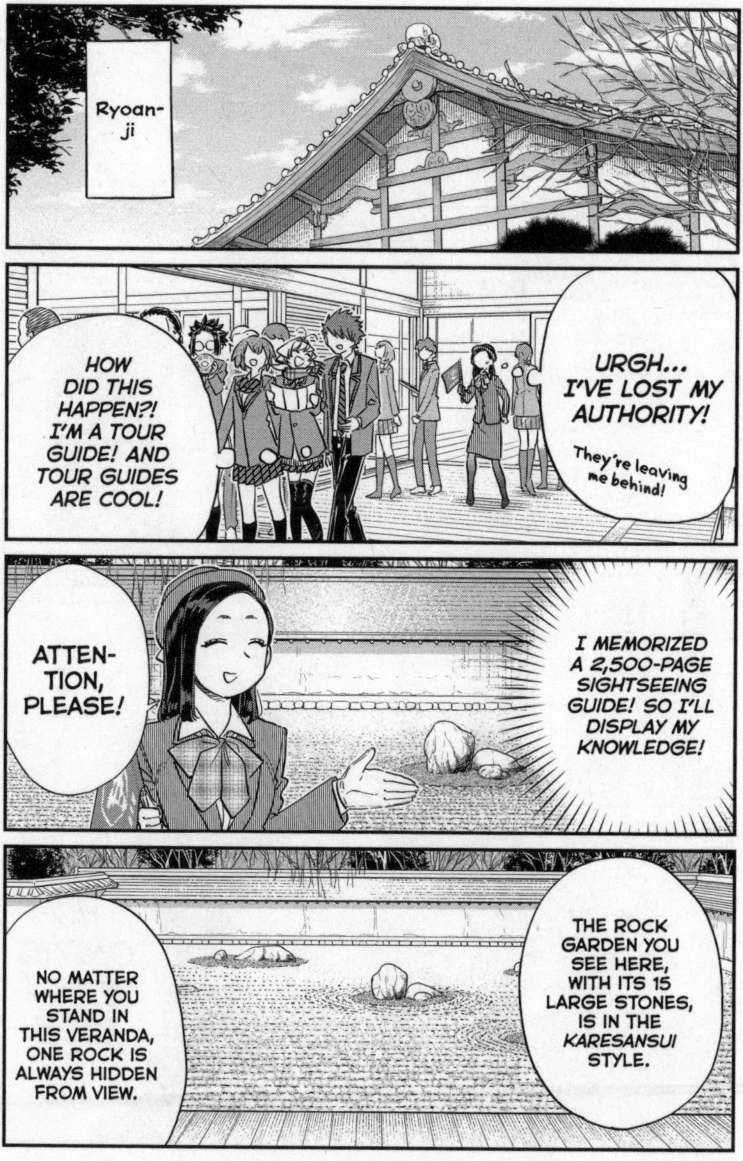
Ryoan-ji
URGH... I'VE LOST MY AUTHORITY!
They're leaving me behind!
HOW DID THIS HAPPEN?! I'M A TOUR GUIDE! AND TOUR GUIDES ARE COOL!
I MEMORIZED A 2,500-PAGE SIGHTSEEING GUIDE! SO I'LL DISPLAY MY KNOWLEDGE!
ATTEN-TION, PLEASE!
THE ROCK GARDEN YOU SEE HERE, WITH ITS 15 LARGE STONES, IS IN THE *KARESANSUI* STYLE.
NO MATTER WHERE YOU STAND IN THIS VERANDA, ONE ROCK IS ALWAYS HIDDEN FROM VIEW.

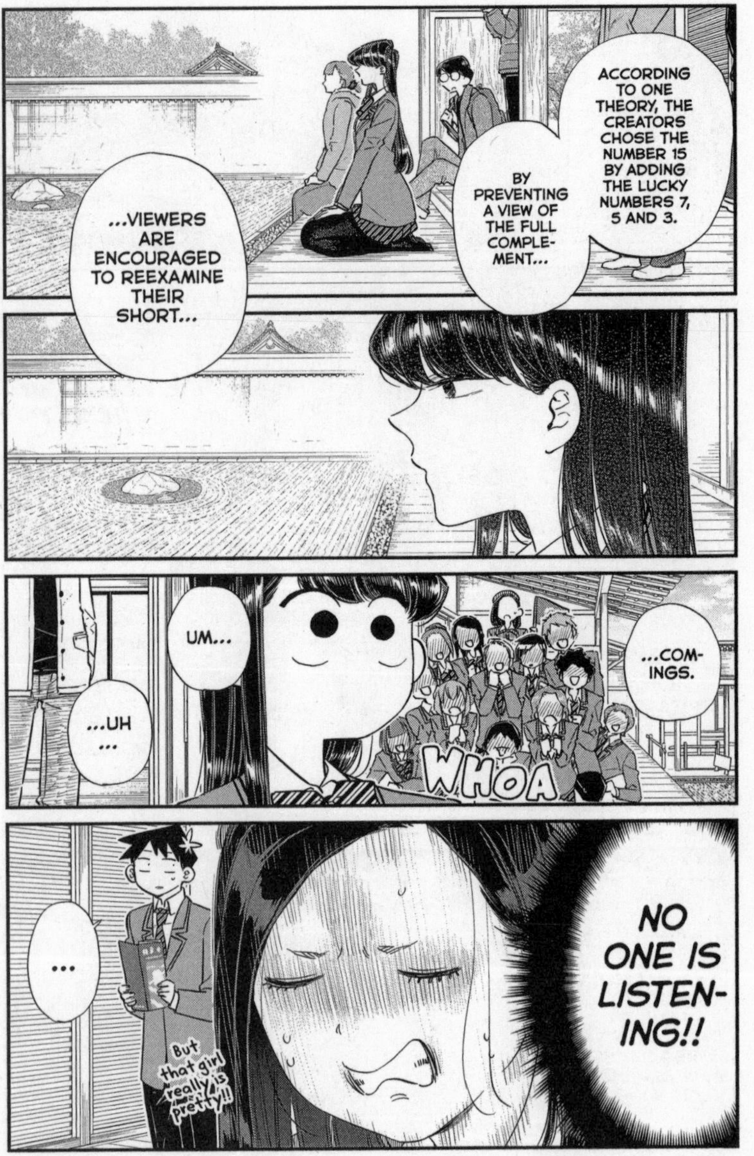
ACCORDING TO ONE THEORY, THE CREATORS CHOSE THE NUMBER 15 BY ADDING THE LUCKY NUMBERS 7, 5 AND 3.
BY PREVENTING A VIEW OF THE FULL COMPLEMENT...
...VIEWERS ARE ENCOURAGED TO REEXAMINE THEIR SHORT...
...COMINGS.
UM...
...UH ...
WHOA
NO ONE IS LISTENING!!
...
But that girl really is pretty!!

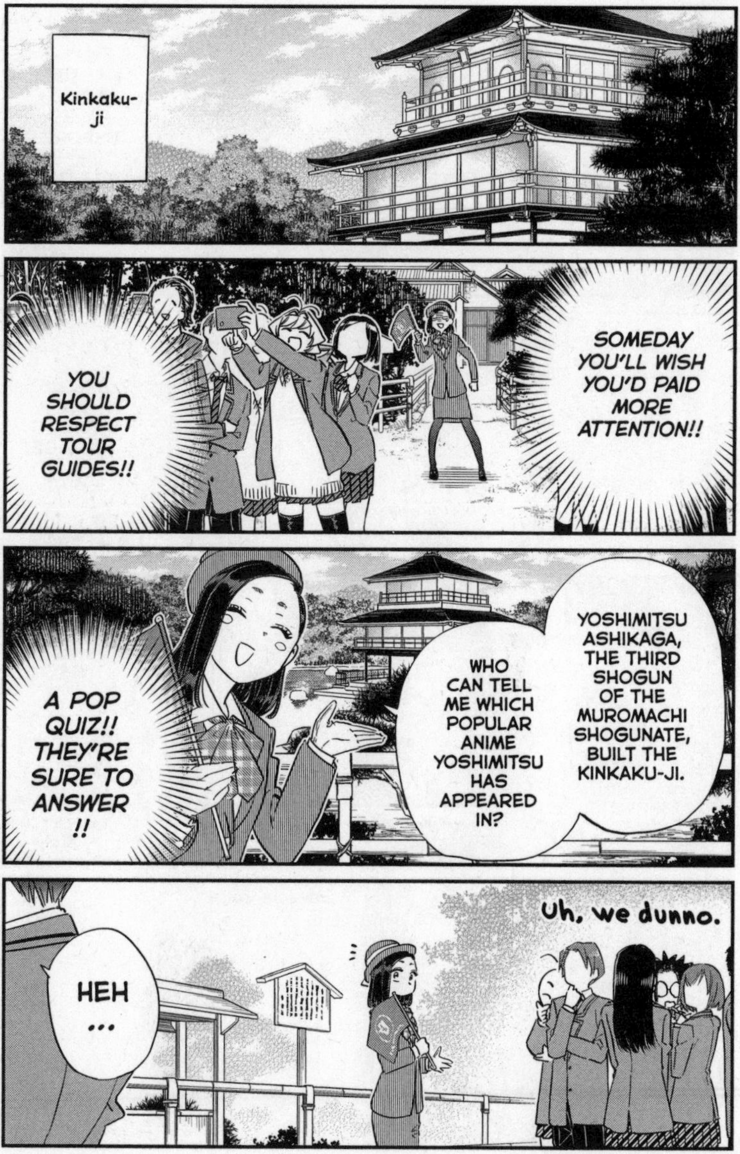
Kinkaku-ji
SOMEDAY YOU'LL WISH YOU'D PAID MORE ATTENTION!!
YOU SHOULD RESPECT TOUR GUIDES!!
YOSHIMITSU ASHIKAGA, THE THIRD SHOGUN OF THE MUROMACHI SHOGUNATE, BUILT THE KINKAKU-JI.
WHO CAN TELL ME WHICH POPULAR ANIME YOSHIMITSU HAS APPEARED IN?
A POP QUIZ!! THEY'RE SURE TO ANSWER !!
Uh, we dunno.
HEH ...

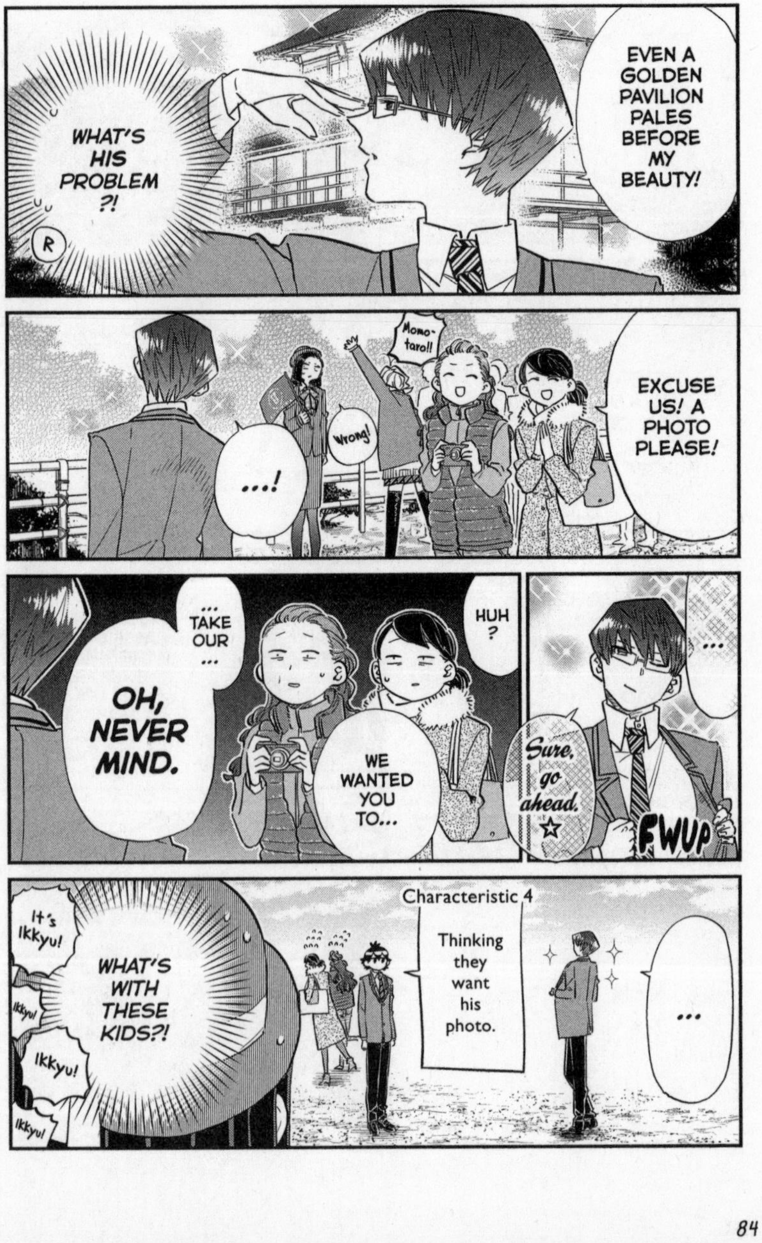
EVEN A GOLDEN PAVILION PALES BEFORE MY BEAUTY!
WHAT'S HIS PROBLEM ?!
R
EXCUSE US! A PHOTO PLEASE!
Momo-taro!!
Wrong!
...!
...
Sure, go ahead. ☆
FWUP
HUH ?
... TAKE OUR ...
WE WANTED YOU TO...
OH, NEVER MIND.
...
Characteristic 4
Thinking they want his photo.
It's Ikkyu!
WHAT'S WITH THESE KIDS?!
Ikkyu!
Ikkyu!
Ikkyu!

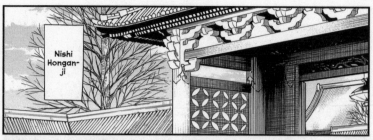

Nishi Hongan-ji
THIS IS THE HEAD TEMPLE OF THE JODO SHINSHU HONGAN-JI SECT OF BUDDHISM. IT WAS CONSTRUCTED AROUND THE MAUSOLEUM FOR THE MONK KNOWN AS SHINRAN.
INSIDE IS THE HIUNKAKU, A NATIONAL TREASURE. ALONG WITH THE KINKAKU AND GINKAKU, IT IS ONE OF KYOTO'S THREE GREAT PAVILIONS.
BLUUUUUUUUH
NO INTEREST ?!
They'll never get into college!
LOOK, KOMI! THEY WERE SELLING THIS STUFF!
TADAAAAH
Complete Shin-sengumi costume
That's extra luggage!
SHE ALREADY BOUGHT A WOODEN SWORD ?!
Scary!

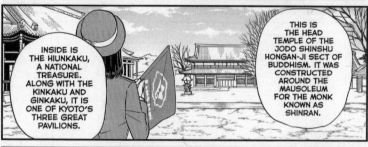

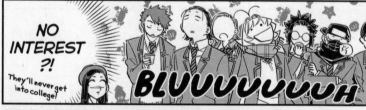

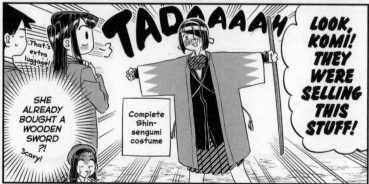

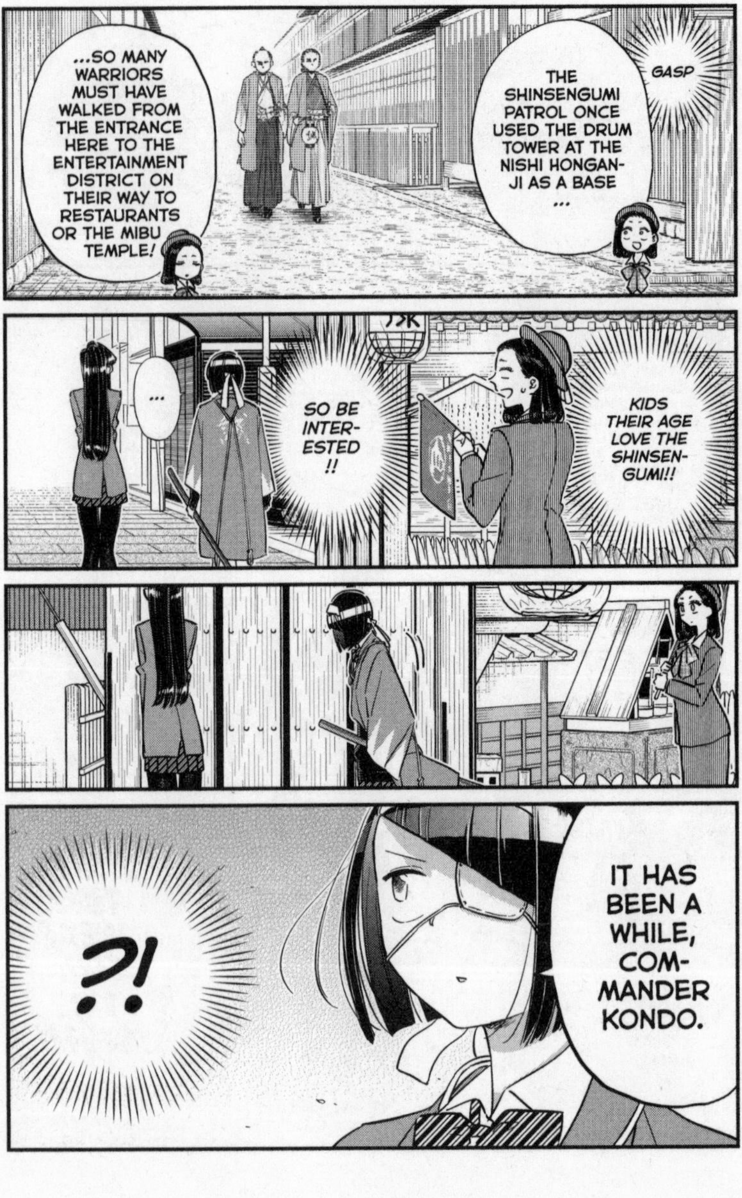
GASP
THE SHINSENGUMI PATROL ONCE USED THE DRUM TOWER AT THE NISHI HONGAN-JI AS A BASE ...
...SO MANY WARRIORS MUST HAVE WALKED FROM THE ENTRANCE HERE TO THE ENTERTAINMENT DISTRICT ON THEIR WAY TO RESTAURANTS OR THE MIBU TEMPLE!
KIDS THEIR AGE LOVE THE SHINSEN-GUMI!!
SO BE INTER-ESTED !!
...
IT HAS BEEN A WHILE, COM-MANDER KONDO.
?!

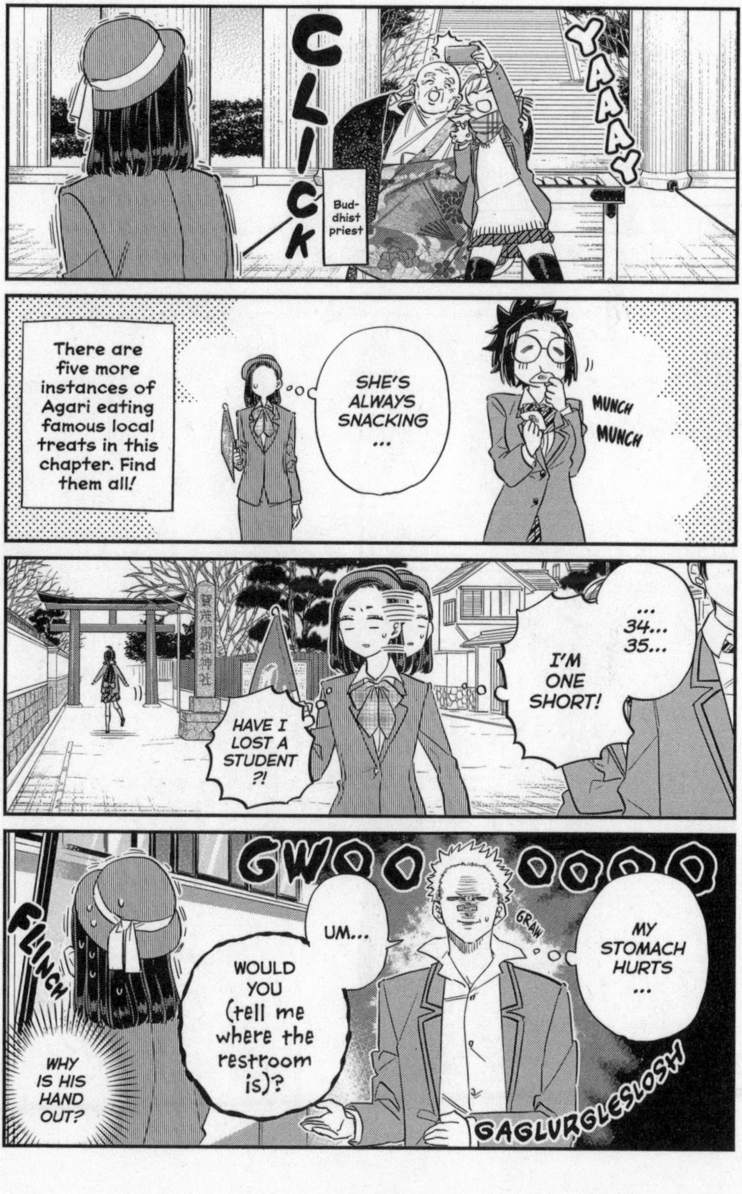
YAAAAY
CLICK
Bud-dhist priest
MUNCH
MUNCH
SHE'S ALWAYS SNACKING ...
There are five more instances of Agari eating famous local treats in this chapter. Find them all!
... 34... 35...
I'M ONE SHORT!
HAVE I LOST A STUDENT ?!
GWOOOOOO
MY STOMACH HURTS ...
GRAW
GAGLURGLESLOSH
UM...
WOULD YOU (tell me where the restroom is)?
FLINCH
WHY IS HIS HAND OUT?

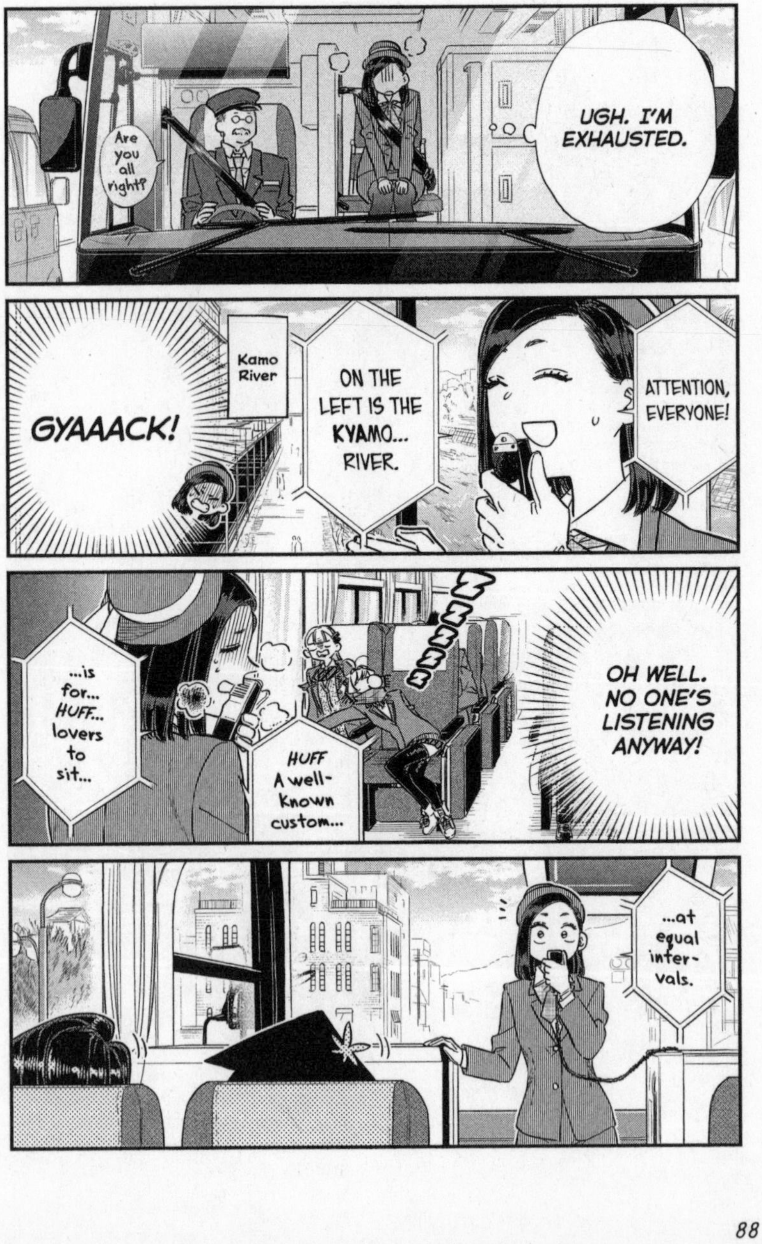
UGH. I'M EXHAUSTED.
Are you all right?
ATTENTION, EVERYONE!
ON THE LEFT IS THE KYAMO... RIVER.
Kamo River
GYAAACK!
OH WELL. NO ONE'S LISTENING ANYWAY!
HUFF A well-known custom...
...is for... HUFF... lovers to sit...
...at equal inter-vals.

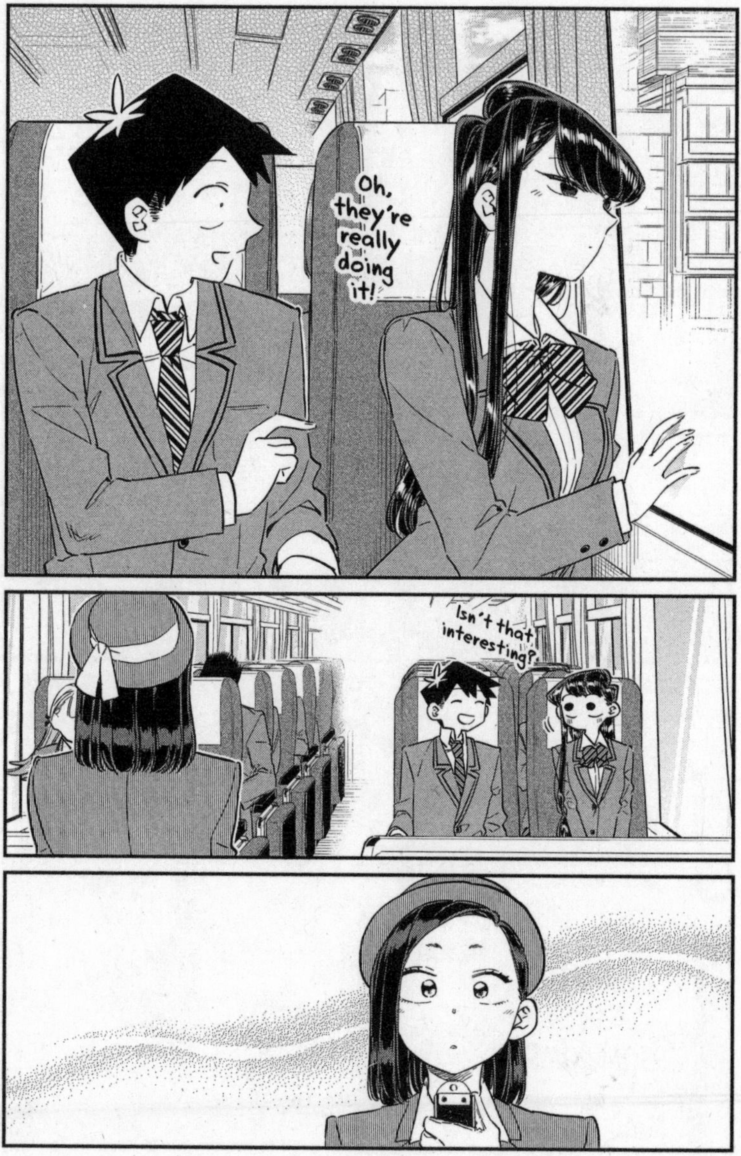
Oh, they're really doing it!
Isn't that interesting?

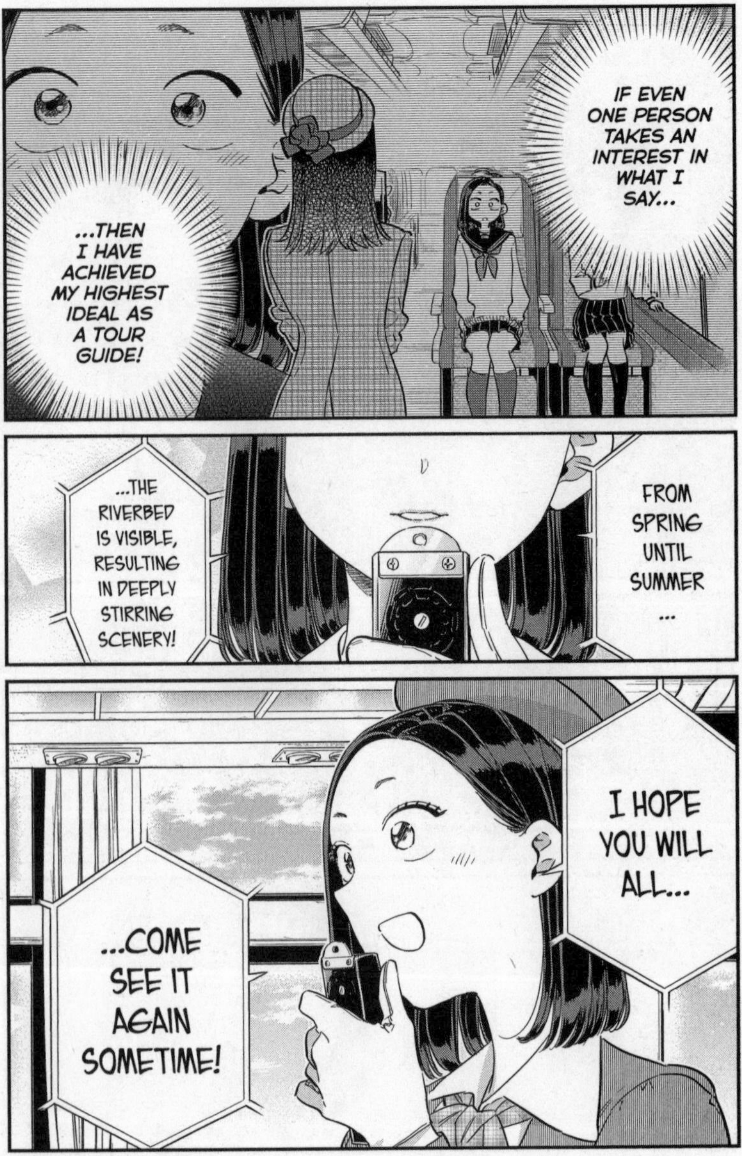
IF EVEN ONE PERSON TAKES AN INTEREST IN WHAT I SAY...
...THEN I HAVE ACHIEVED MY HIGHEST IDEAL AS A TOUR GUIDE!
FROM SPRING UNTIL SUMMER ...
...THE RIVERBED IS VISIBLE, RESULTING IN DEEPLY STIRRING SCENERY!
I HOPE YOU WILL ALL...
...COME SEE IT AGAIN SOMETIME!

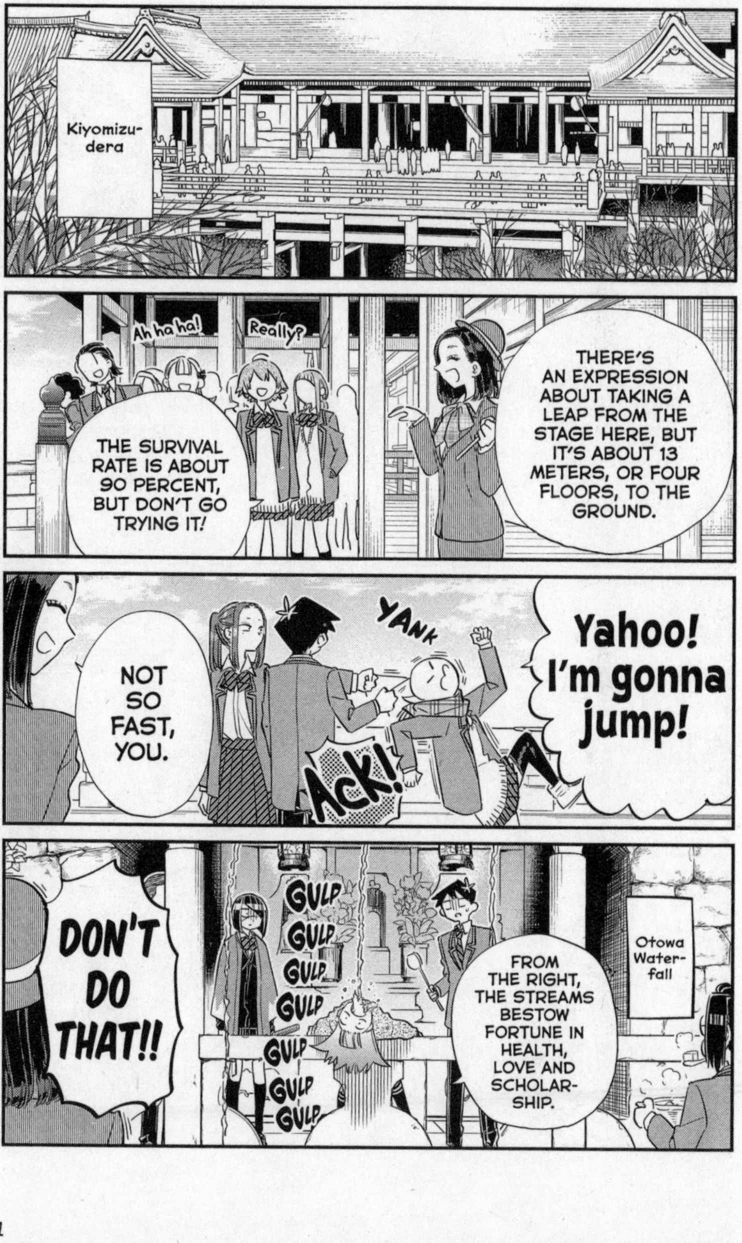
Kiyomizu-dera
THERE'S AN EXPRESSION ABOUT TAKING A LEAP FROM THE STAGE HERE, BUT IT'S ABOUT 13 METERS, OR FOUR FLOORS, TO THE GROUND.
Really?
Ah ha ha!
THE SURVIVAL RATE IS ABOUT 90 PERCENT, BUT DON'T GO TRYING IT!
Yahoo! I'm gonna jump!
YANK
NOT SO FAST, YOU.
ACK!
Otowa Waterfall
FROM THE RIGHT, THE STREAMS BESTOW FORTUNE IN HEALTH, LOVE AND SCHOLARSHIP.
GULP GULP GULP GULP GULP GULP GULP
DON'T DO THAT!!

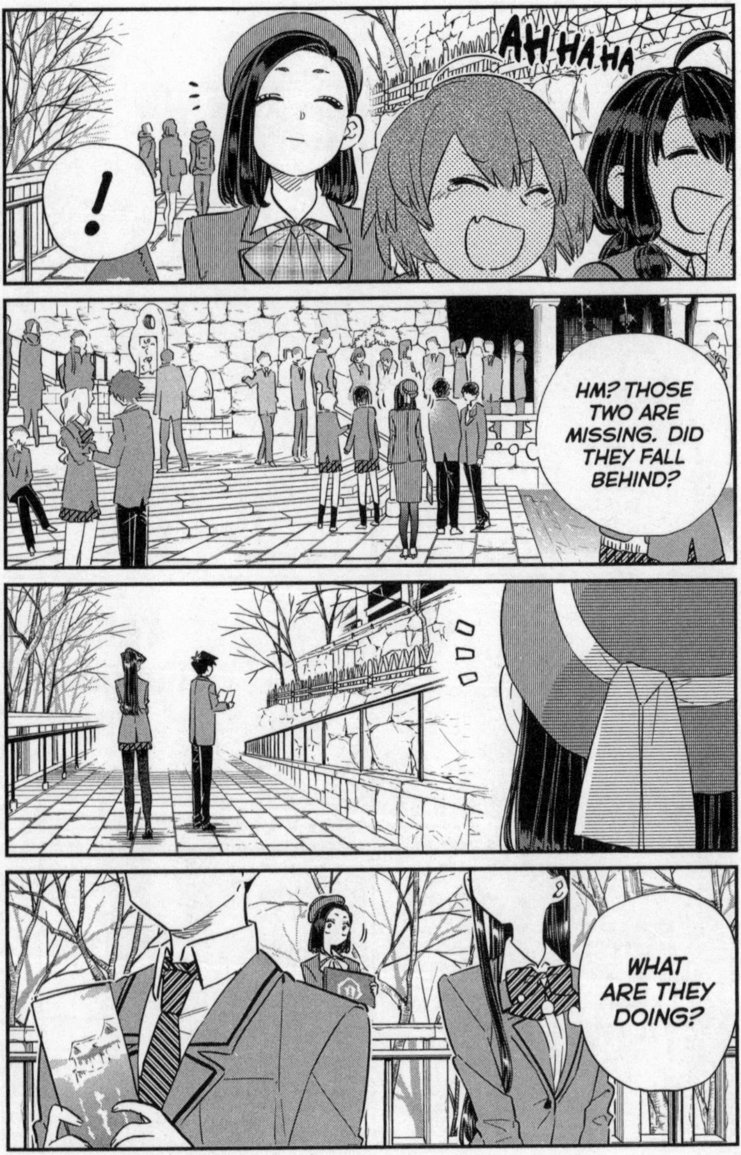
AH HA HA
!
HM? THOSE TWO ARE MISSING. DID THEY FALL BEHIND?
WHAT ARE THEY DOING?

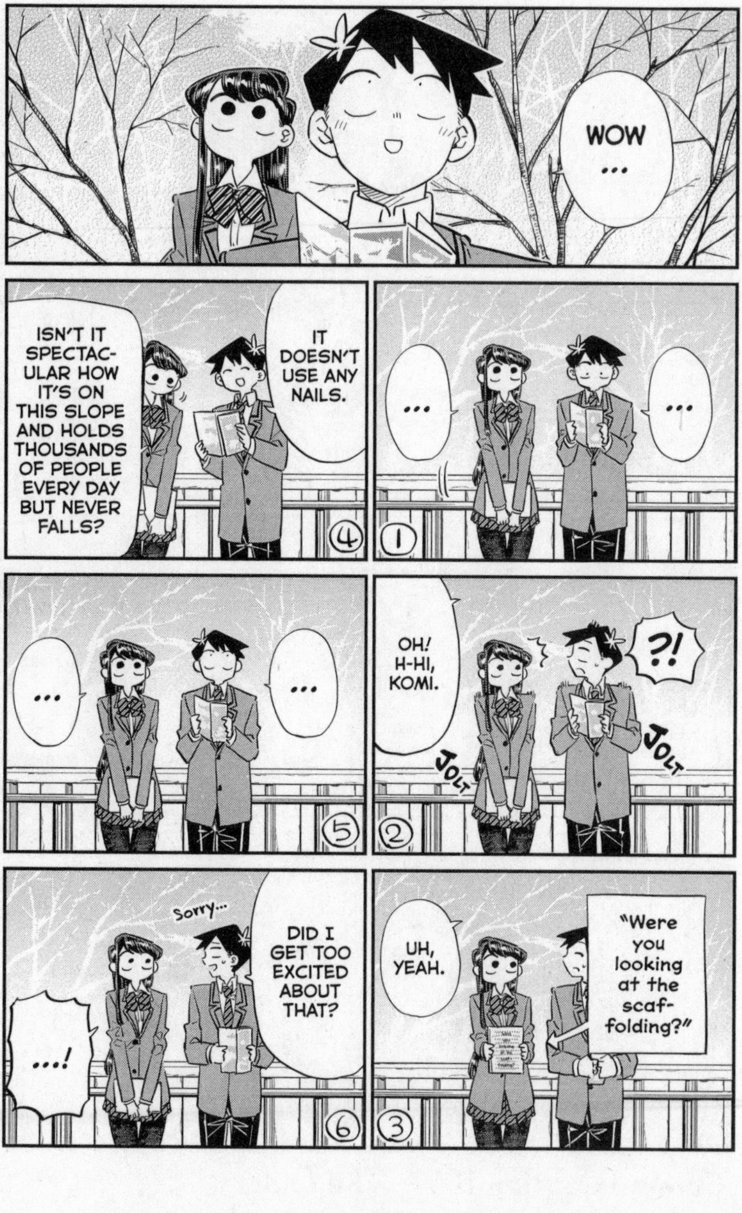

WOW ...
...
...
?!
OH! H-HI, KOMI.
JOLT
JOLT
"Were you looking at the scaf-folding?"
UH, YEAH.
IT DOESN'T USE ANY NAILS.
ISN'T IT SPECTAC-ULAR HOW IT'S ON THIS SLOPE AND HOLDS THOUSANDS OF PEOPLE EVERY DAY BUT NEVER FALLS?
...
...
DID I GET TOO EXCITED ABOUT THAT?
Sorry...
...!

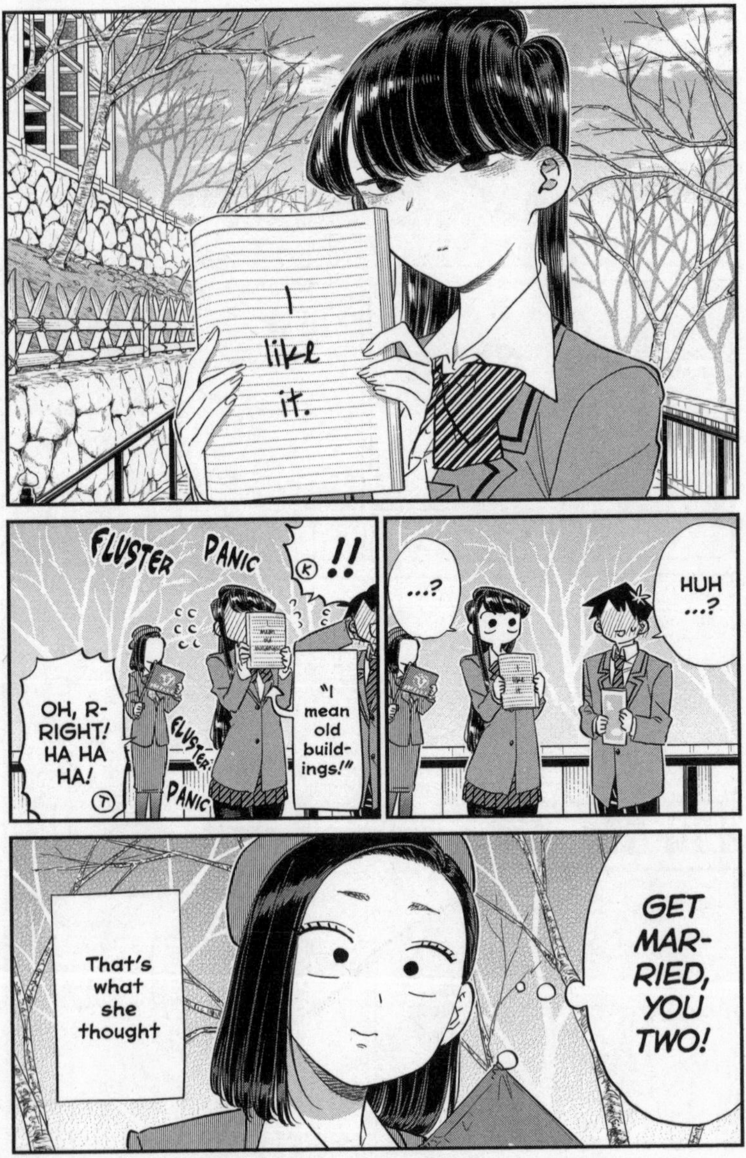
I like it.
HUH ...?
...?
!!
PANIC
FLUSTER
"I mean old buildings!"
FLUSTER
PANIC
OH, R-RIGHT! HA HA HA!
GET MAR-RIED, YOU TWO!
That's what she thought

Communication 105 – The End

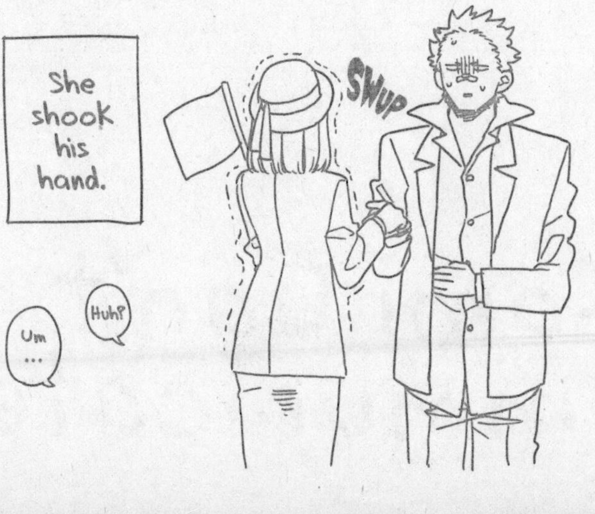
SWUP
She shook his hand.
Huh?
Um...

Komi Can't
Communicate

Komi Can't Communicate

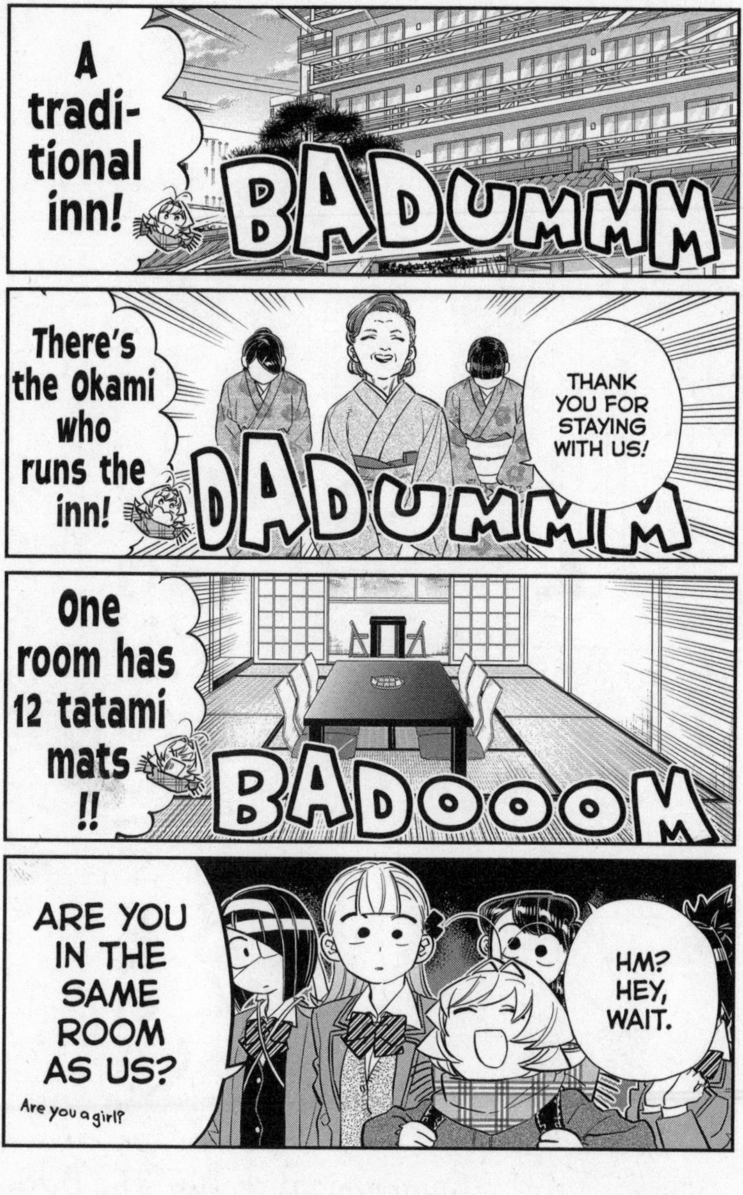
A traditional inn!
BADUMMM
THANK YOU FOR STAYING WITH US!
There's the Okami who runs the inn!
DADUMMM
One room has 12 tatami mats!!
BADOOOM
HM? HEY, WAIT.
ARE YOU IN THE SAME ROOM AS US?
Are you a girl?

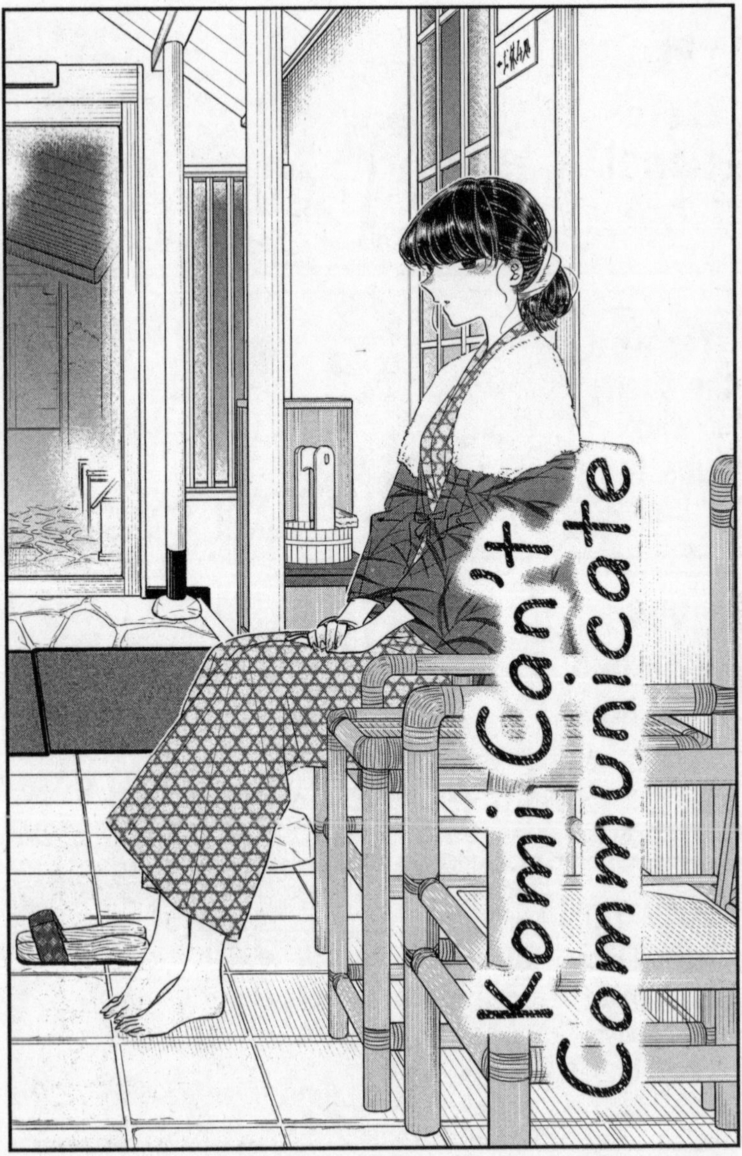
Komi Can't Communicate

Communication 106: The Bath

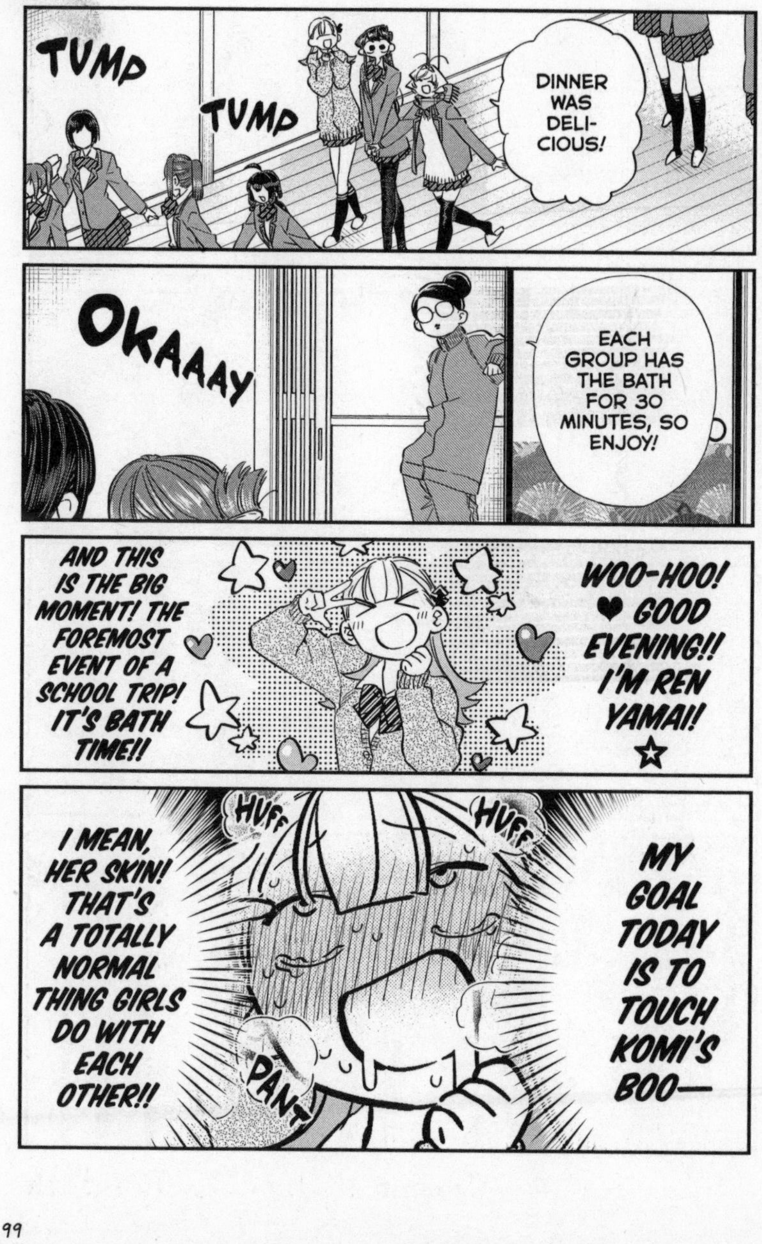
DINNER WAS DELICIOUS!
TUMP
TUMP
EACH GROUP HAS THE BATH FOR 30 MINUTES, SO ENJOY!
OKAAAY
WOO-HOO! ❤ GOOD EVENING!! I'M REN YAMAI! ☆
AND THIS IS THE BIG MOMENT! THE FOREMOST EVENT OF A SCHOOL TRIP! IT'S BATH TIME!!
MY GOAL TODAY IS TO TOUCH KOMI'S BOO—
HUFF
HUFF
I MEAN, HER SKIN! THAT'S A TOTALLY NORMAL THING GIRLS DO WITH EACH OTHER!!
PANT

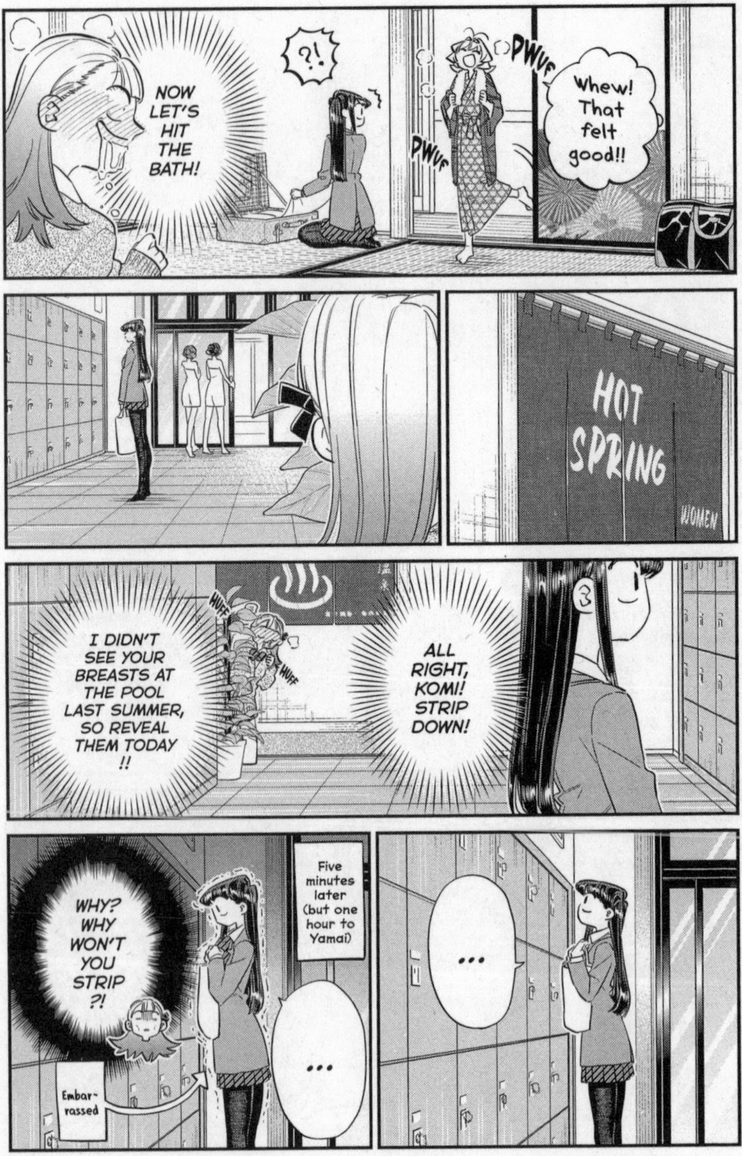
Whew! That felt good!!
PWUF
PWUF
?!
NOW LET'S HIT THE BATH!
HOT SPRING
WOMEN
ALL RIGHT, KOMI! STRIP DOWN!
HUFF
HUFF
I DIDN'T SEE YOUR BREASTS AT THE POOL LAST SUMMER, SO REVEAL THEM TODAY !!
...
Five minutes later (but one hour to Yamai)
...
WHY? WHY WON'T YOU STRIP ?!
Embar-rassed

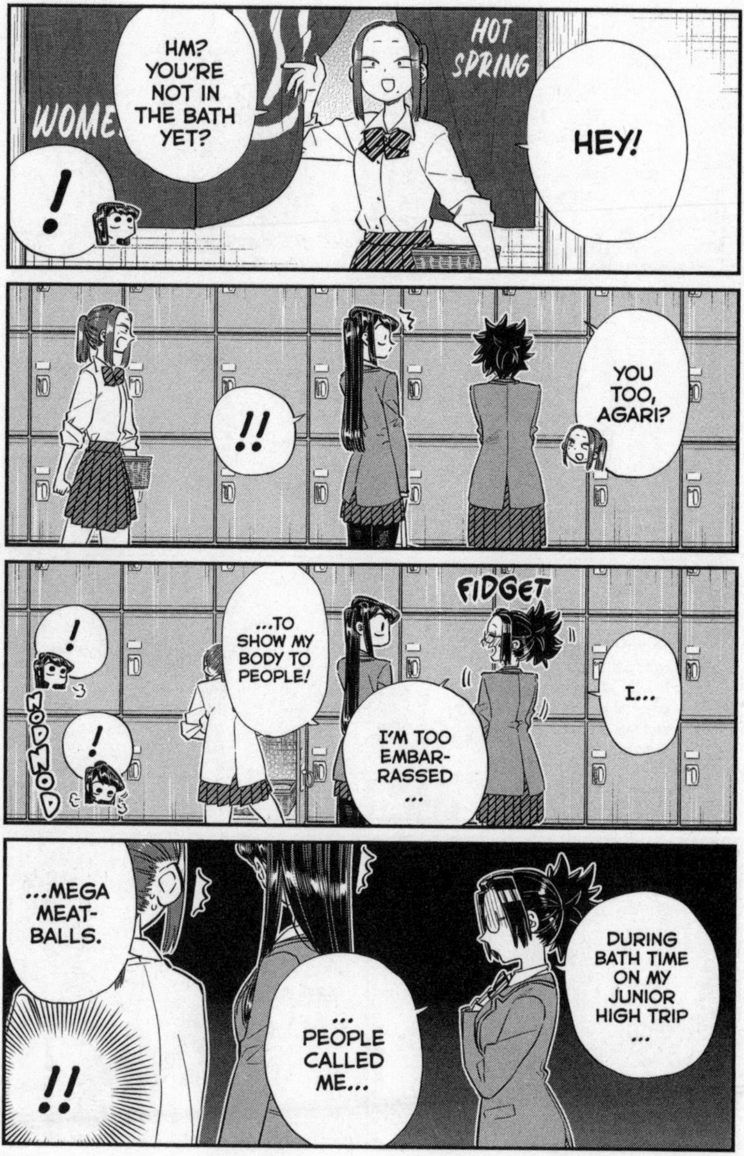
HOT SPRING
HEY!
HM? YOU'RE NOT IN THE BATH YET?
!
YOU TOO, AGARI?
!!
FIDGET
I...
I'M TOO EMBAR-RASSED ...
...TO SHOW MY BODY TO PEOPLE!
!
NODNOD
!
DURING BATH TIME ON MY JUNIOR HIGH TRIP ...
... PEOPLE CALLED ME...
...MEGA MEAT-BALLS.
!!

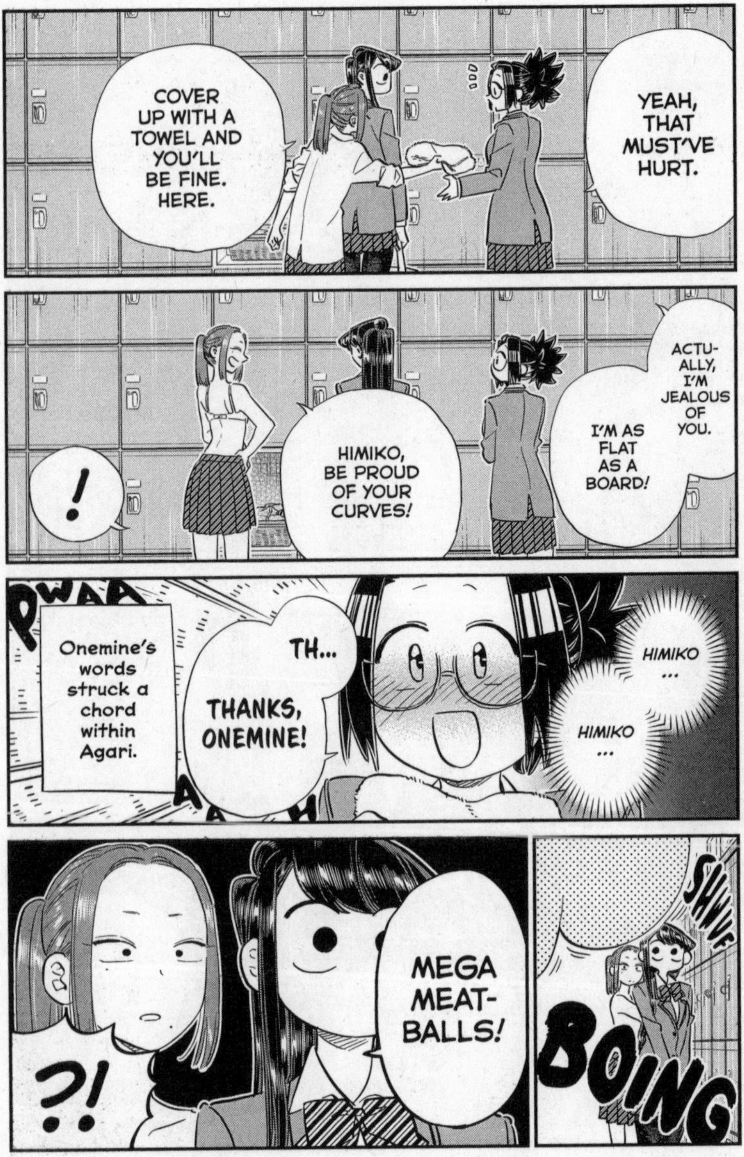
YEAH, THAT MUST'VE HURT.
COVER UP WITH A TOWEL AND YOU'LL BE FINE. HERE.
ACTU-ALLY, I'M JEALOUS OF YOU.
I'M AS FLAT AS A BOARD!
HIMIKO, BE PROUD OF YOUR CURVES!
!
HIMIKO...
HIMIKO...
TH...
THANKS, ONEMINE!
Onemine's words struck a chord within Agari.
PWAAAAH
SHWF
BOING
MEGA MEAT-BALLS!
?!

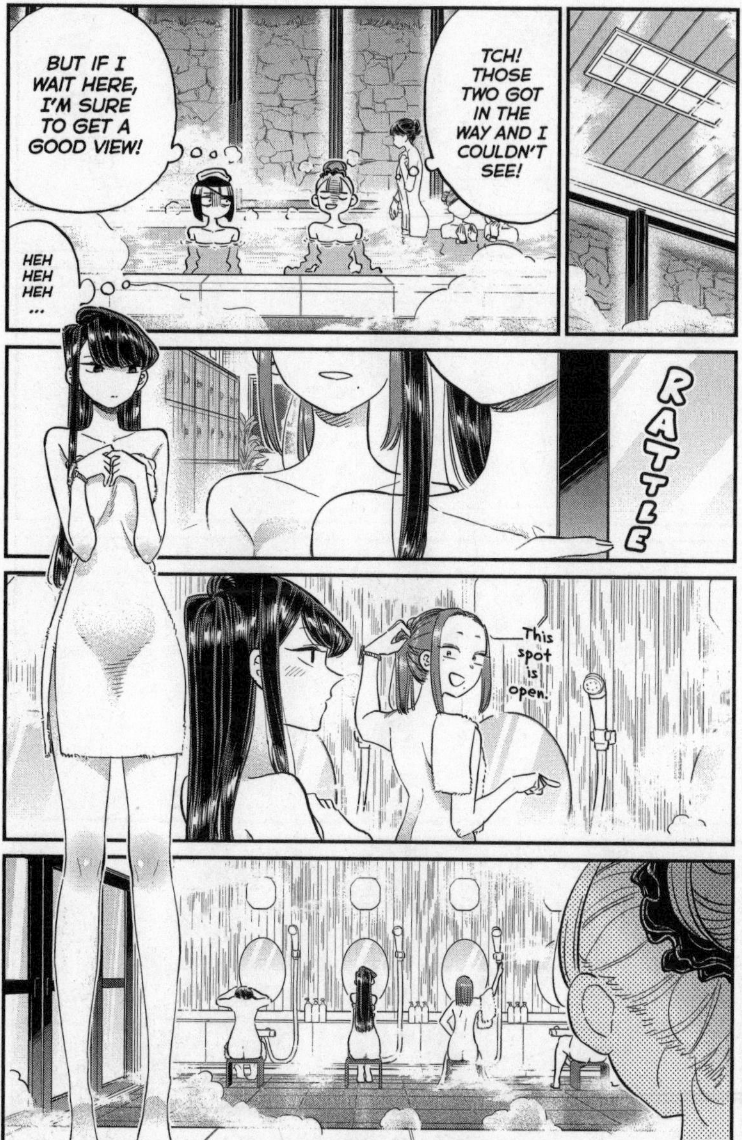
TCH! THOSE TWO GOT IN THE WAY AND I COULDN'T SEE!
BUT IF I WAIT HERE, I'M SURE TO GET A GOOD VIEW!
HEH HEH HEH ...
RATTLE
This spot is open.

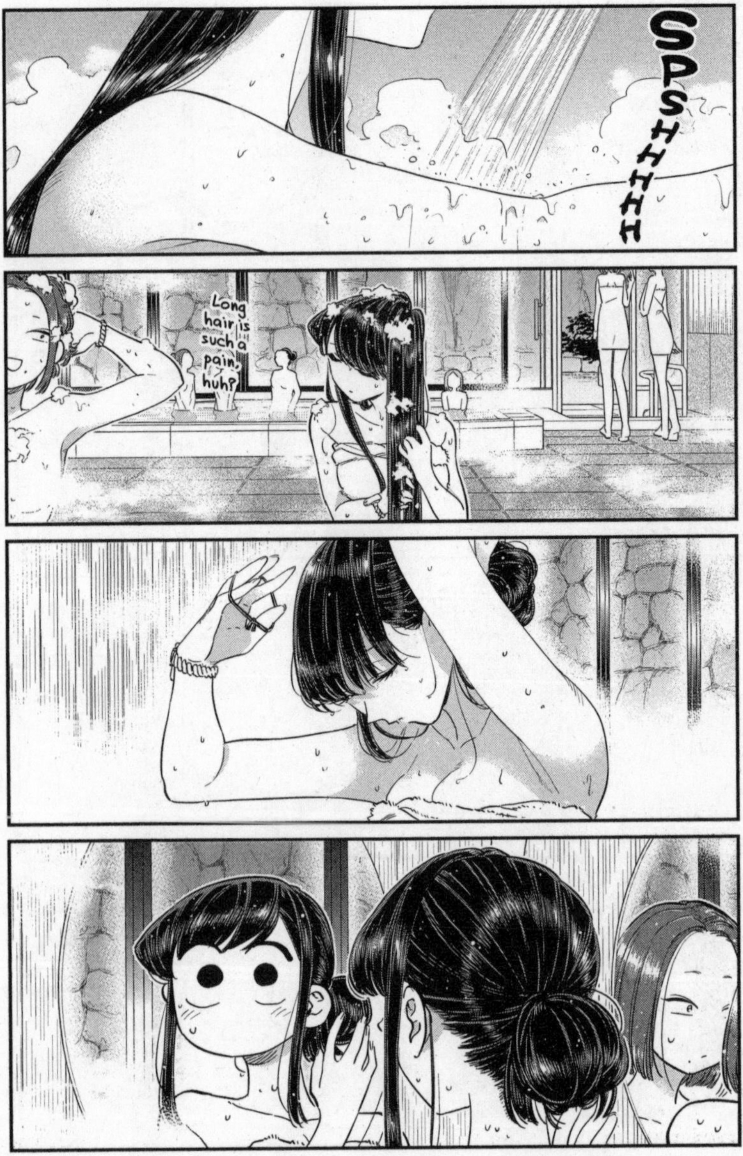
SPSHHHHHH
Long hair is such a pain, huh?

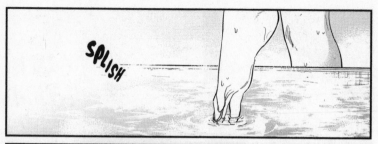

SPLISH

AHHH

KOMI, KOMI...

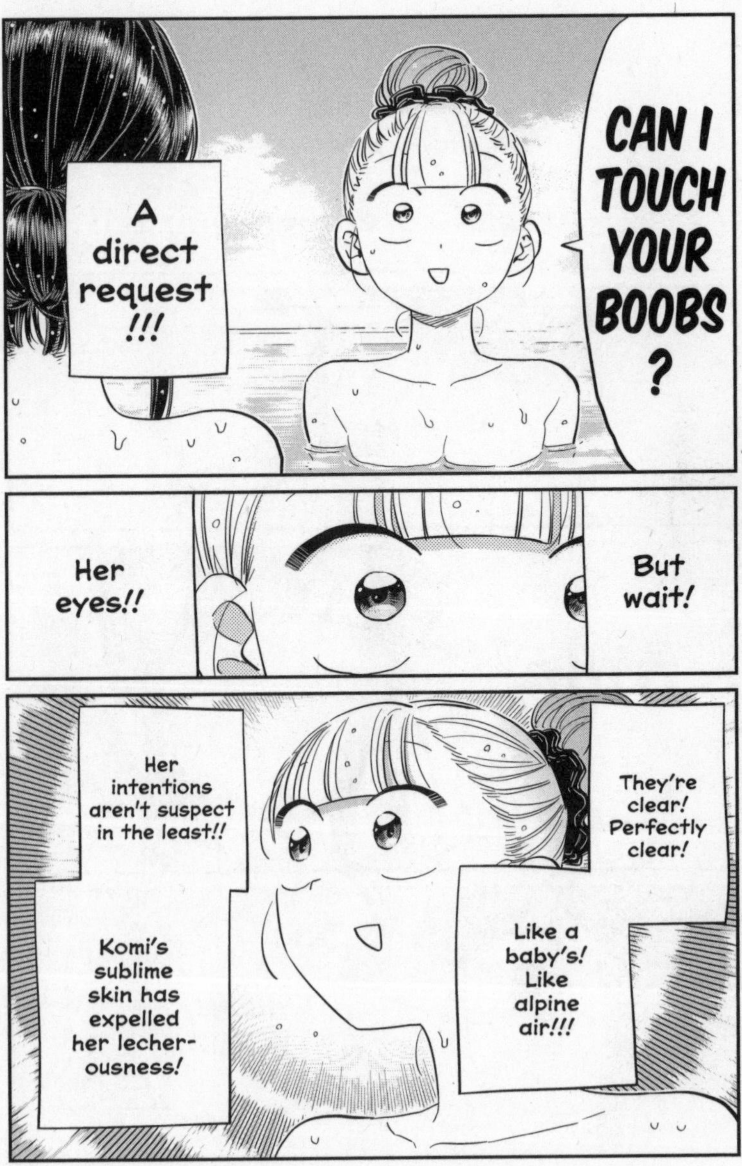
CAN I TOUCH YOUR BOOBS?
A direct request!!!
But wait!
Her eyes!!
They're clear! Perfectly clear!
Her intentions aren't suspect in the least!!
Like a baby's! Like alpine air!!!
Komi's sublime skin has expelled her lecher-ousness!

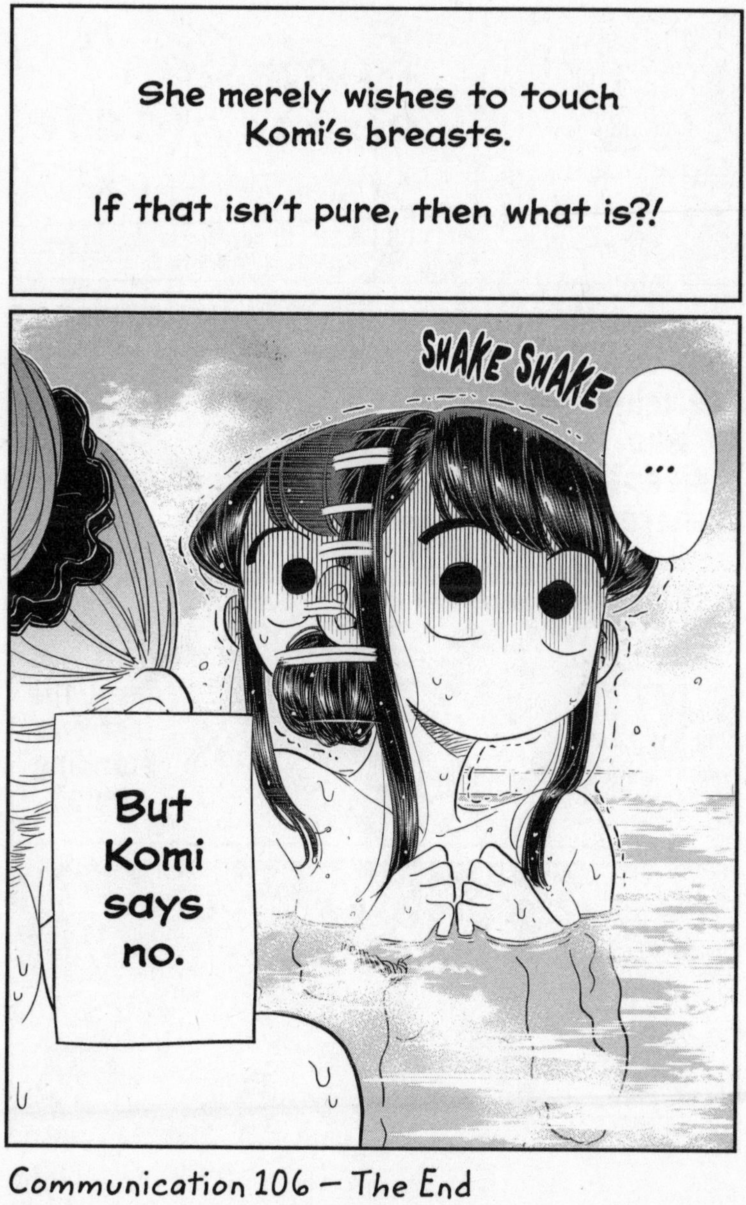
She merely wishes to touch Komi's breasts.
If that isn't pure, then what is?!
SHAKE SHAKE
...
But Komi says no.

Communication 106 – The End

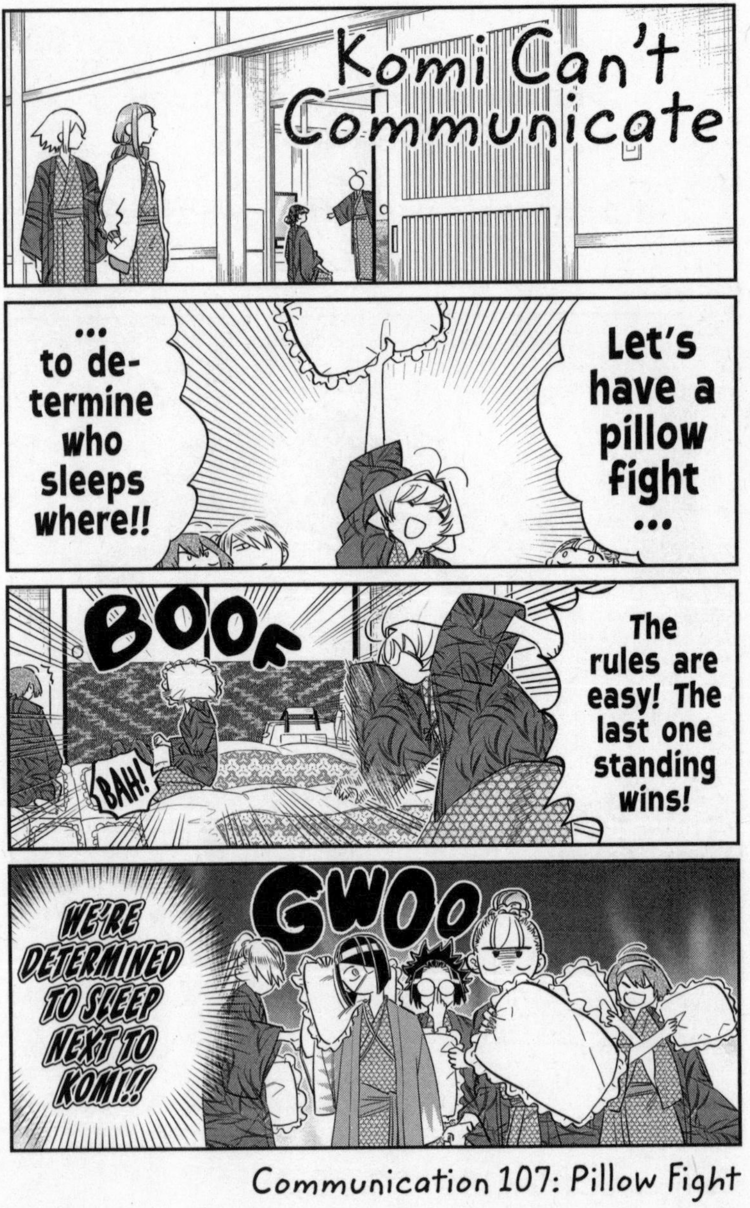
Komi Can't Communicate
Let's have a pillow fight ...
... to de-termine who sleeps where!!
The rules are easy! The last one standing wins!
BOOF
BAH!
GWOO
WE'RE DETERMINED TO SLEEP NEXT TO KOMI!!

Communication 107: Pillow Fight

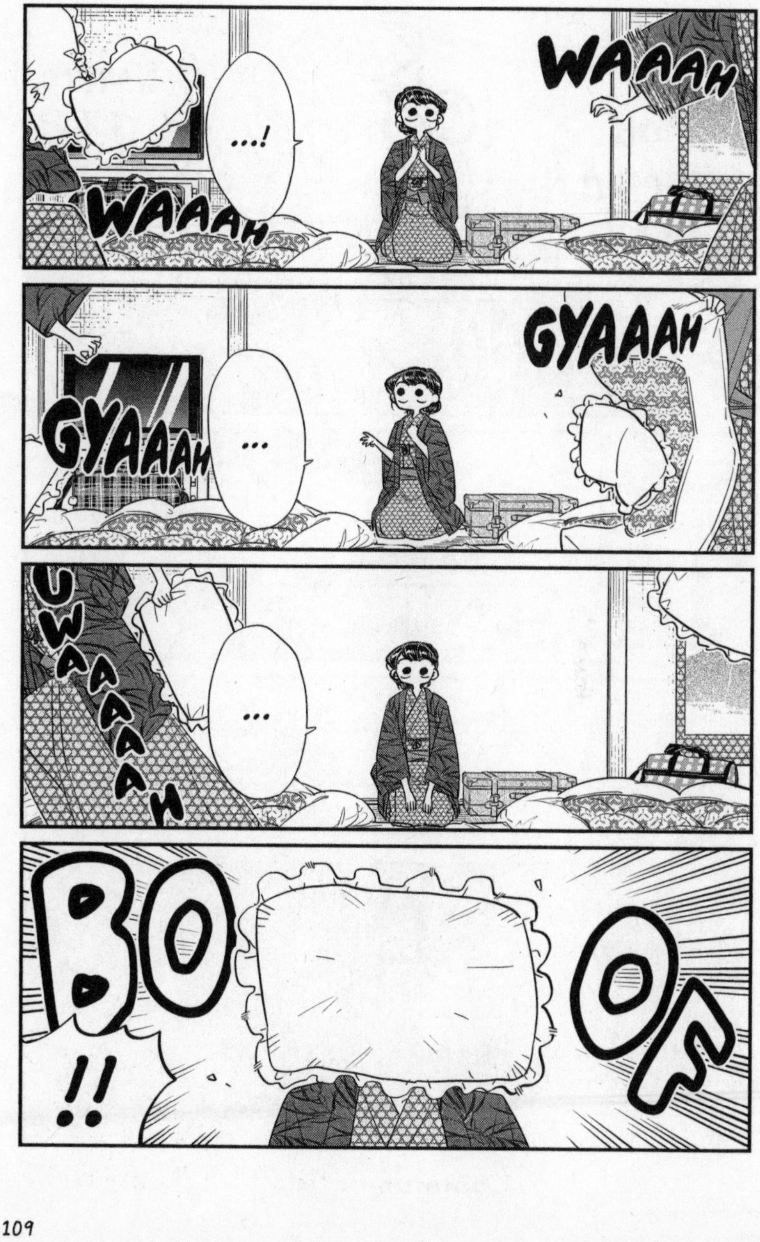
WAAAH
...!
WAAAH
GYAAAH
...
GYAAAH
...
UWAAAAAAH
BOOF!!

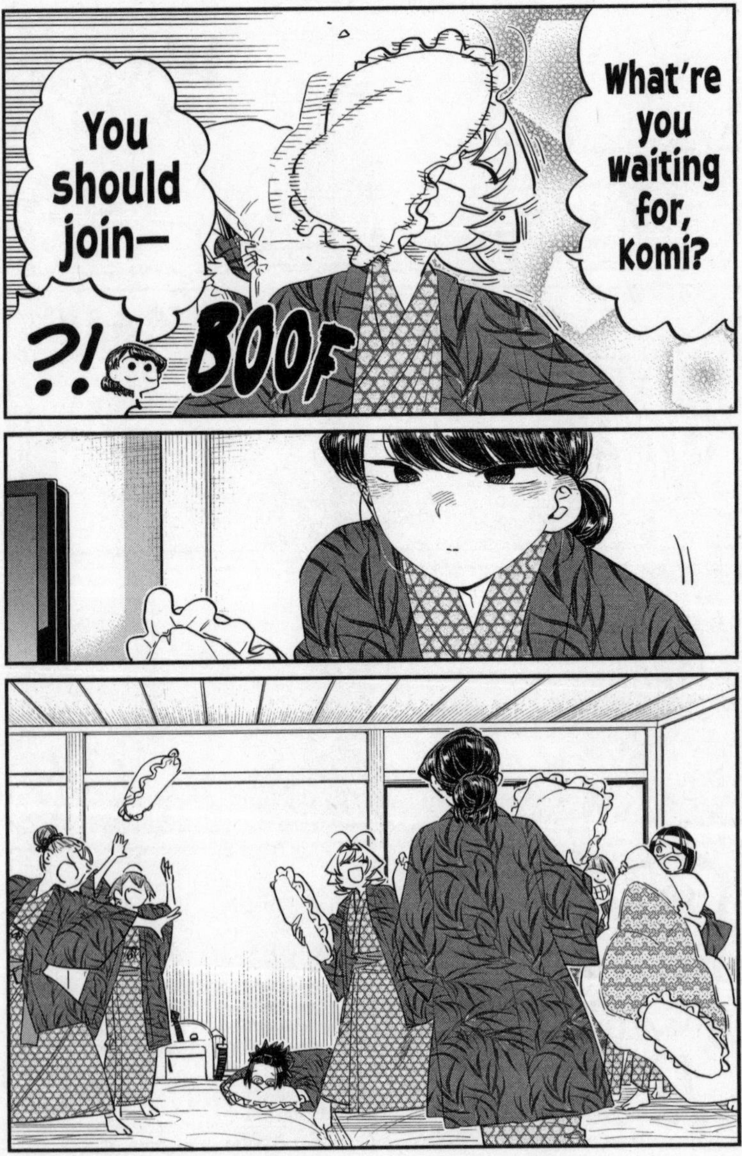
What're you waiting for, Komi?
You should join—
BOOF
?!

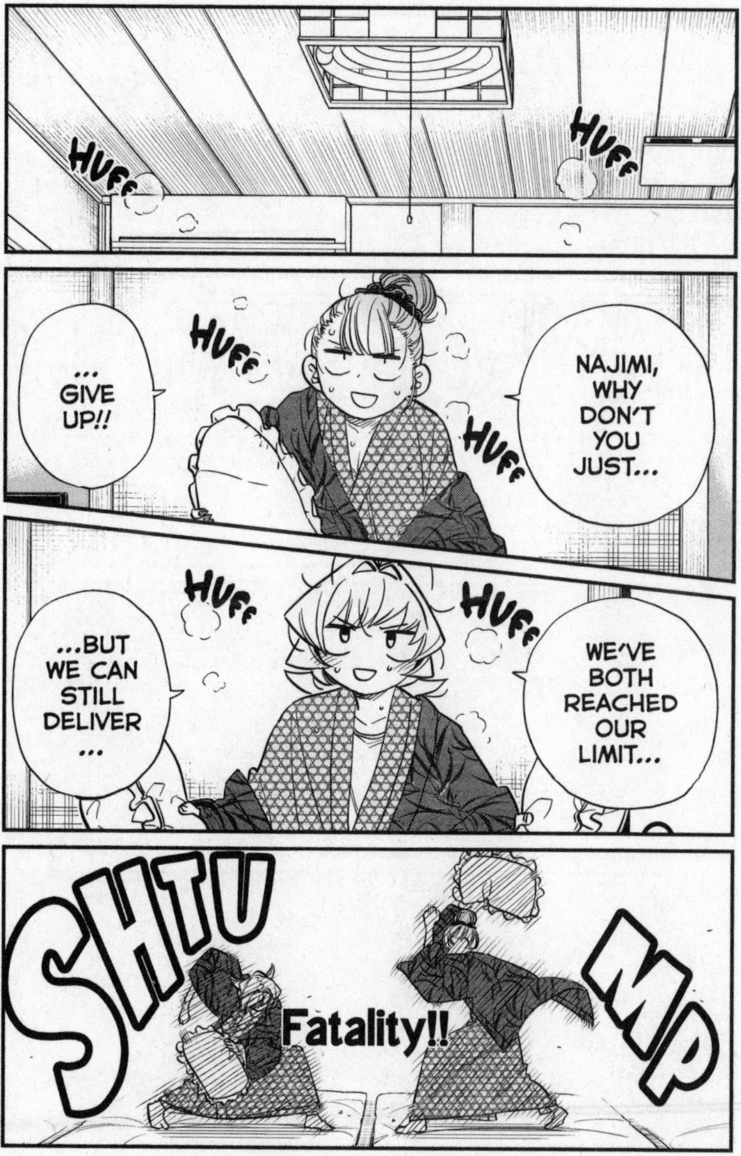

HUFF
HUFF
NAJIMI, WHY DON'T YOU JUST...
HUFF
HUFF
...GIVE UP!!
WE'VE BOTH REACHED OUR LIMIT...
HUFF
HUFF
...BUT WE CAN STILL DELIVER ...
SHTU
MP
Fatality!!

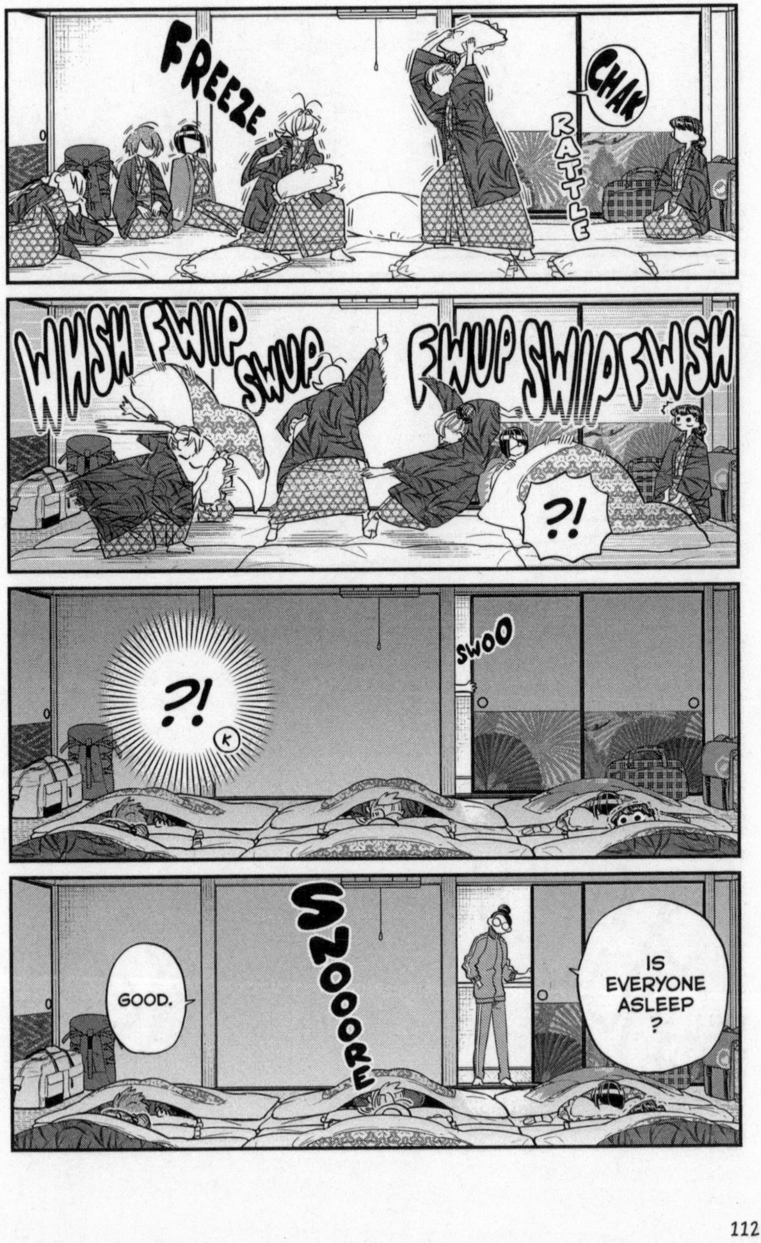
CHAK
RATTLE
FREEZE
FWSH
SWIP
FWUP
?!
SWUP
FWIP
WHSH
SWOO
?!
K
IS EVERYONE ASLEEP?
SNOOORE
GOOD.

...
ARE YOU ASLEEP, YAMAI?
OF COURSE NOT! HOW COULD I FALL ASLEEP THAT FAST?!
...
HEH ...
TEE-HEE ...
SHWAP
?!
JOLT

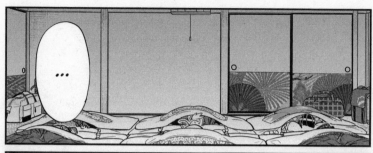

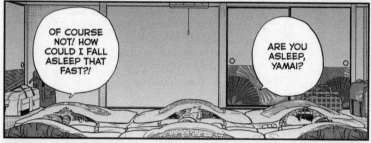

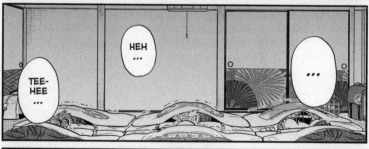

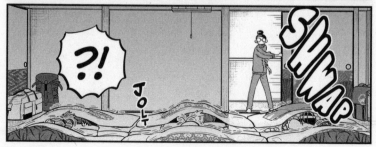

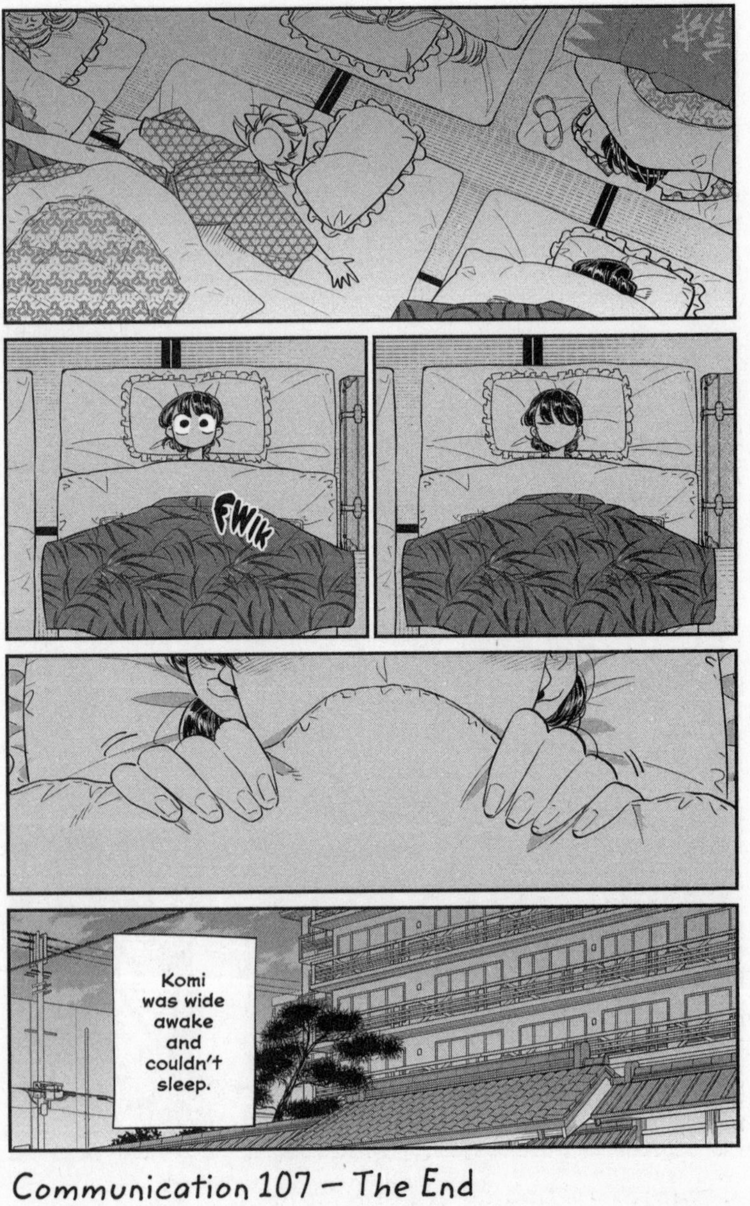
FWIK
Komi was wide awake and couldn't sleep.

Communication 107 – The End

Komi Can't Communicate

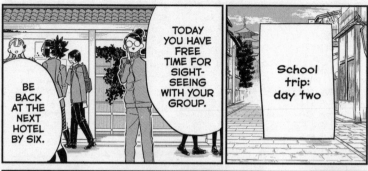

School trip: day two
TODAY YOU HAVE FREE TIME FOR SIGHT-SEEING WITH YOUR GROUP.
BE BACK AT THE NEXT HOTEL BY SIX.
KOMI!
Ayami Sasaki
Mikuni Kato
!
W-WELL, LET'S GO!
AWK
WARD
WILL THEY BE ALL RIGHT?

Communication 108: Free Time

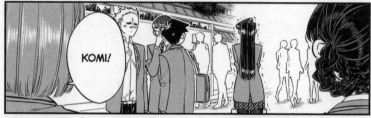

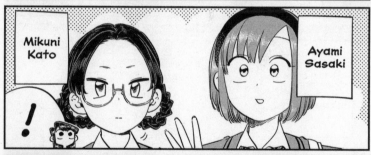

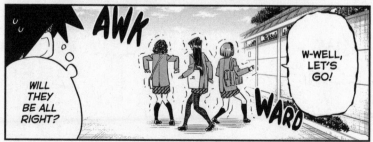

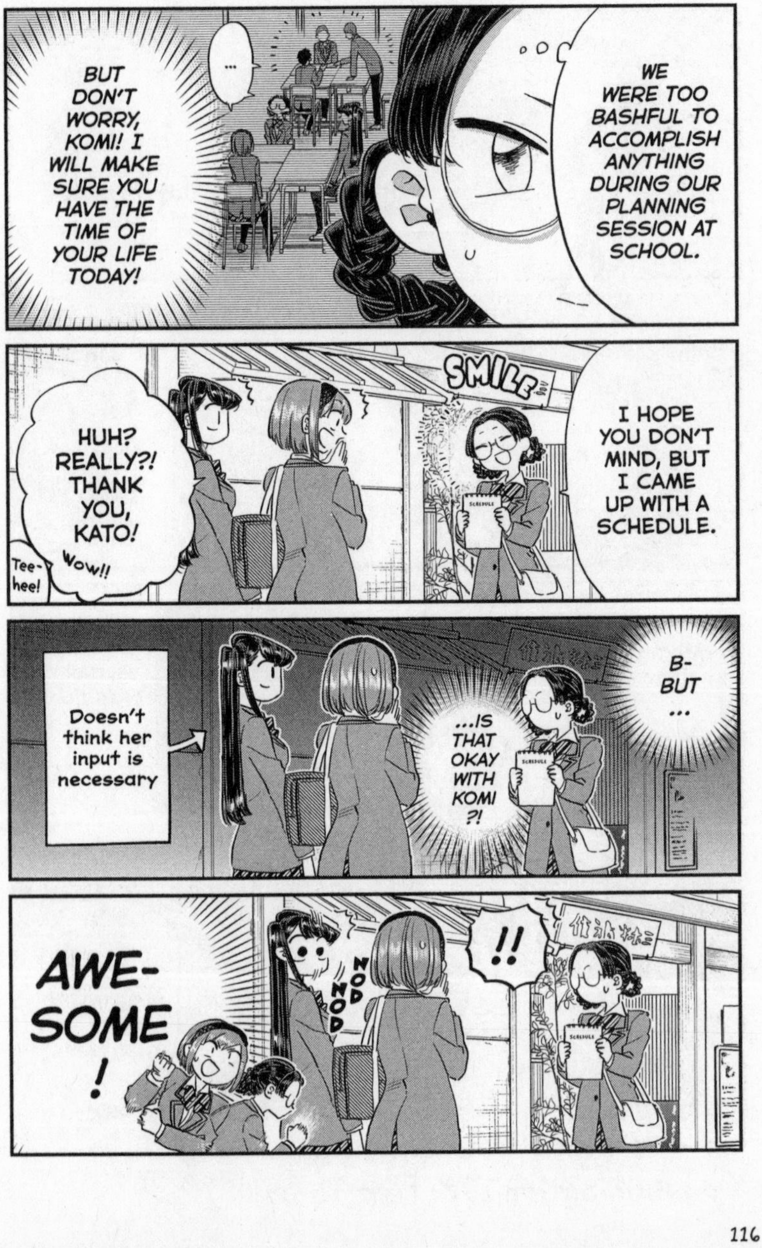
WE WERE TOO BASHFUL TO ACCOMPLISH ANYTHING DURING OUR PLANNING SESSION AT SCHOOL.
...
BUT DON'T WORRY, KOMI! I WILL MAKE SURE YOU HAVE THE TIME OF YOUR LIFE TODAY!
I HOPE YOU DON'T MIND, BUT I CAME UP WITH A SCHEDULE.
SMILE
SCHEDULE
HUH? REALLY?! THANK YOU, KATO!
Wow!!
Tee-hee!
B-BUT...
...IS THAT OKAY WITH KOMI?!
Doesn't think her input is necessary
!!
NOD NOD
AWESOME!

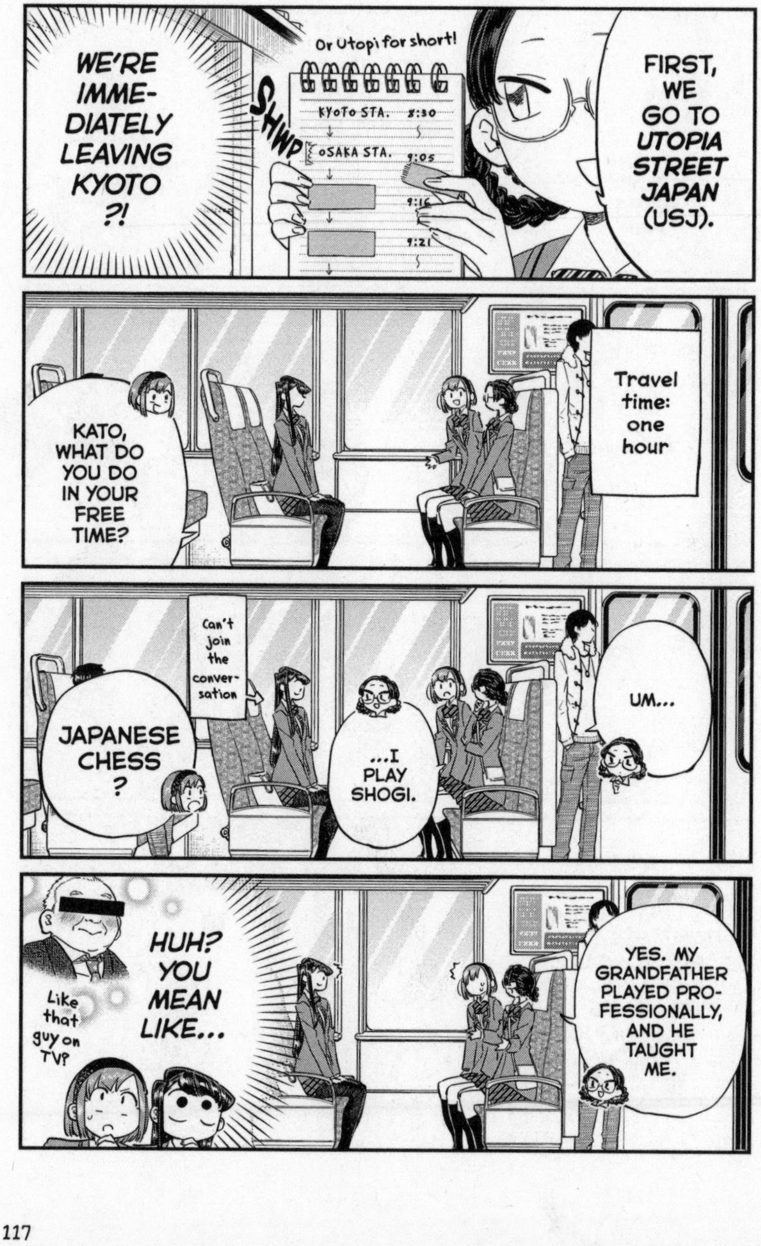
FIRST, WE GO TO UTOPIA STREET JAPAN (USJ).
Or Utopi for short!
KYOTO STA. 8:30
OSAKA STA. 9:05
9:16
9:21
SHWP
WE'RE IMMEDIATELY LEAVING KYOTO?!
Travel time: one hour
KATO, WHAT DO YOU DO IN YOUR FREE TIME?
UM...
...I PLAY SHOGI.
Can't join the conversation
JAPANESE CHESS?
YES. MY GRANDFATHER PLAYED PROFESSIONALLY, AND HE TAUGHT ME.
HUH? YOU MEAN LIKE...
Like that guy on TV?

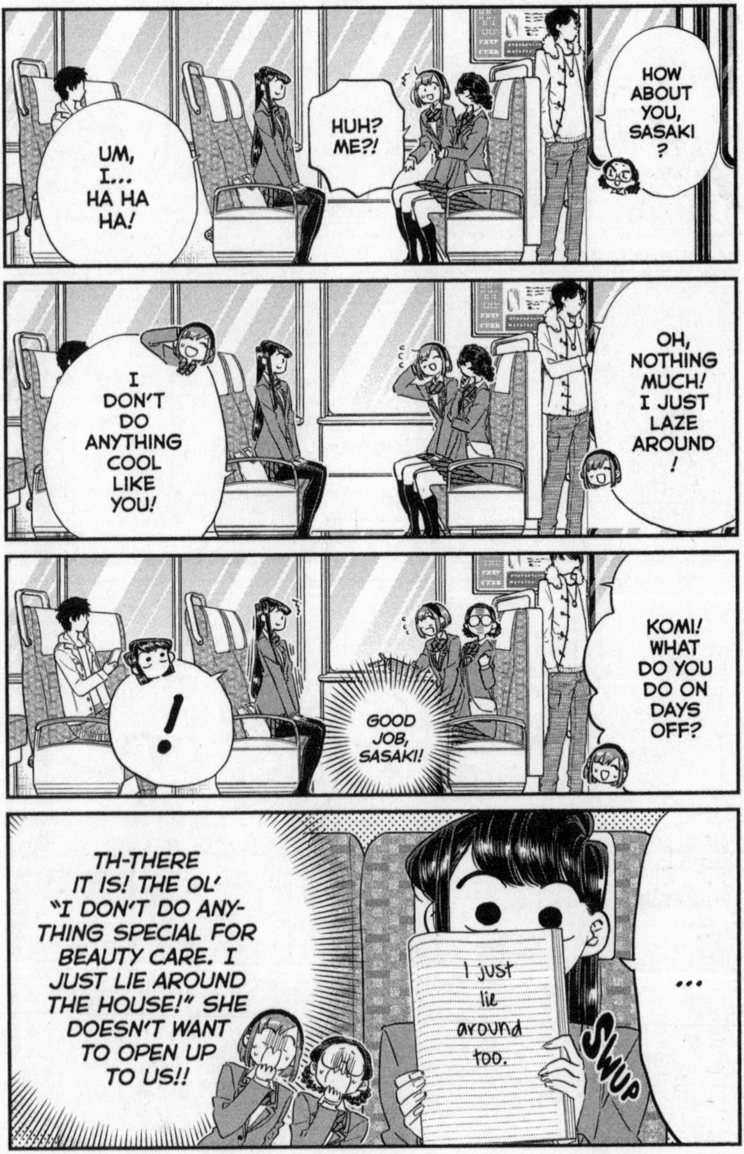
HOW ABOUT YOU, SASAKI?
HUH? ME?!
UM, I... HA HA HA!
OH, NOTHING MUCH! I JUST LAZE AROUND!
I DON'T DO ANYTHING COOL LIKE YOU!
KOMI! WHAT DO YOU DO ON DAYS OFF?
GOOD JOB, SASAKI!
!
...
SWUP
I just lie around too.
TH-THERE IT IS! THE OL' "I DON'T DO ANYTHING SPECIAL FOR BEAUTY CARE. I JUST LIE AROUND THE HOUSE!" SHE DOESN'T WANT TO OPEN UP TO US!!

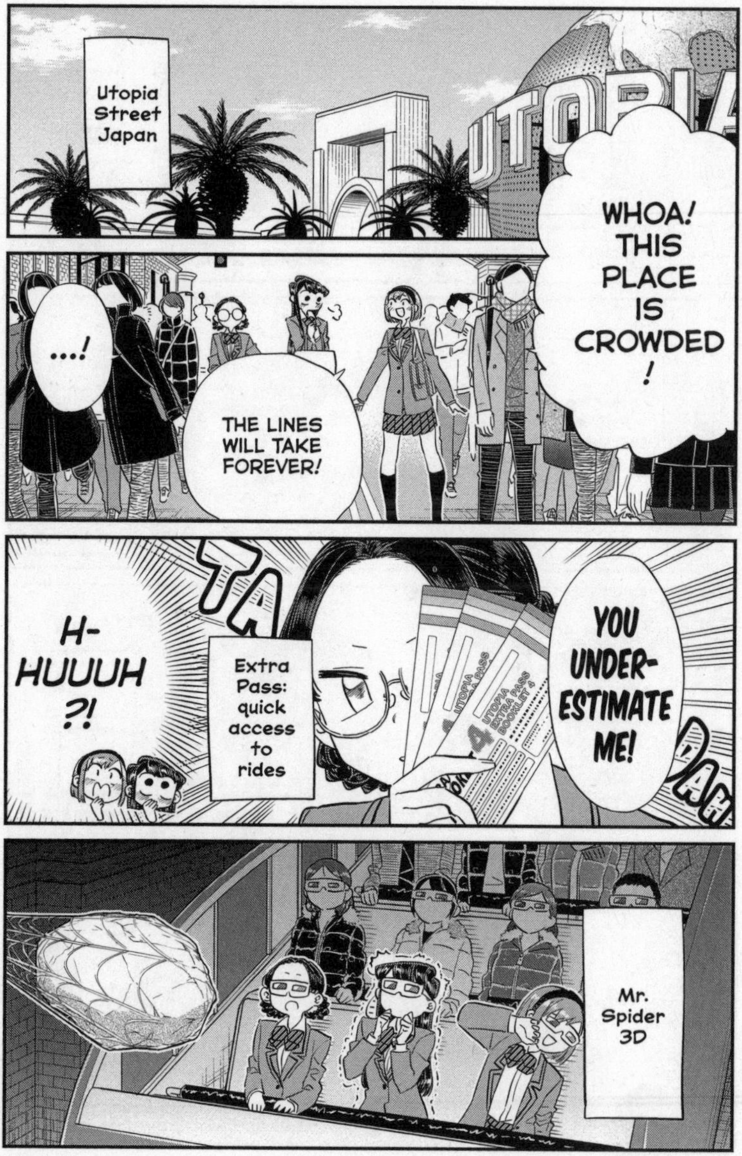
Utopia Street Japan
WHOA! THIS PLACE IS CROWDED!
THE LINES WILL TAKE FOREVER!
...!
YOU UNDER-ESTIMATE ME!
DAH
UTOPIA EXTRA PASS BOOKLET 4
Extra Pass: quick access to rides
TA
H-HUUUH?!
Mr. Spider 3D

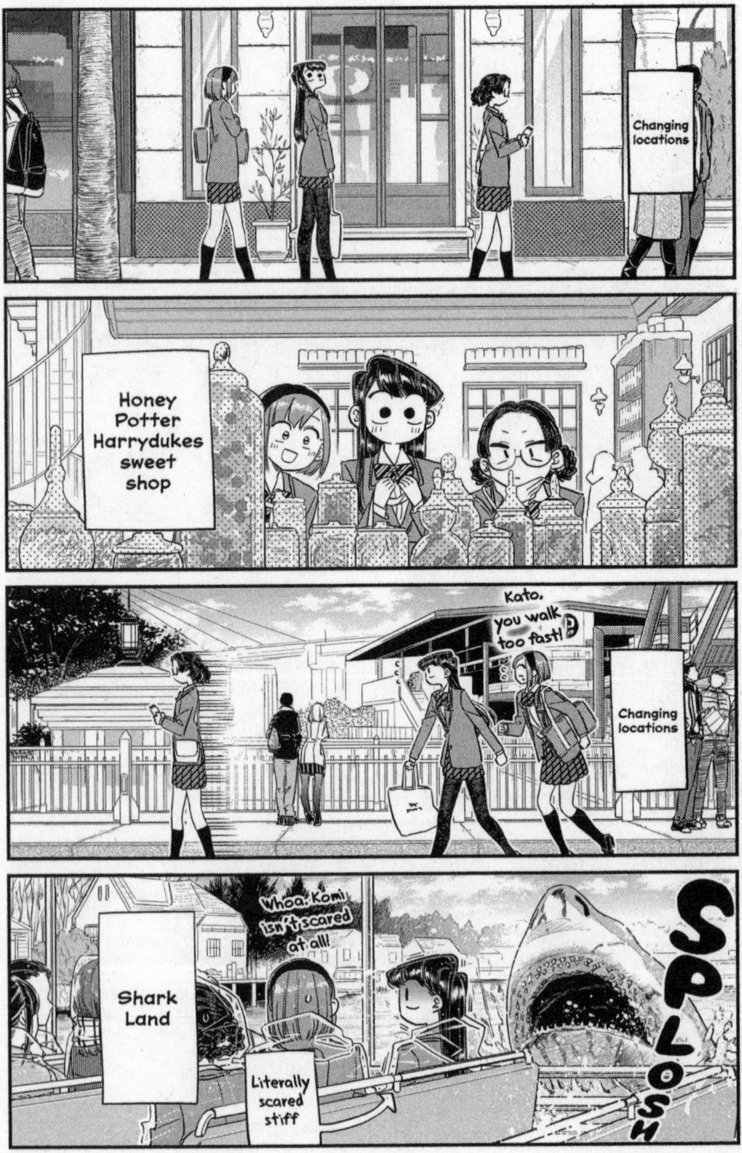

Changing locations
Honey Potter Harrydukes sweet shop
Changing locations
Kato, you walk too fast!
SPLOSH
Whoa. Komi isn't scared at all!
Shark Land
Literally scared stiff

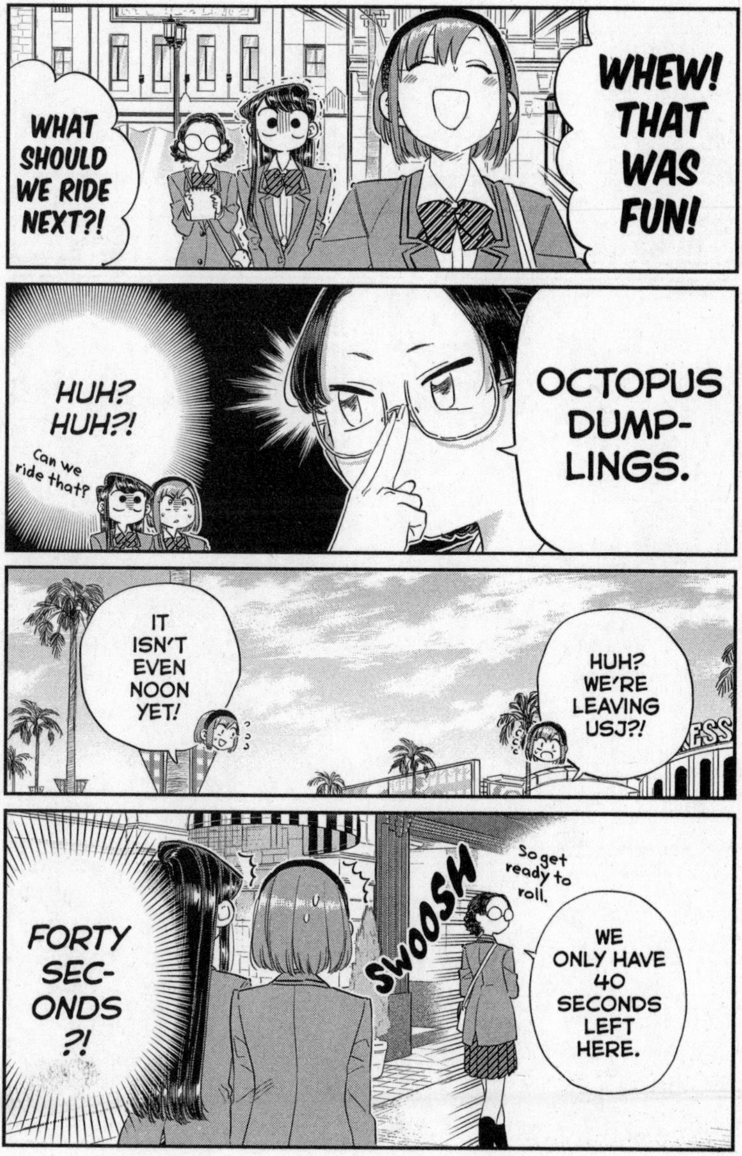
WHEW! THAT WAS FUN!
WHAT SHOULD WE RIDE NEXT?!
OCTOPUS DUMP-LINGS.
HUH? HUH?!
Can we ride that?
HUH? WE'RE LEAVING USJ?!
IT ISN'T EVEN NOON YET!
WE ONLY HAVE 40 SECONDS LEFT HERE.
So get ready to roll.
SWOOSH
FORTY SEC-ONDS?!

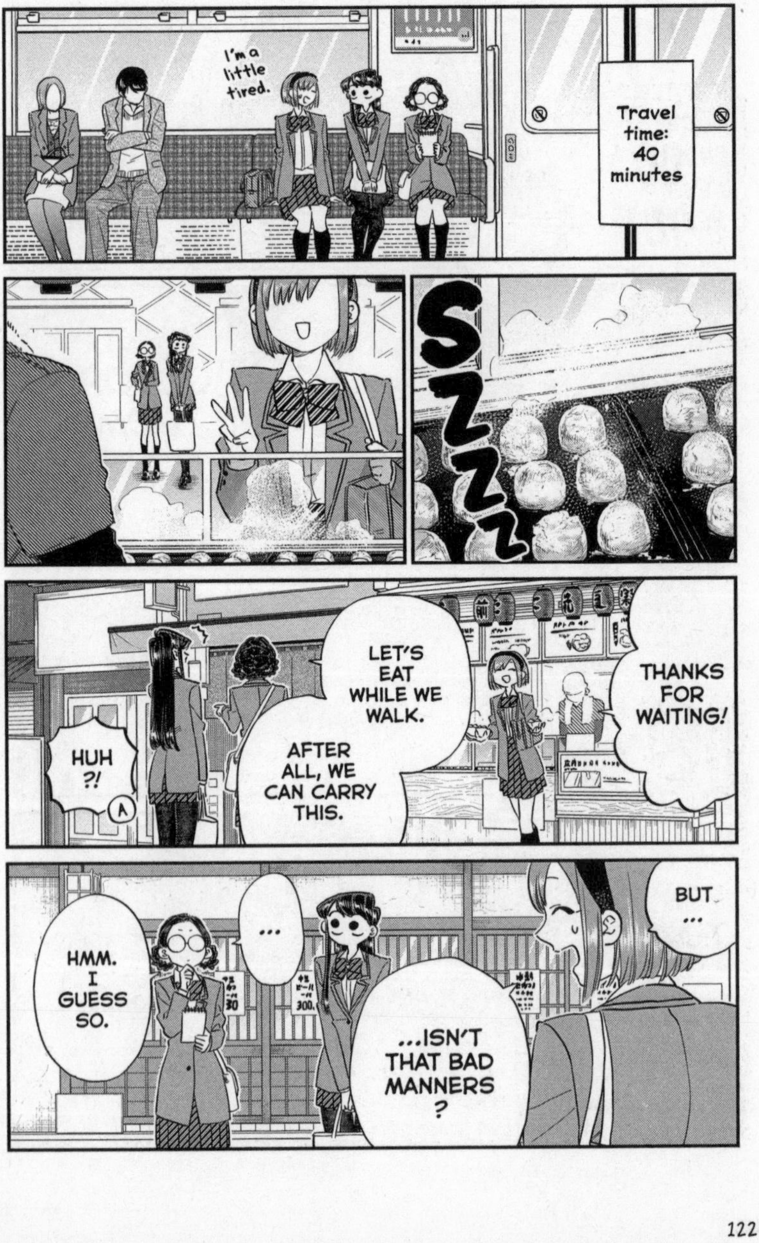
Travel time: 40 minutes
I'm a little tired.
SZZZ
THANKS FOR WAITING!
LET'S EAT WHILE WE WALK.
AFTER ALL, WE CAN CARRY THIS.
HUH ?!
A
BUT ...
...ISN'T THAT BAD MANNERS ?
...
HMM. I GUESS SO.

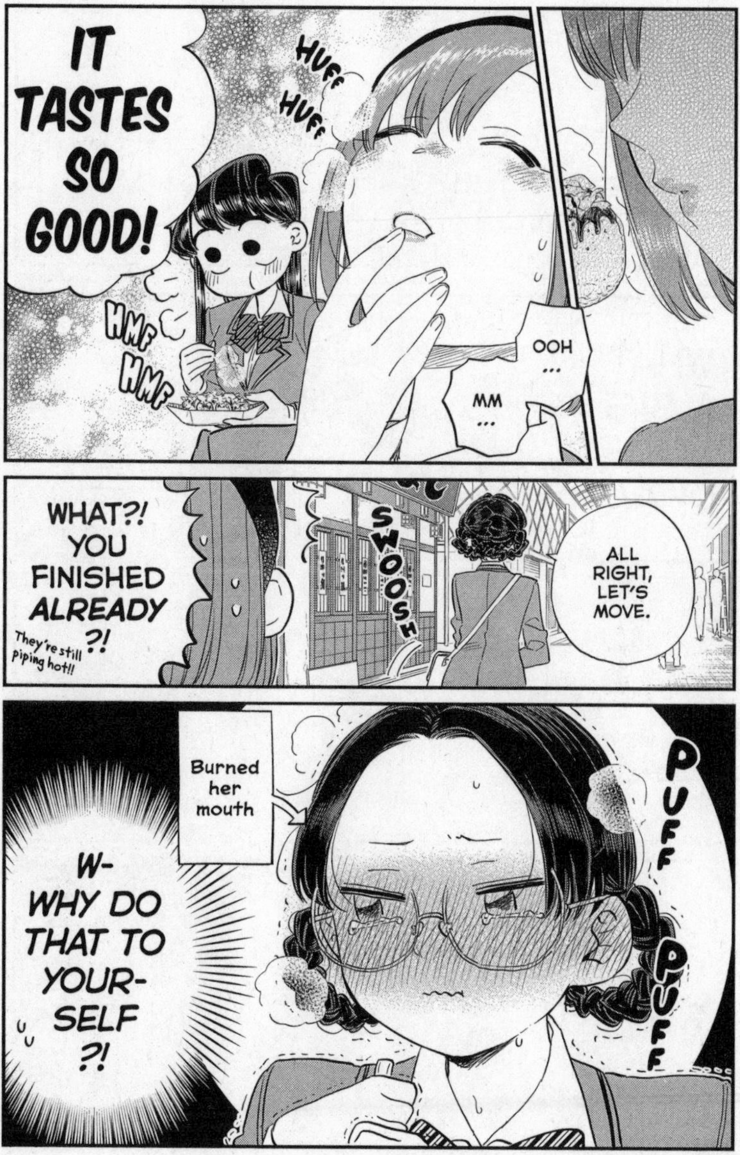
HUFF HUFF
IT TASTES SO GOOD!
OOH ...
MM ...
HMF HMF
ALL RIGHT, LET'S MOVE.
SWOOSH
WHAT?! YOU FINISHED ALREADY?!
They're still piping hot!!
PUFF PUFF PUFF
Burned her mouth
W- WHY DO THAT TO YOURSELF?!

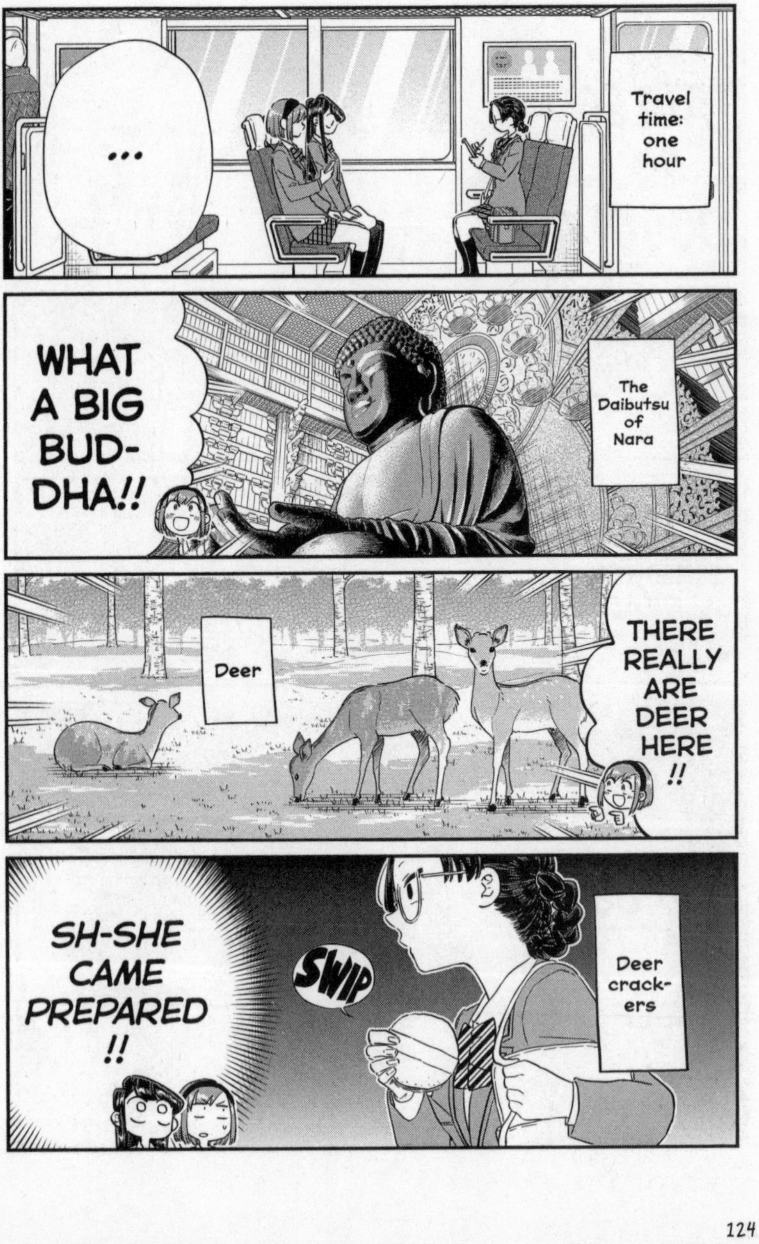
Travel time: one hour
...
The Daibutsu of Nara
WHAT A BIG BUD-DHA!!
THERE REALLY ARE DEER HERE !!
Deer
Deer crack-ers
SWIP
SH-SHE CAME PREPARED !!

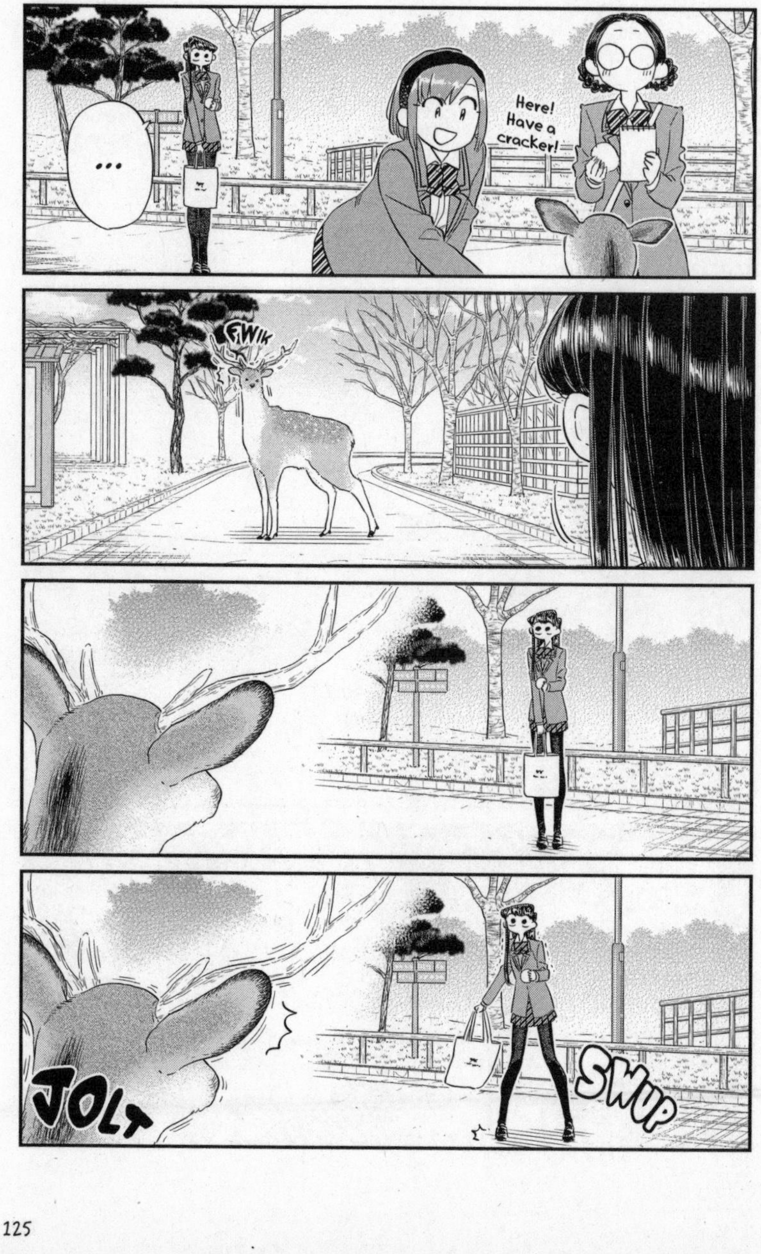
Here! Have a cracker!
...
FWIK
SWUP
JOLT

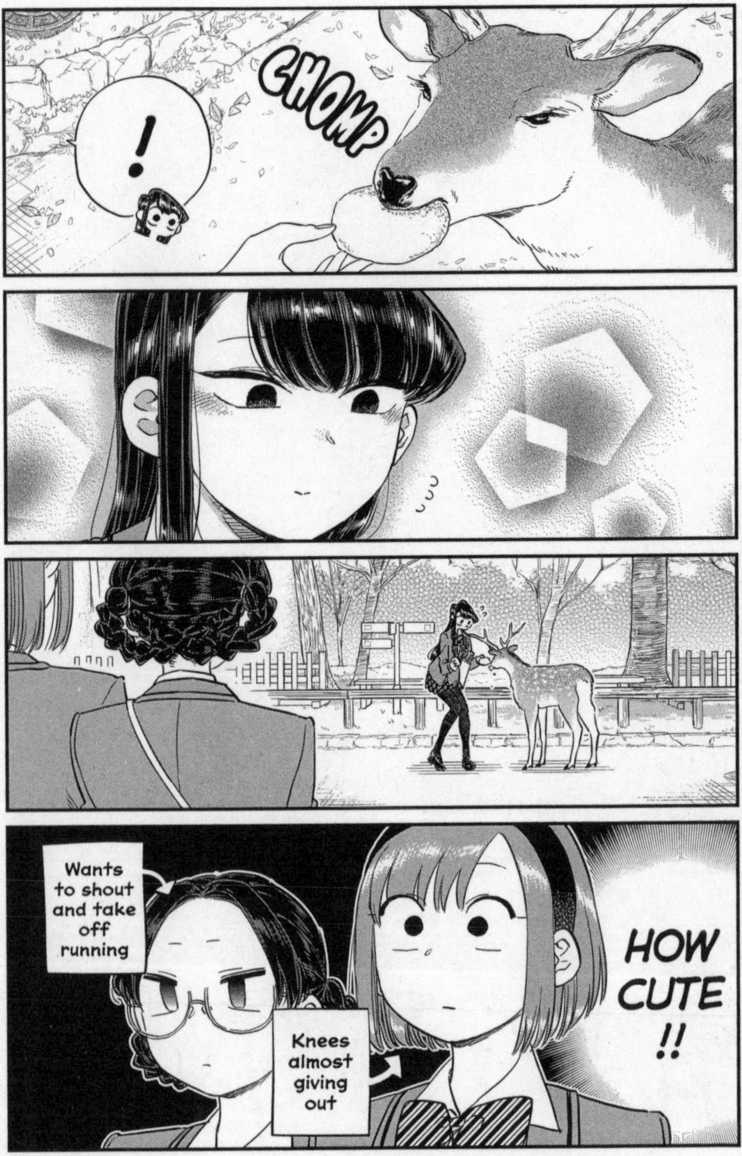
CHOMP
!
HOW CUTE !!
Knees almost giving out
Wants to shout and take off running

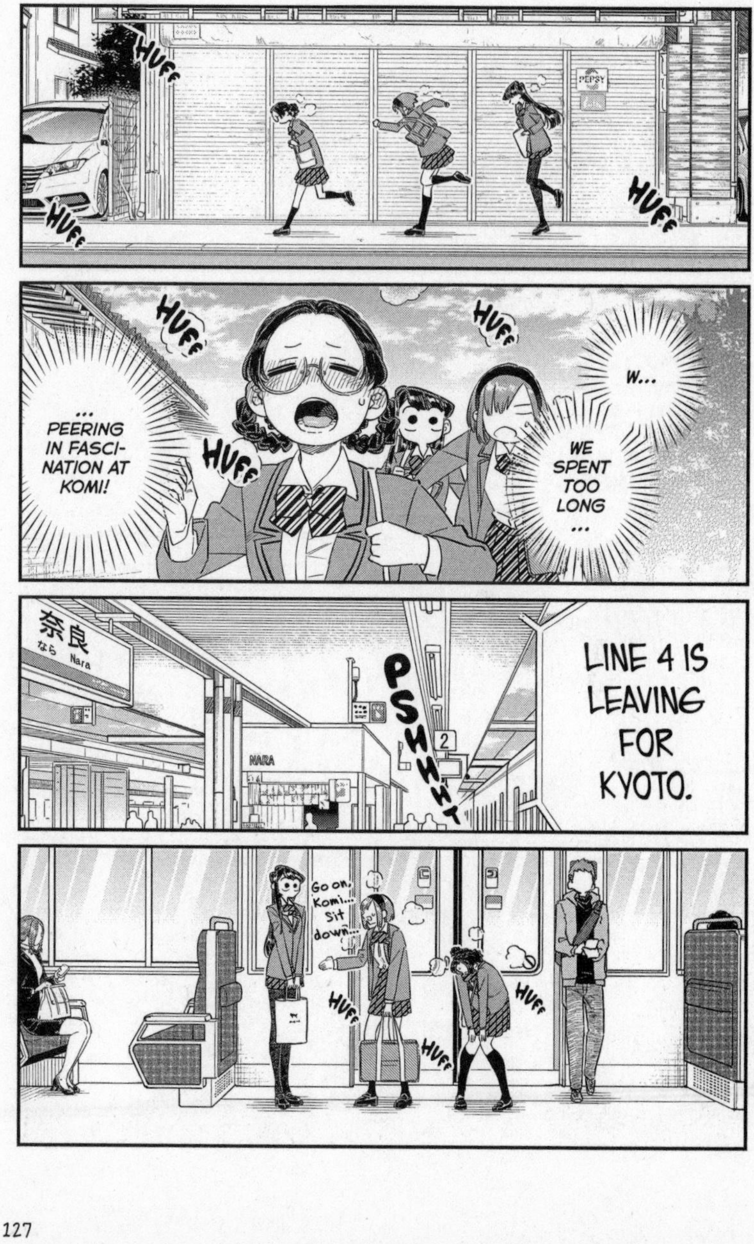

HUFF
HUFF
HUFF
W...
WE SPENT TOO LONG ...
HUFF
HUFF
... PEERING IN FASCINATION AT KOMI!
HUFF
LINE 4 IS LEAVING FOR KYOTO.
PSHHHT
2
奈良 なら Nara
NARA
HUFF
Go on, Komi... Sit down...
HUFF
HUFF

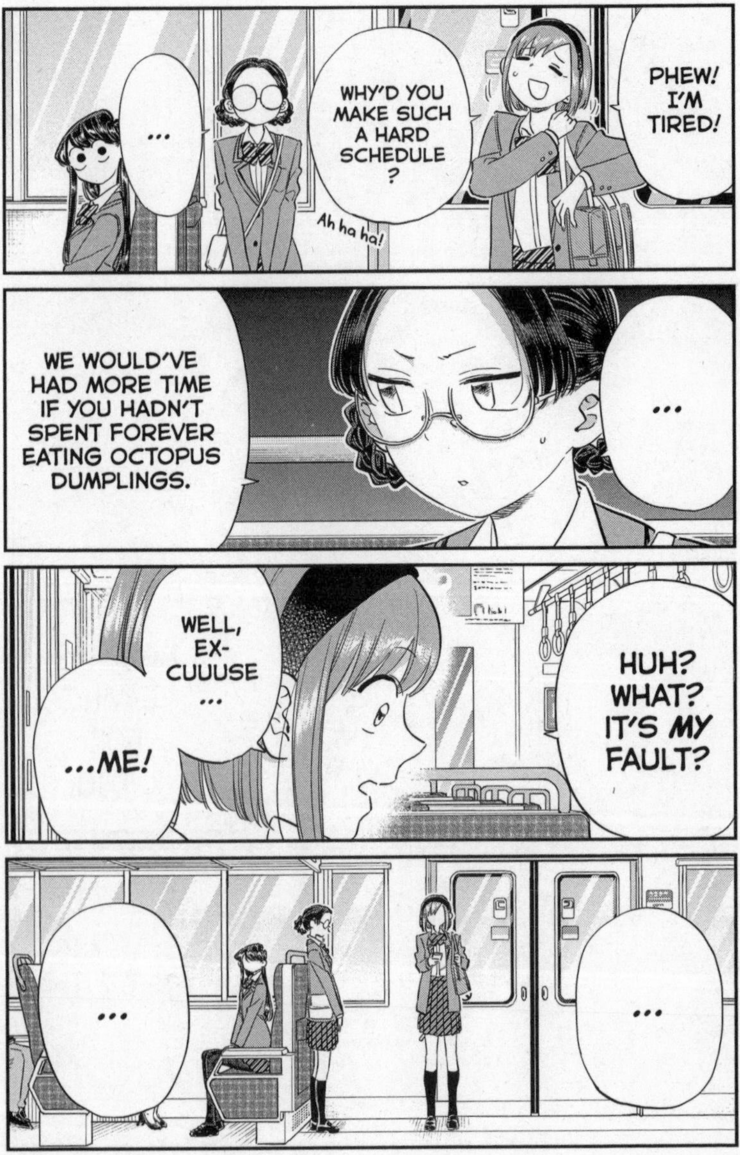
PHEW! I'M TIRED!
Ah ha ha!
WHY'D YOU MAKE SUCH A HARD SCHEDULE ?
...
...
WE WOULD'VE HAD MORE TIME IF YOU HADN'T SPENT FOREVER EATING OCTOPUS DUMPLINGS.
HUH? WHAT? IT'S *MY* FAULT?
WELL, EX-CUUUSE ...
...ME!
...
...

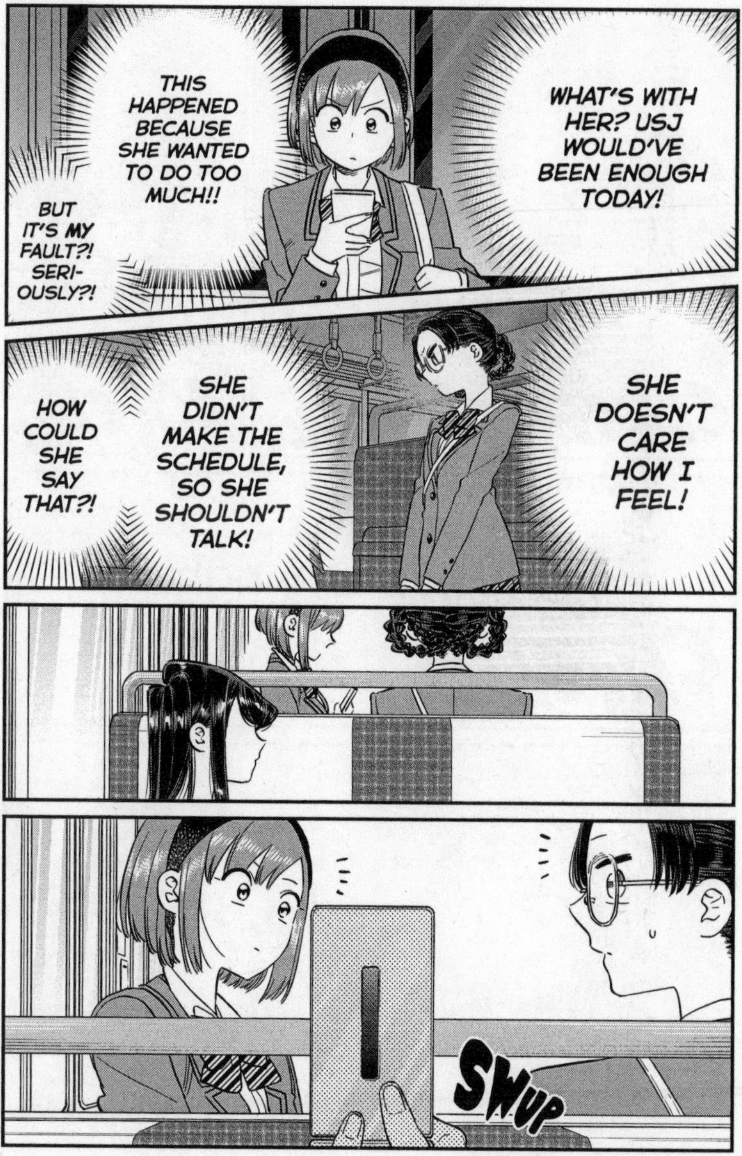
WHAT'S WITH HER? USJ WOULD'VE BEEN ENOUGH TODAY!
THIS HAPPENED BECAUSE SHE WANTED TO DO TOO MUCH!!
BUT IT'S MY FAULT?! SERI-OUSLY?!
SHE DOESN'T CARE HOW I FEEL!
SHE DIDN'T MAKE THE SCHEDULE, SO SHE SHOULDN'T TALK!
HOW COULD SHE SAY THAT?!
SWUP

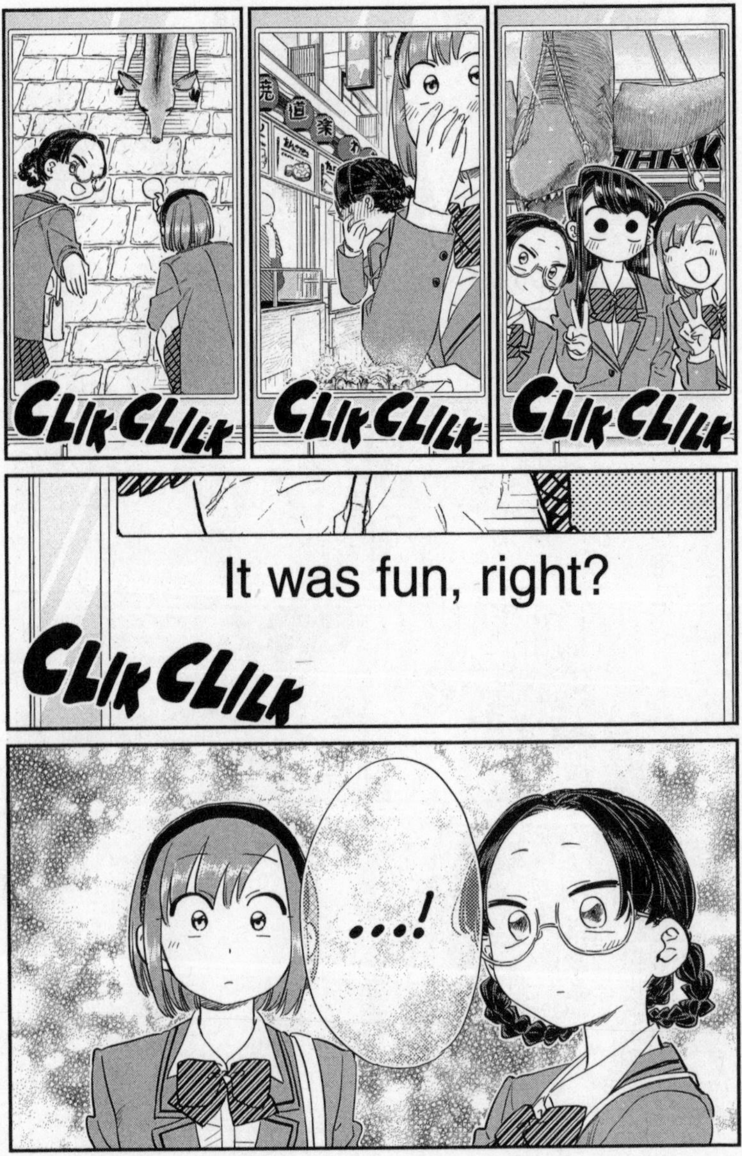
CLIK CLILK
CLIK CLILK
CLIK CLILK
It was fun, right?
CLIK CLILK
...!

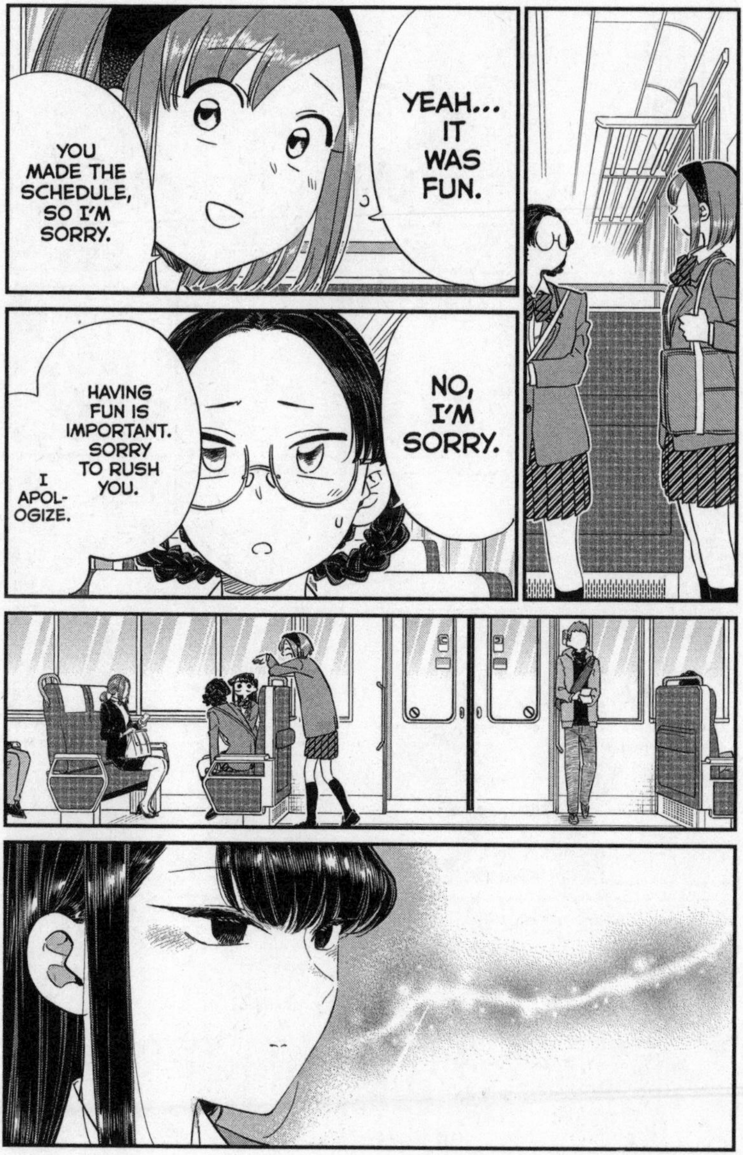
YEAH... IT WAS FUN.
YOU MADE THE SCHEDULE, SO I'M SORRY.
NO, I'M SORRY.
HAVING FUN IS IMPORTANT. SORRY TO RUSH YOU.
I APOLOGIZE.

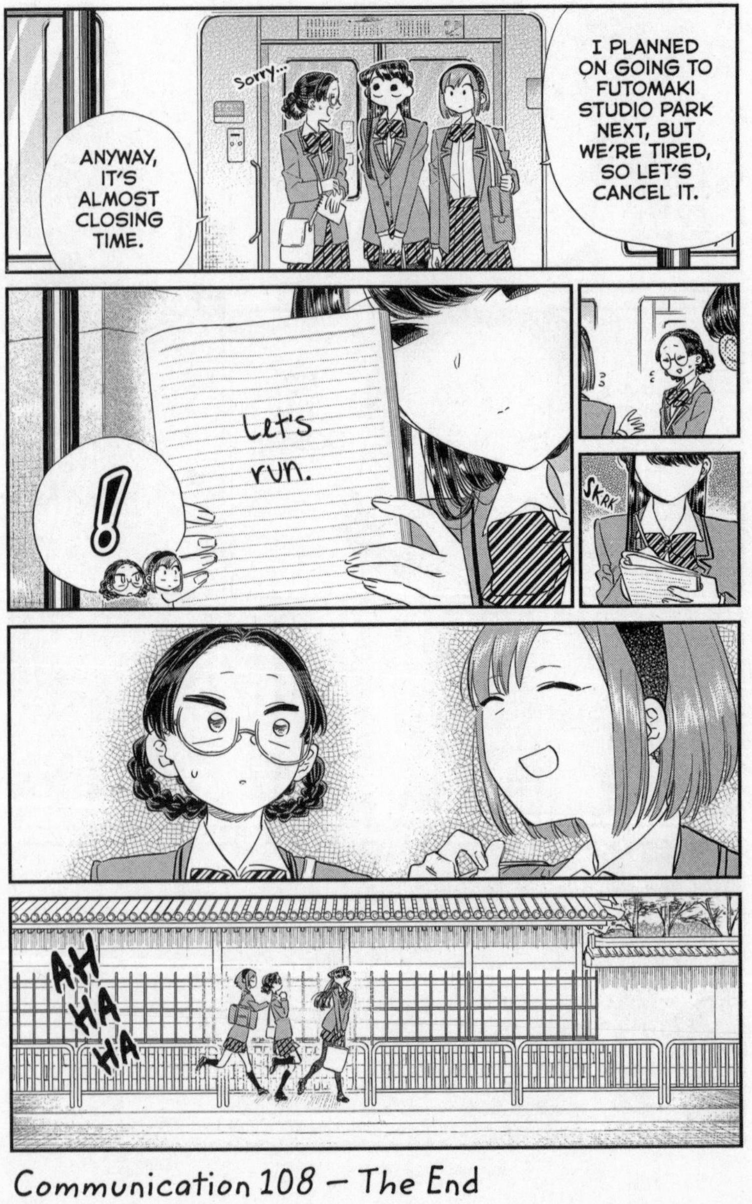
I PLANNED ON GOING TO FUTOMAKI STUDIO PARK NEXT, BUT WE'RE TIRED, SO LET'S CANCEL IT.
Sorry...
ANYWAY, IT'S ALMOST CLOSING TIME.
SKRK
Let's run.
!
AH HA HA HA

Communication 108 – The End

Komi Can't Communicate

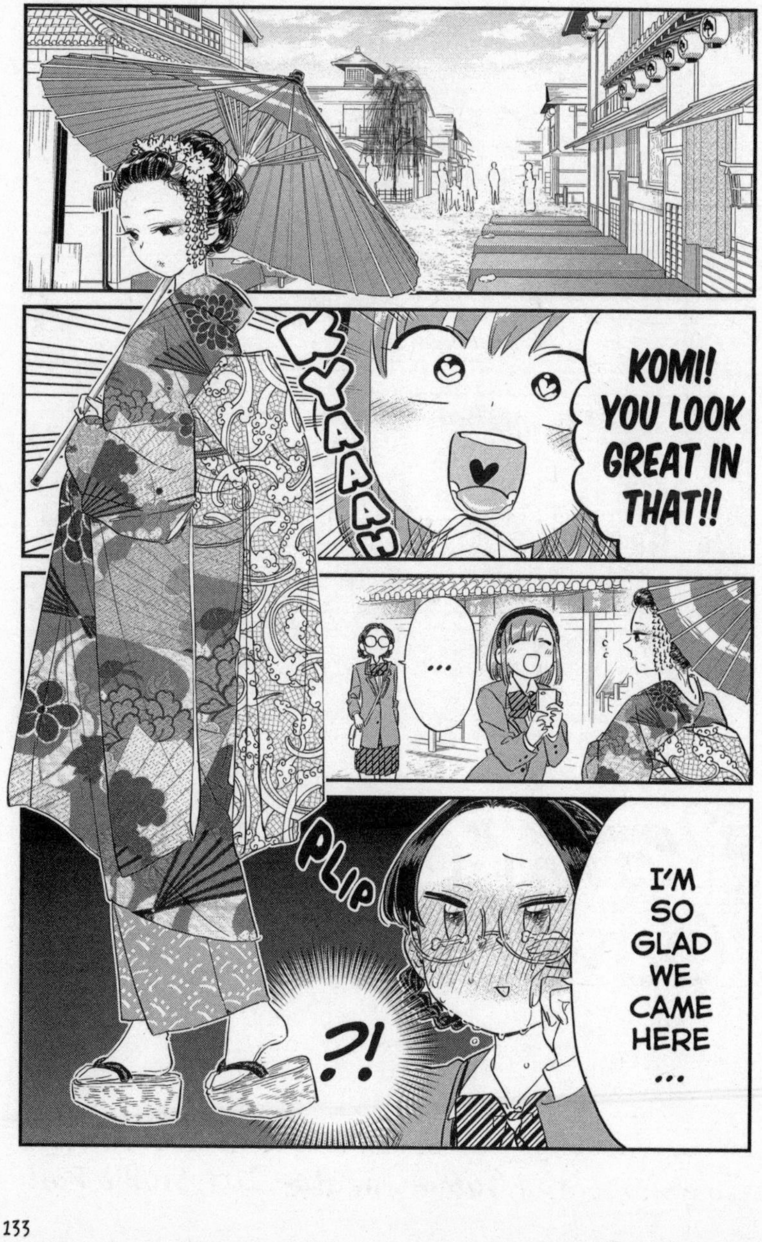
KOMI! YOU LOOK GREAT IN THAT!!
KYAAAAH
...
I'M SO GLAD WE CAME HERE ...
PLIP
?!

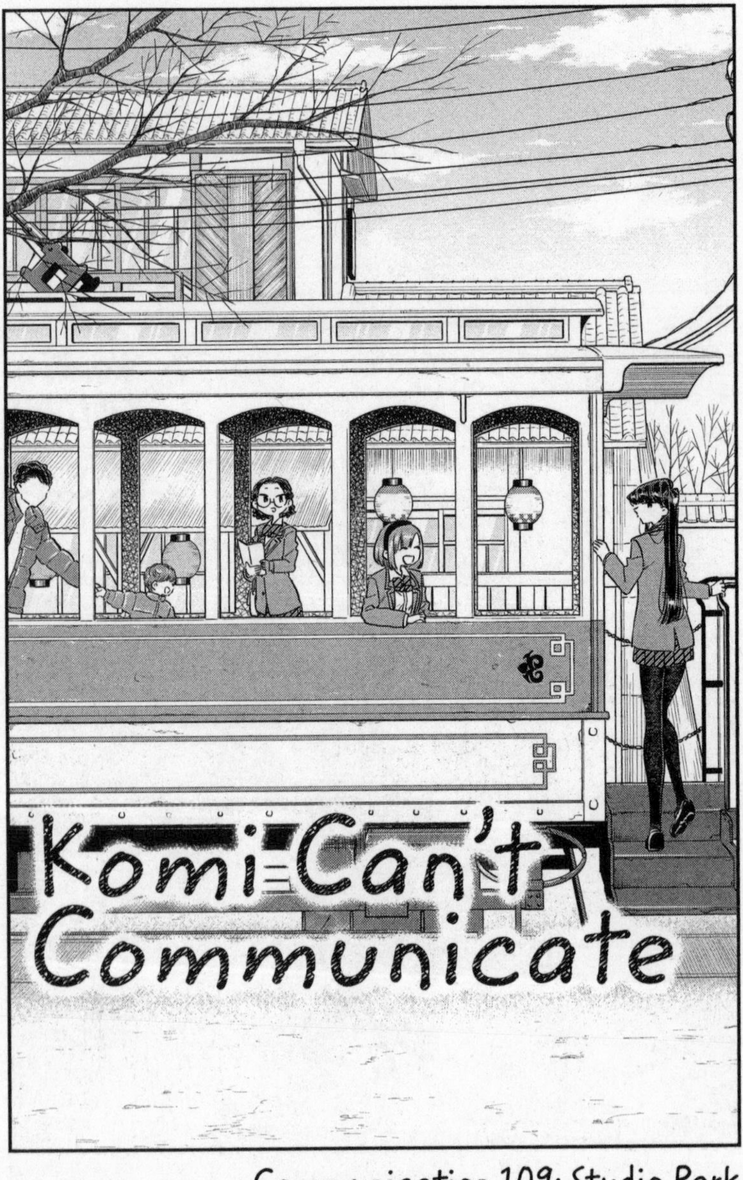
Komi Can't Communicate

Communication 109: Studio Park

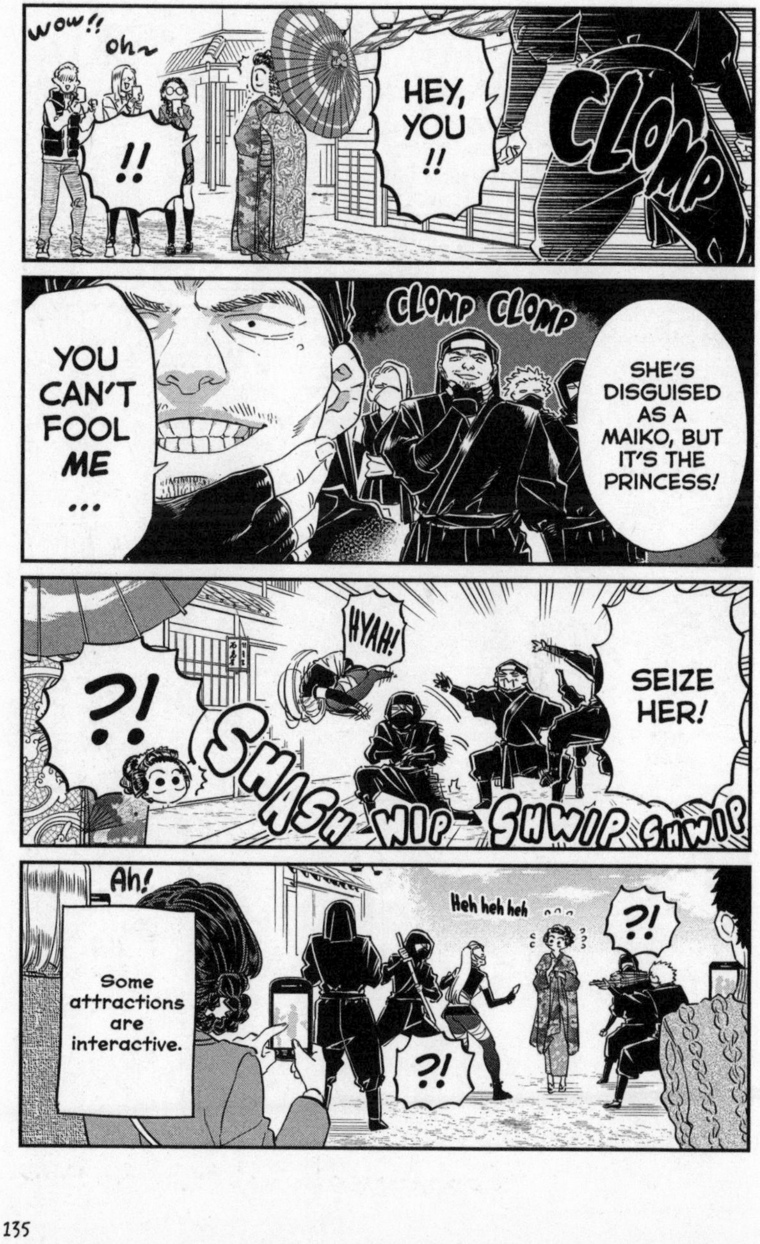
CLOMP
HEY, YOU !!
oh~
wow!!
!!
SHE'S DISGUISED AS A MAIKO, BUT IT'S THE PRINCESS!
CLOMP CLOMP
YOU CAN'T FOOL ME ...
SEIZE HER!
HYAH!
?!
SHASH WIP SHWIP SHWIP
?!
Heh heh heh
Ah!
Some attractions are interactive.
?!

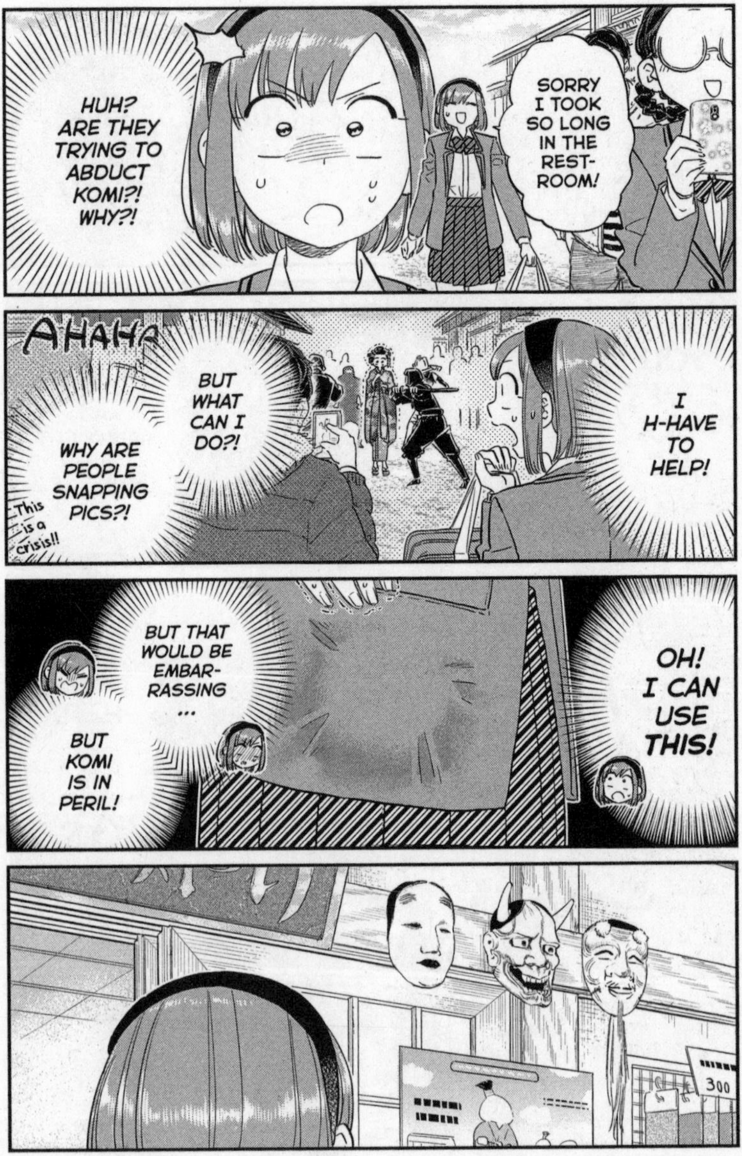

SORRY I TOOK SO LONG IN THE REST-ROOM!
HUH? ARE THEY TRYING TO ABDUCT KOMI?! WHY?!
I H-HAVE TO HELP!
BUT WHAT CAN I DO?!
AHAHA
WHY ARE PEOPLE SNAPPING PICS?!
This is a crisis!!
OH! I CAN USE THIS!
BUT THAT WOULD BE EMBAR-RASSING...
BUT KOMI IS IN PERIL!
300

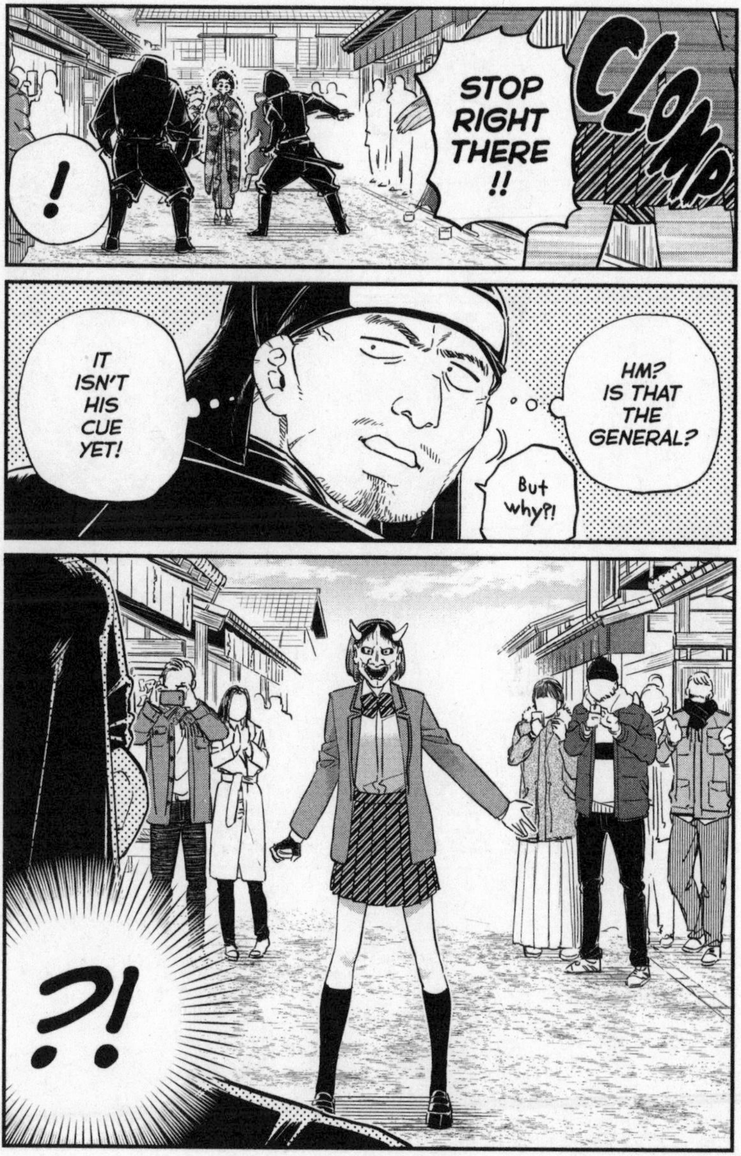
CLOMP
STOP RIGHT THERE !!
!
HM? IS THAT THE GENERAL?
But why?!
IT ISN'T HIS CUE YET!
?!

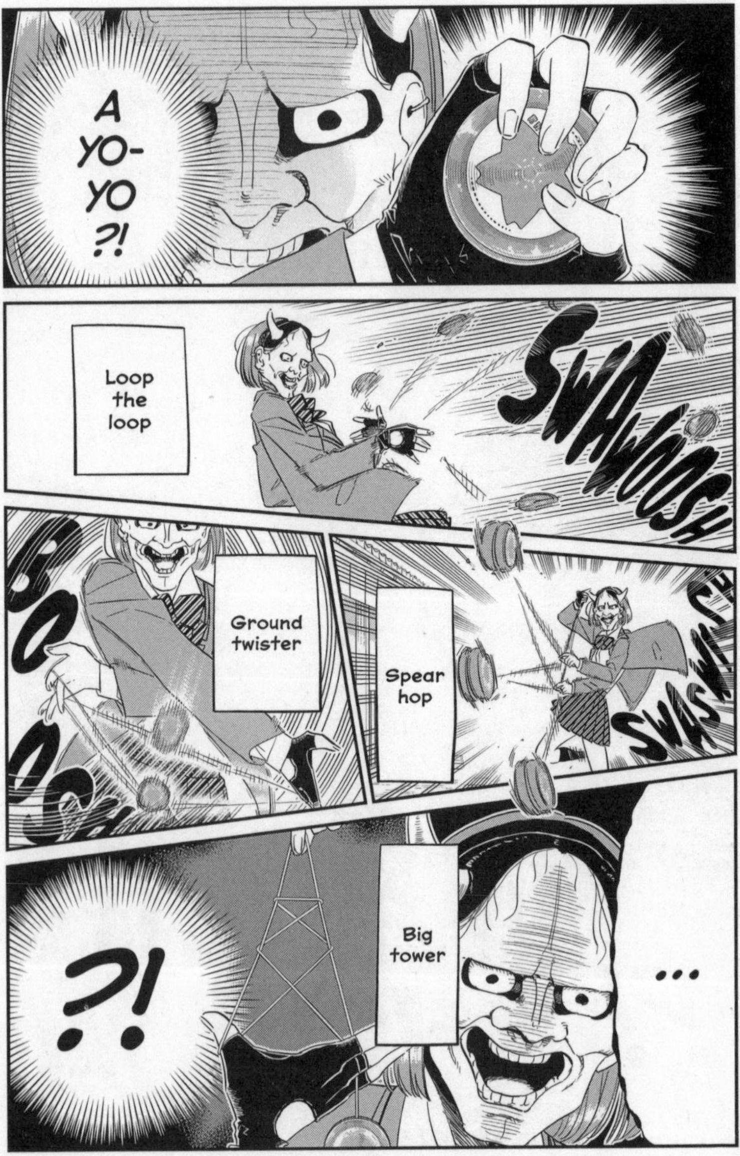
A YO-YO?!
Loop the loop
Spear hop
SWASH SWASH
Ground twister
BOOSH
Big tower
...
?!

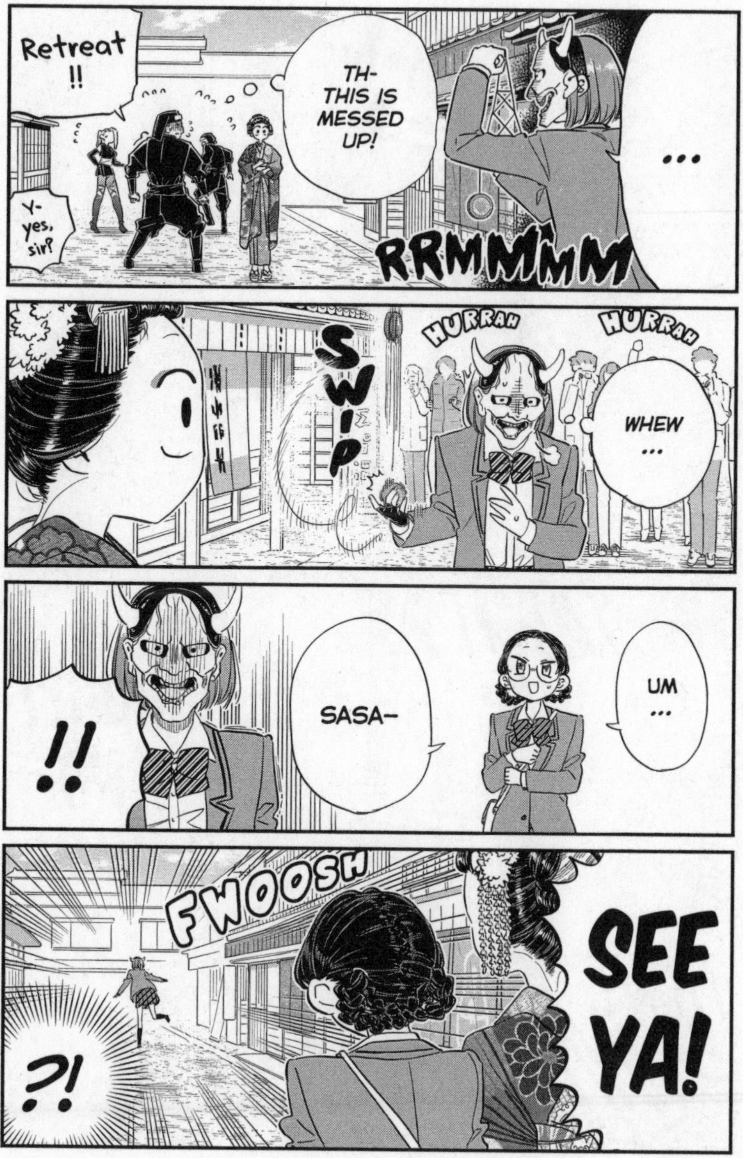
...
RRMMMM
TH- THIS IS MESSED UP!
Retreat !!
Y- yes, sir?
HURRAH
HURRAH
WHEW ...
SWIP
UM ...
SASA-
!!
SEE YA!
FWOOSH
?!

KOMI! ARE YOU ALL RIGHT?!
TMP TMP TMP
I JUST PASSED SOME WEIRDO IN A MASK...
UH, YEAH.
S...
SOMEONE WITH A YO-YO...
...CAME TO HER RESCUE.
...
HUH?! NO WAY!!
DA DUM
...

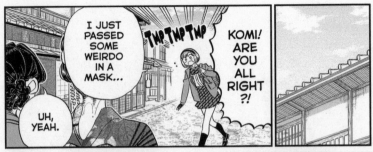

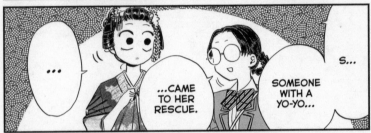

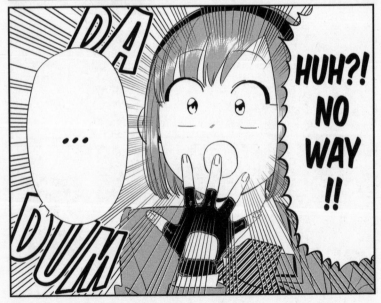

Communication 109 – The End

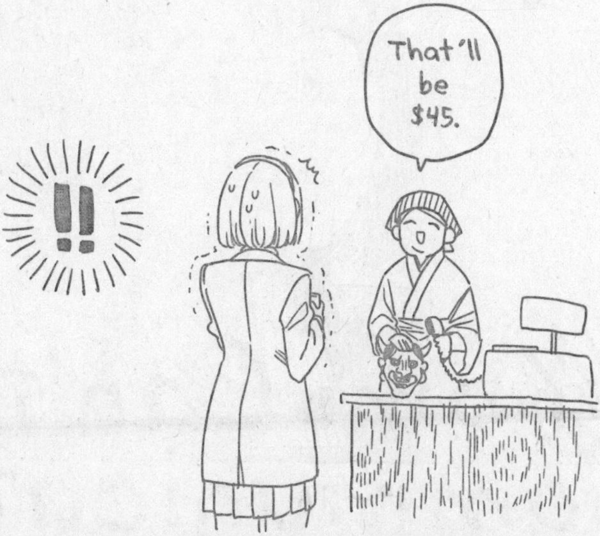
That'll be $45.
!!

Komi Can't
Communicate

Komi Can't Communicate

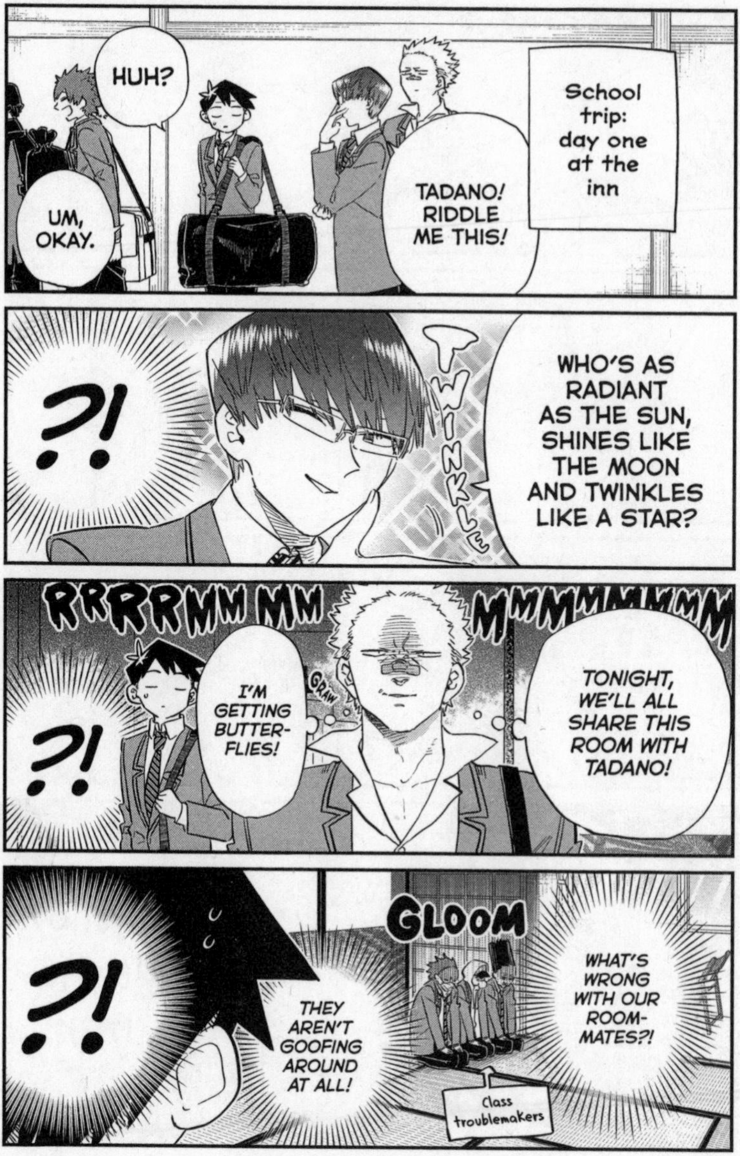
School trip: day one at the inn
TADANO! RIDDLE ME THIS!
HUH?
UM, OKAY.
WHO'S AS RADIANT AS THE SUN, SHINES LIKE THE MOON AND TWINKLES LIKE A STAR?
TWINKLE
?!
RRRRMM MM MMMMMMMMM
TONIGHT, WE'LL ALL SHARE THIS ROOM WITH TADANO!
GRAW
I'M GETTING BUTTER-FLIES!
?!
WHAT'S WRONG WITH OUR ROOM-MATES?!
GLOOM
Class troublemakers
THEY AREN'T GOOFING AROUND AT ALL!
?!

Communication 110: The Universe

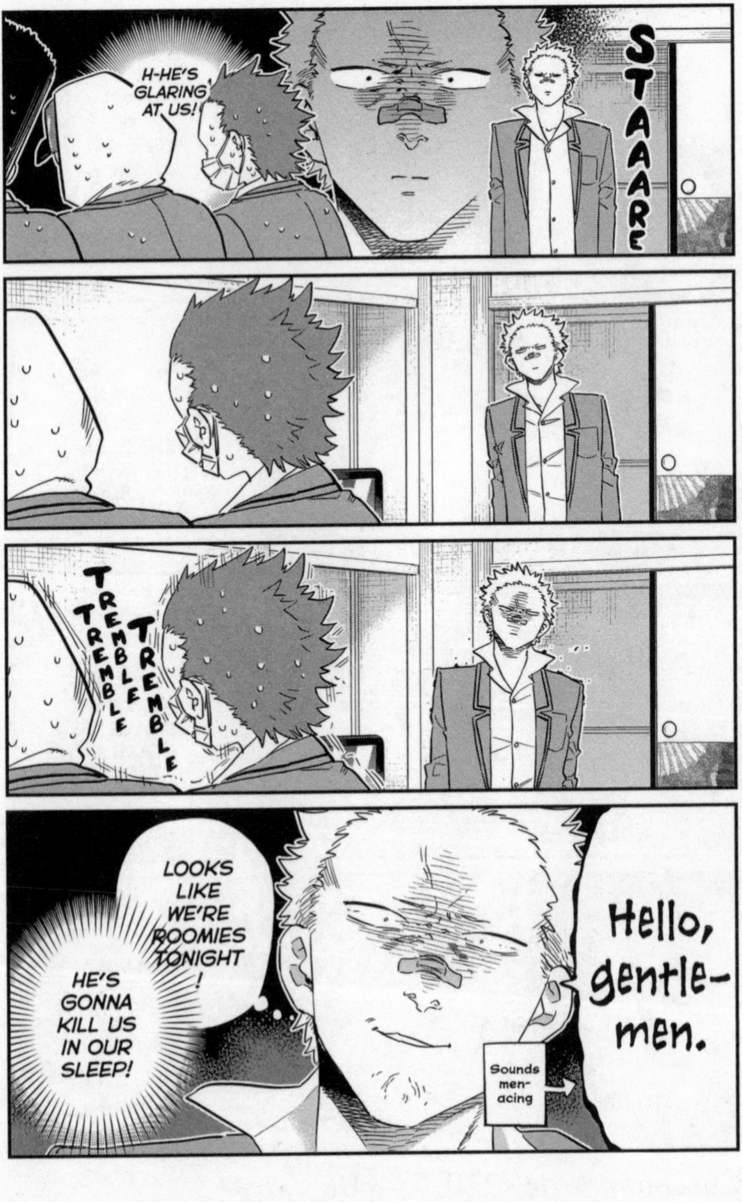
STAAARE
H-HE'S GLARING AT US!
TREMBLE TREMBLE TREMBLE
Hello, gentle-men.
Sounds men-acing
LOOKS LIKE WE'RE ROOMIES TONIGHT!
HE'S GONNA KILL US IN OUR SLEEP!

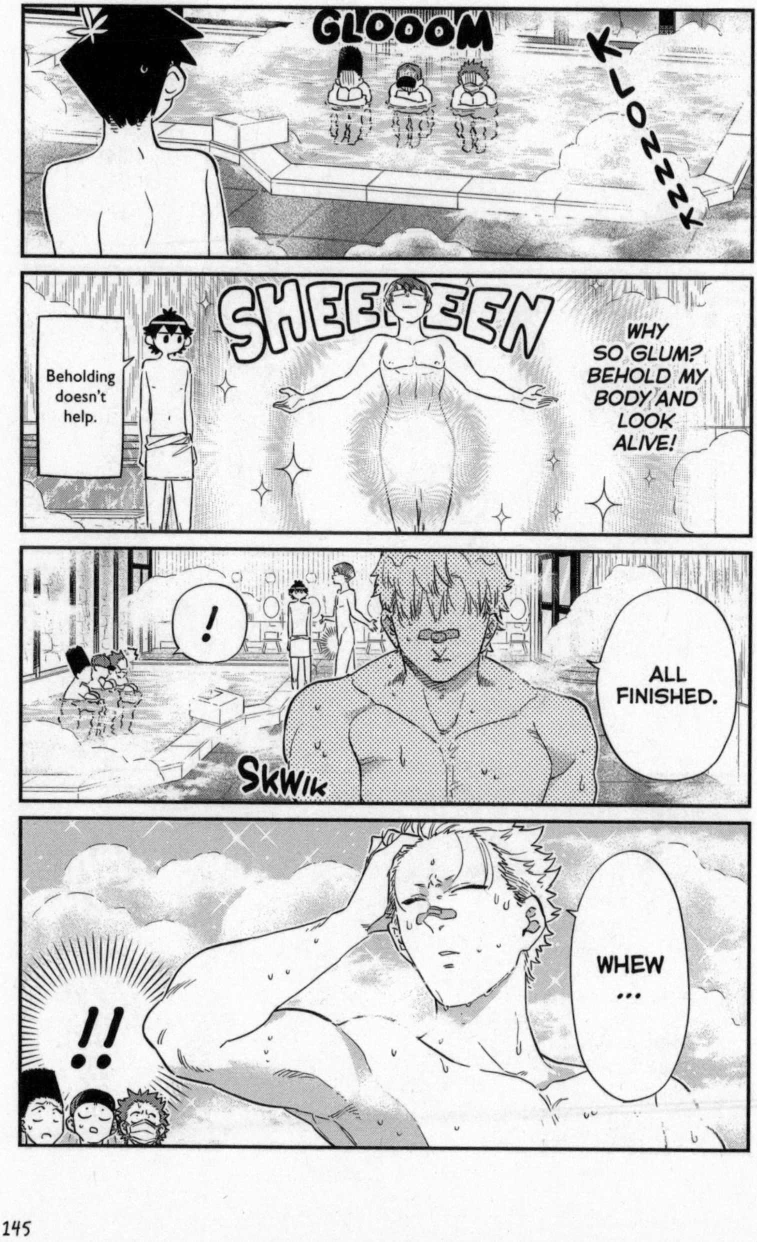
KLONNNK
GLOOOM
WHY SO GLUM? BEHOLD MY BODY AND LOOK ALIVE!
SHEEEEN
Beholding doesn't help.
ALL FINISHED.
!
SKWIK
WHEW...
!!

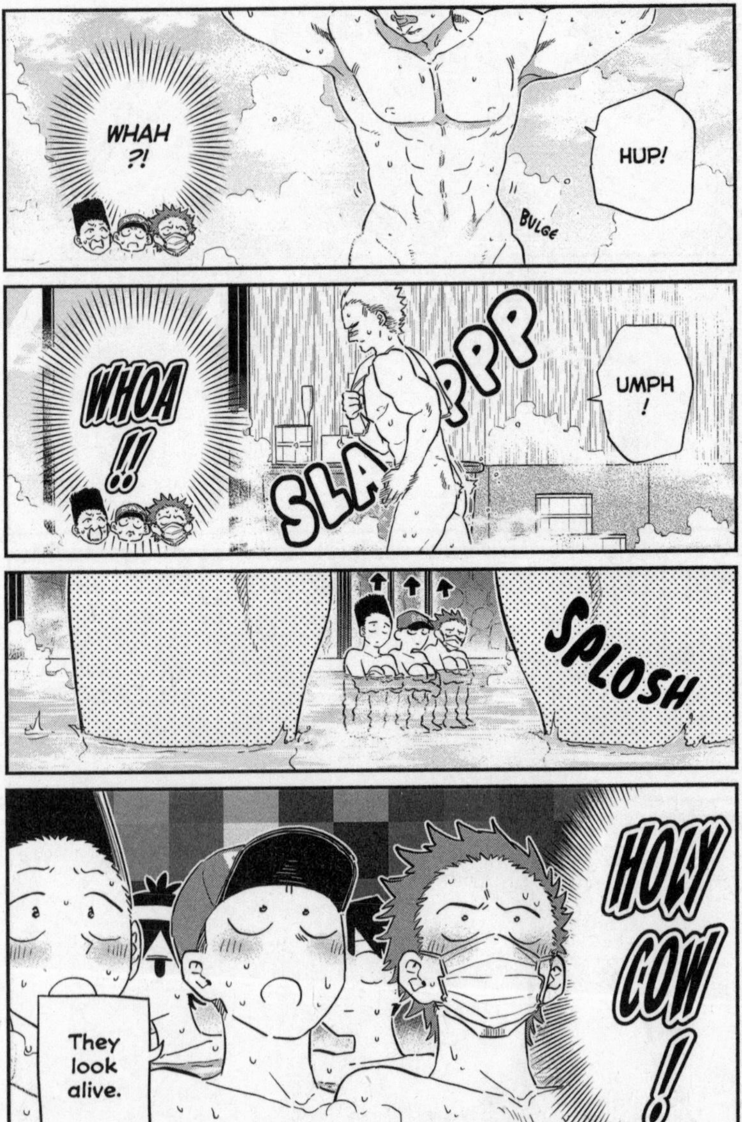
HUP!
BULGE
WHAH ?!
UMPH !
SLAPPP
WHOA !!
SPLOSH
HOLY COW !
They look alive.

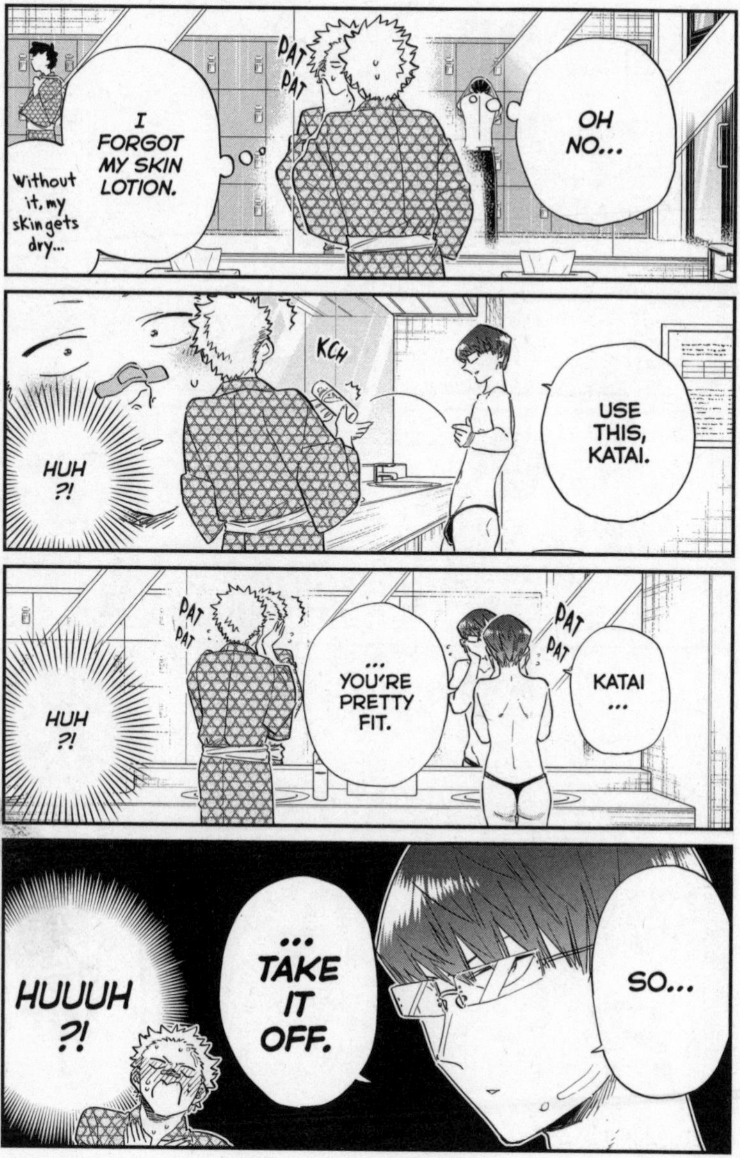
OH NO...
PAT PAT PAT
I FORGOT MY SKIN LOTION.
Without it, my skin gets dry...
USE THIS, KATAI.
KCH
HUH ?!
PAT PAT
KATAI ...
... YOU'RE PRETTY FIT.
PAT PAT
HUH ?!
SO...
... TAKE IT OFF.
HUUUH ?!

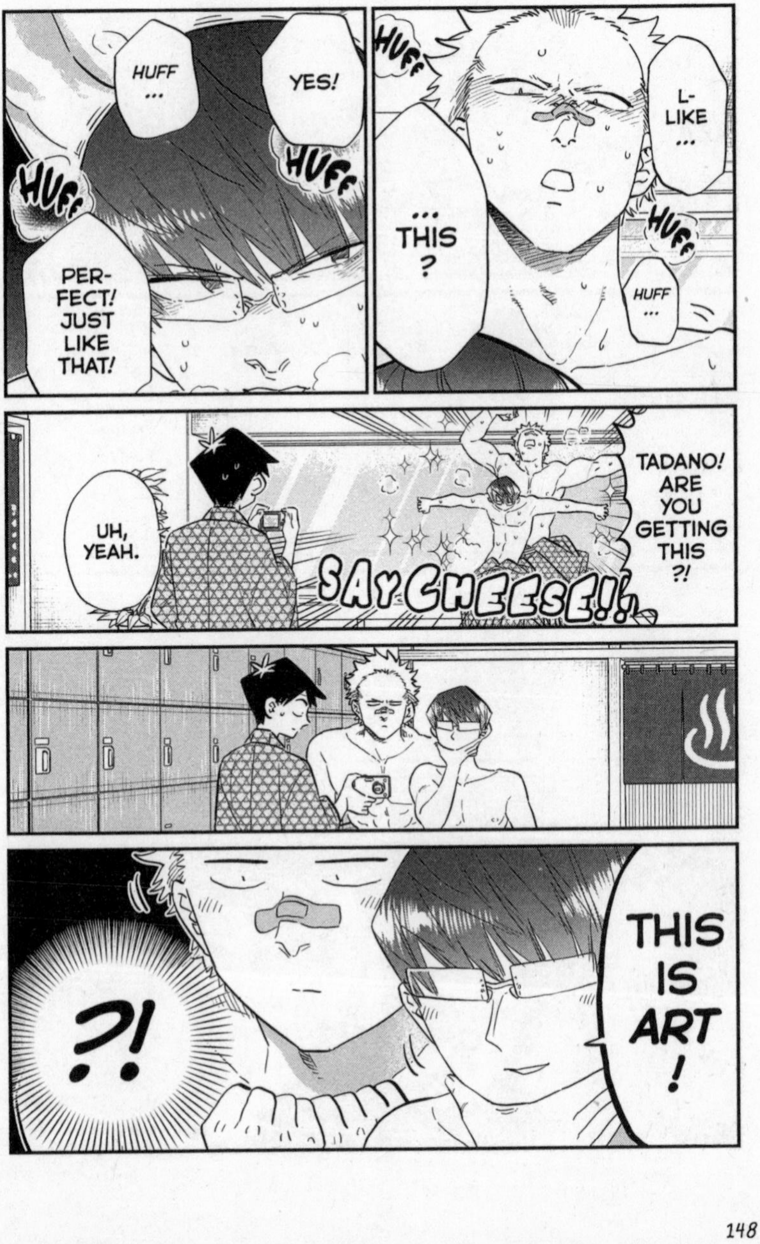

L-LIKE ...
HUFF
... THIS ?
HUFF
HUFF ...
YES!
HUFF ...
HUFF
HUFF
PERFECT! JUST LIKE THAT!
TADANO! ARE YOU GETTING THIS ?!
SAY CHEESE!!
UH, YEAH.
THIS IS ART!
?!

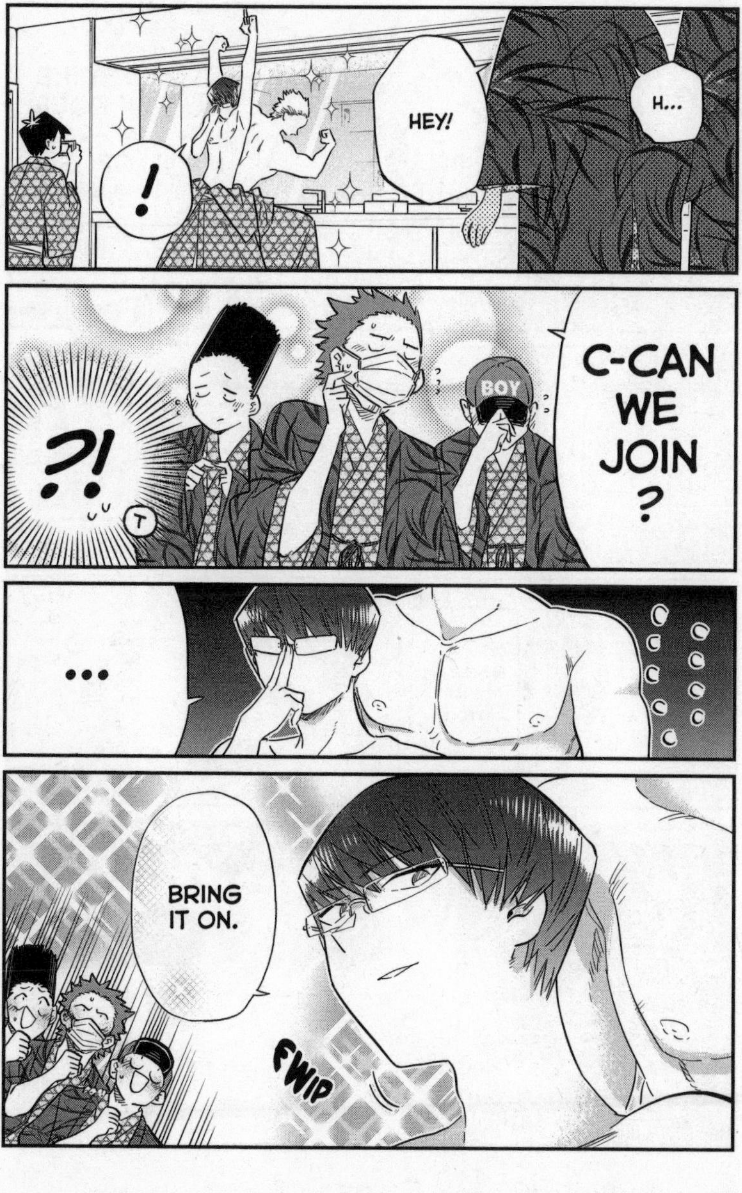
H...
HEY!
!
C-CAN WE JOIN?
T
?!
...
BRING IT ON.
FWIP

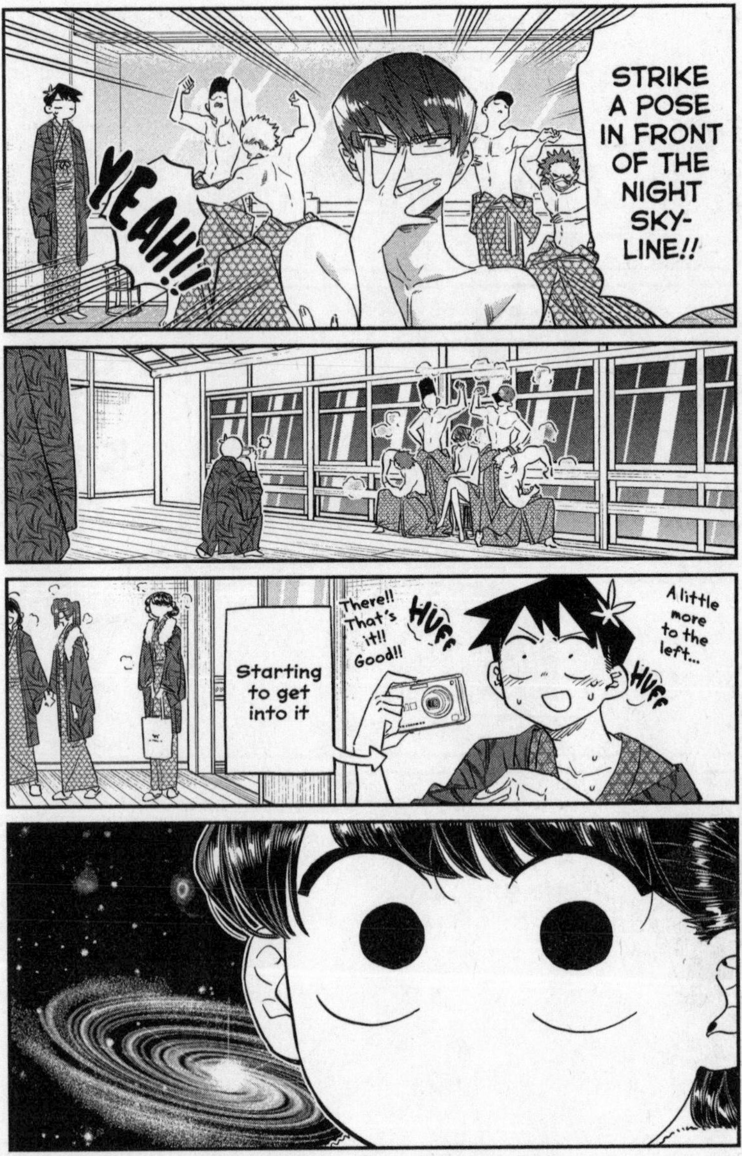
STRIKE A POSE IN FRONT OF THE NIGHT SKY-LINE!!
YEAH!!!
A little more to the left...
HUFF
HUFF
There!! That's it!! Good!!
Starting to get into it

Communication 110 – The End

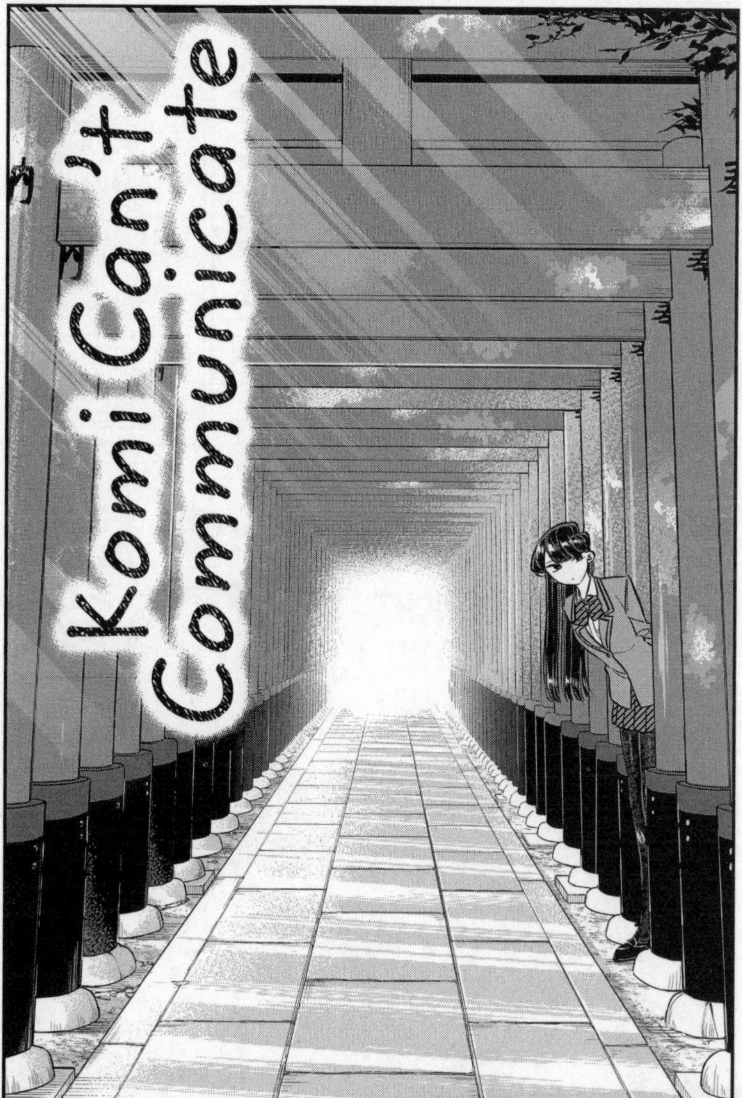
Komi Can't Communicate

Communication 111: Yo-Yo Hannya

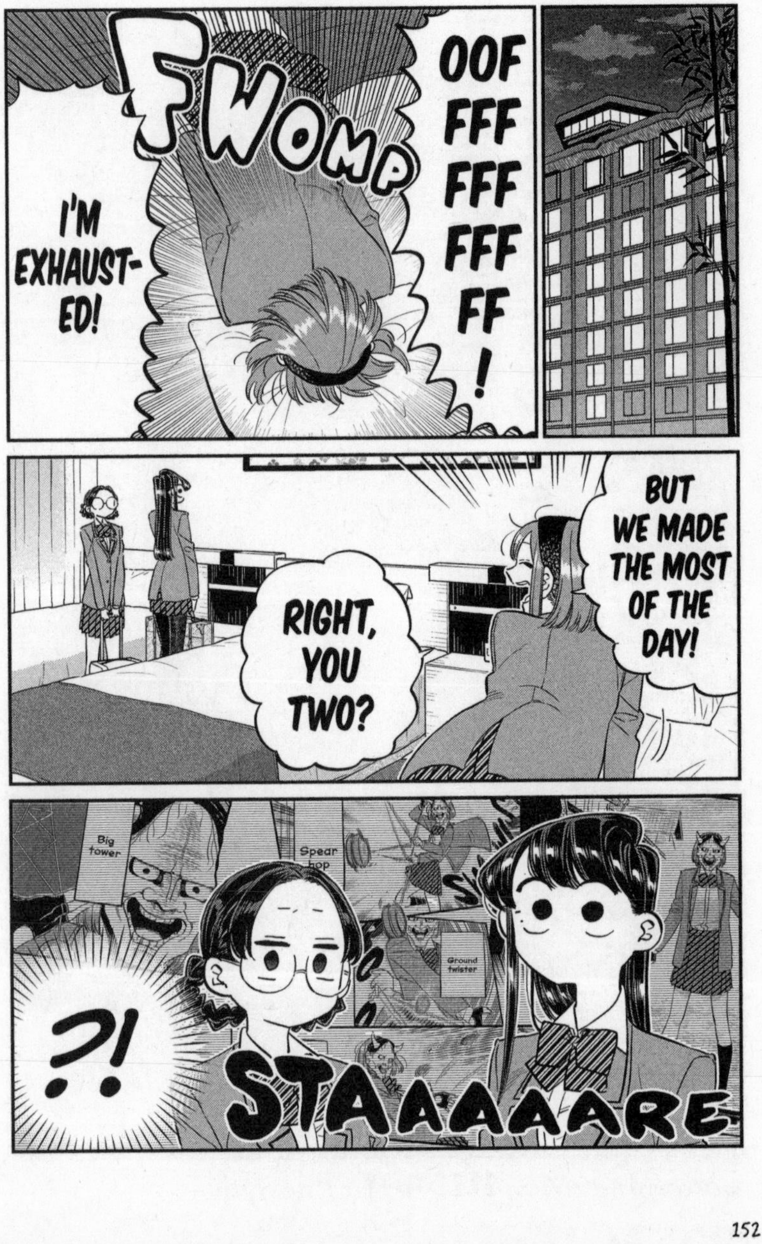
OOF FFF FFF FFF FF !
FWOMP
I'M EXHAUST-ED!
BUT WE MADE THE MOST OF THE DAY!
RIGHT, YOU TWO?
Spear hop
Big tower
Ground twister
STAAAAARE
?!

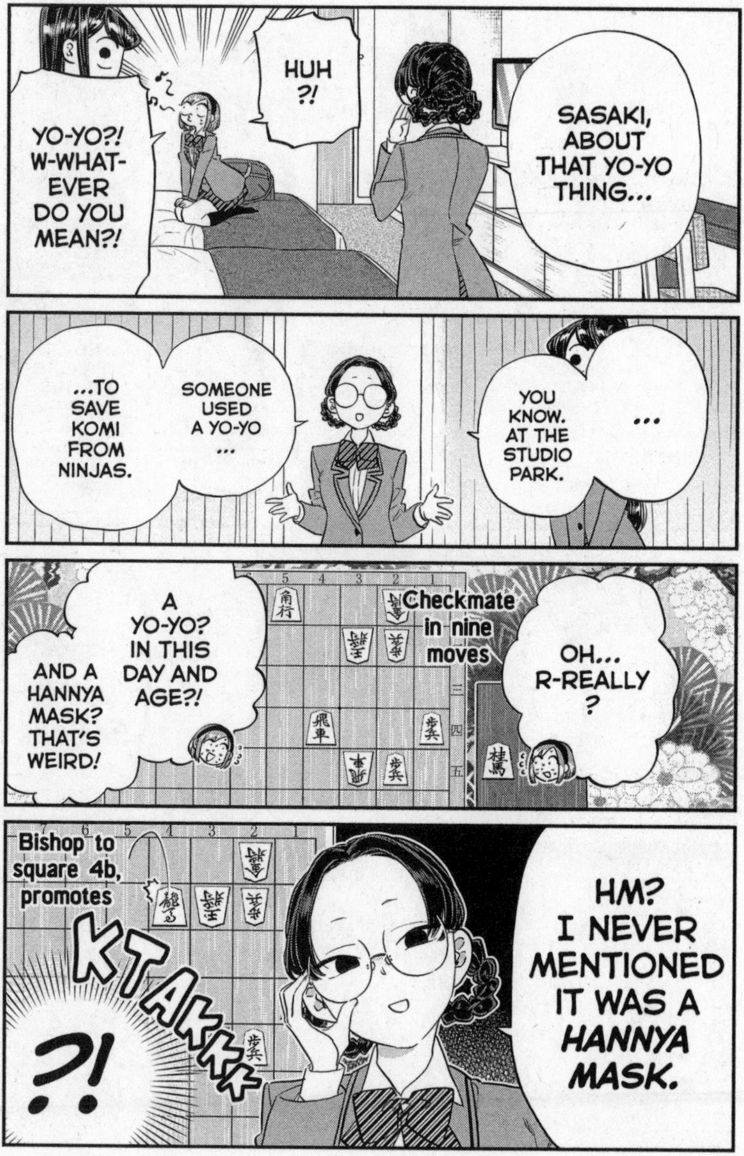

SASAKI, ABOUT THAT YO-YO THING...
HUH ?!
YO-YO?! W-WHATEVER DO YOU MEAN?!
...
YOU KNOW. AT THE STUDIO PARK.
SOMEONE USED A YO-YO ...
...TO SAVE KOMI FROM NINJAS.
OH... R-REALLY ?
Checkmate in nine moves
A YO-YO? IN THIS DAY AND AGE?!
AND A HANNYA MASK? THAT'S WEIRD!
HM? I NEVER MENTIONED IT WAS A *HANNYA MASK.*
Bishop to square 4b, promotes
KTAKKK
?!

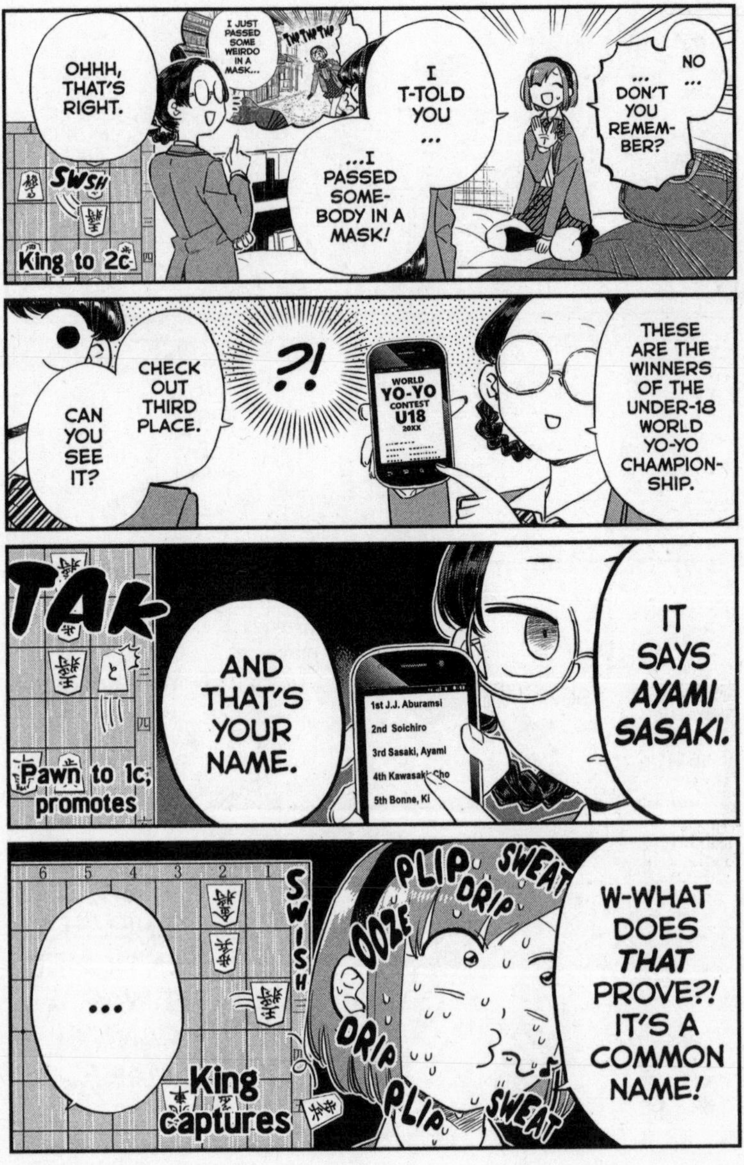
NO ... DON'T YOU REMEMBER?
I T-TOLD YOU ...
...I PASSED SOMEBODY IN A MASK!
TMP TMP TMP
I JUST PASSED SOME WEIRDO IN A MASK...
OHHH, THAT'S RIGHT.
SWSH
King to 2c
THESE ARE THE WINNERS OF THE UNDER-18 WORLD YO-YO CHAMPIONSHIP.
WORLD YO-YO CONTEST U18 20XX
?!
CHECK OUT THIRD PLACE.
CAN YOU SEE IT?
IT SAYS AYAMI SASAKI.
1st J.J. Aburamsi
2nd Soichiro
3rd Sasaki, Ayami
4th Kawasaki Cho
5th Bonne, Ki
AND THAT'S YOUR NAME.
TAK
Pawn to 1c, promotes
W-WHAT DOES THAT PROVE?! IT'S A COMMON NAME!
SWEAT
DRIP
PLIP
OOZE
DRIP
PLIP
SWEAT
SWISH
...
King captures

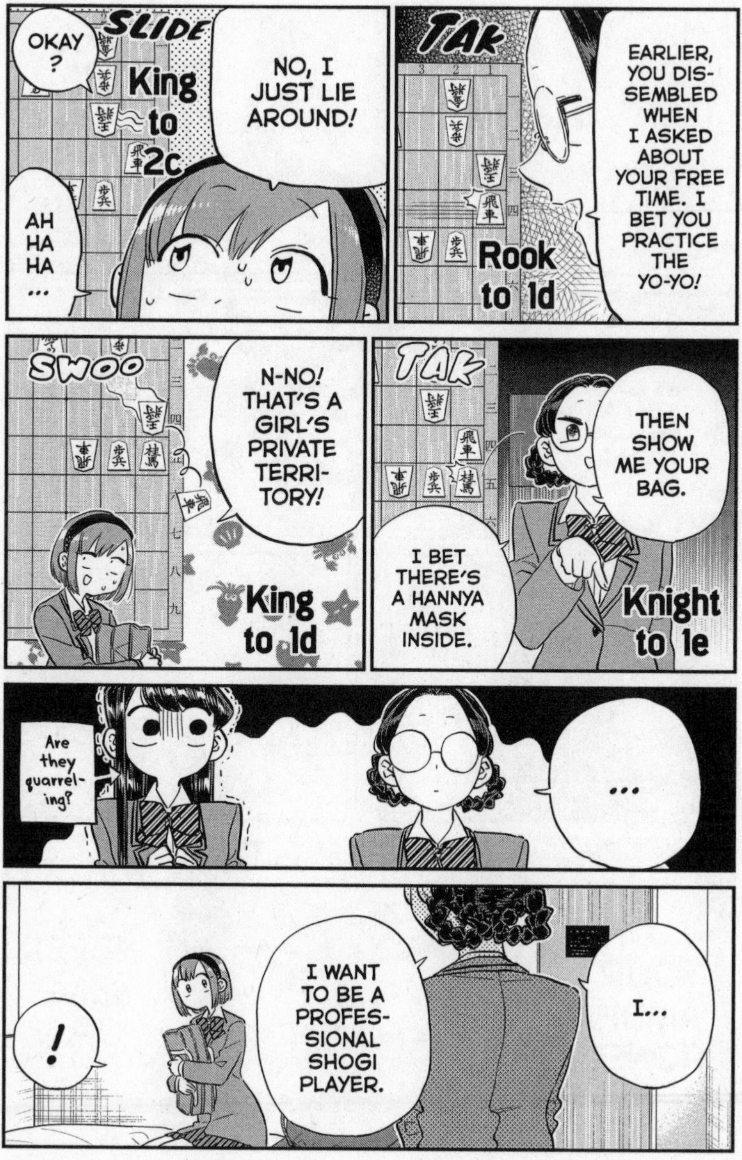
TAK
EARLIER, YOU DISSEMBLED WHEN I ASKED ABOUT YOUR FREE TIME. I BET YOU PRACTICE THE YO-YO!
Rook to 1d
NO, I JUST LIE AROUND!
SLIDE
OKAY?
King to 2c
AH HA HA...
TAK
THEN SHOW ME YOUR BAG.
I BET THERE'S A HANNYA MASK INSIDE.
Knight to 1e
N-NO! THAT'S A GIRL'S PRIVATE TERRITORY!
SWOO
King to 1d
...
Are they quarreling?
I...
I WANT TO BE A PROFESSIONAL SHOGI PLAYER.
!

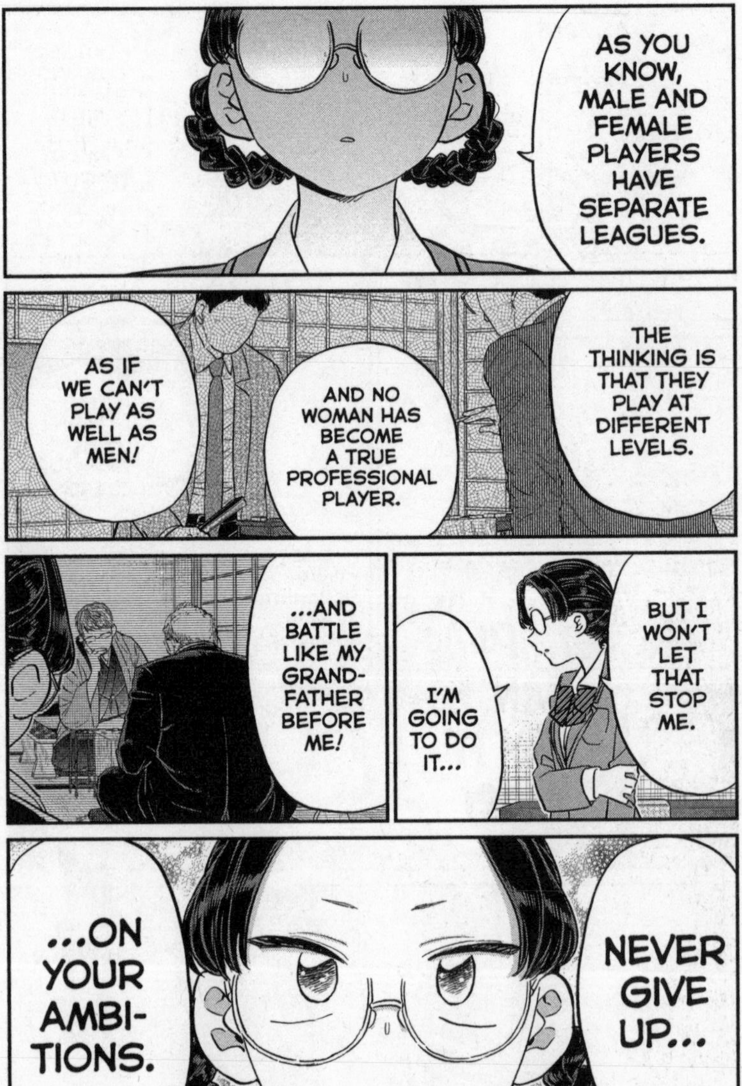
AS YOU KNOW, MALE AND FEMALE PLAYERS HAVE SEPARATE LEAGUES.
THE THINKING IS THAT THEY PLAY AT DIFFERENT LEVELS.
AND NO WOMAN HAS BECOME A TRUE PROFESSIONAL PLAYER.
AS IF WE CAN'T PLAY AS WELL AS MEN!
BUT I WON'T LET THAT STOP ME.
I'M GOING TO DO IT...
...AND BATTLE LIKE MY GRANDFATHER BEFORE ME!
NEVER GIVE UP...
...ON YOUR AMBITIONS.

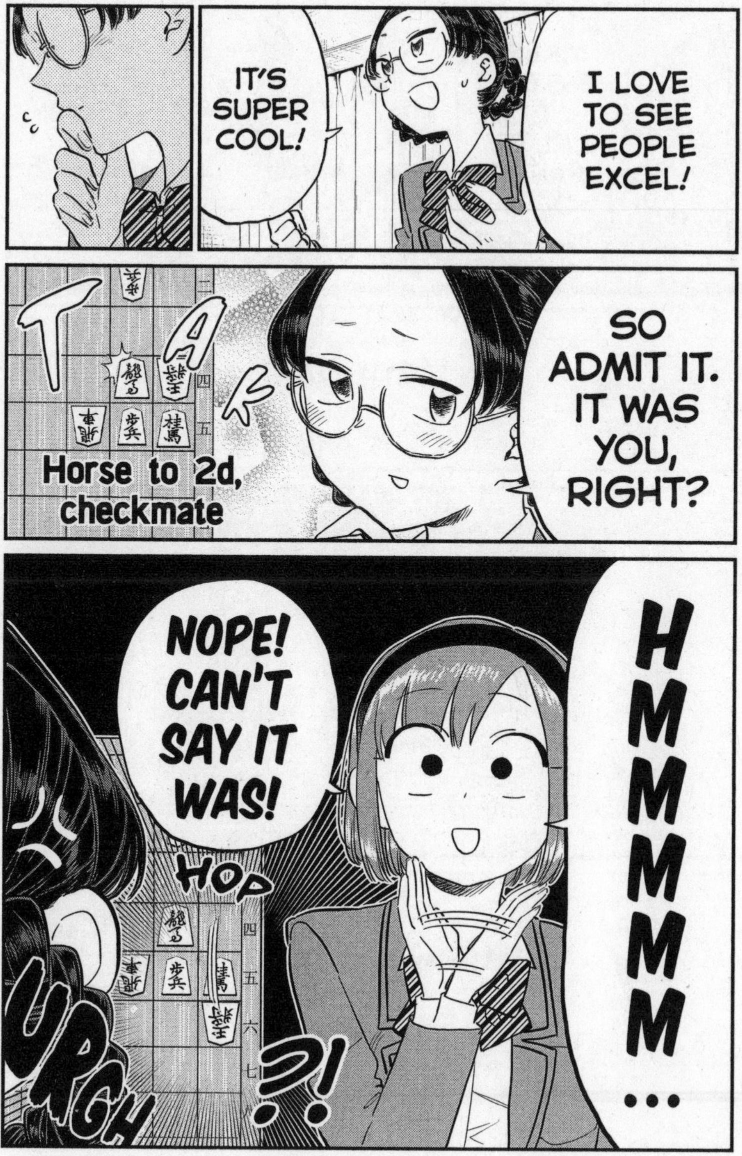
I LOVE TO SEE PEOPLE EXCEL!
IT'S SUPER COOL!
SO ADMIT IT. IT WAS YOU, RIGHT?
TAK
Horse to 2d, checkmate
HMMMMM...
NOPE! CAN'T SAY IT WAS!
HOP
?!
URGH

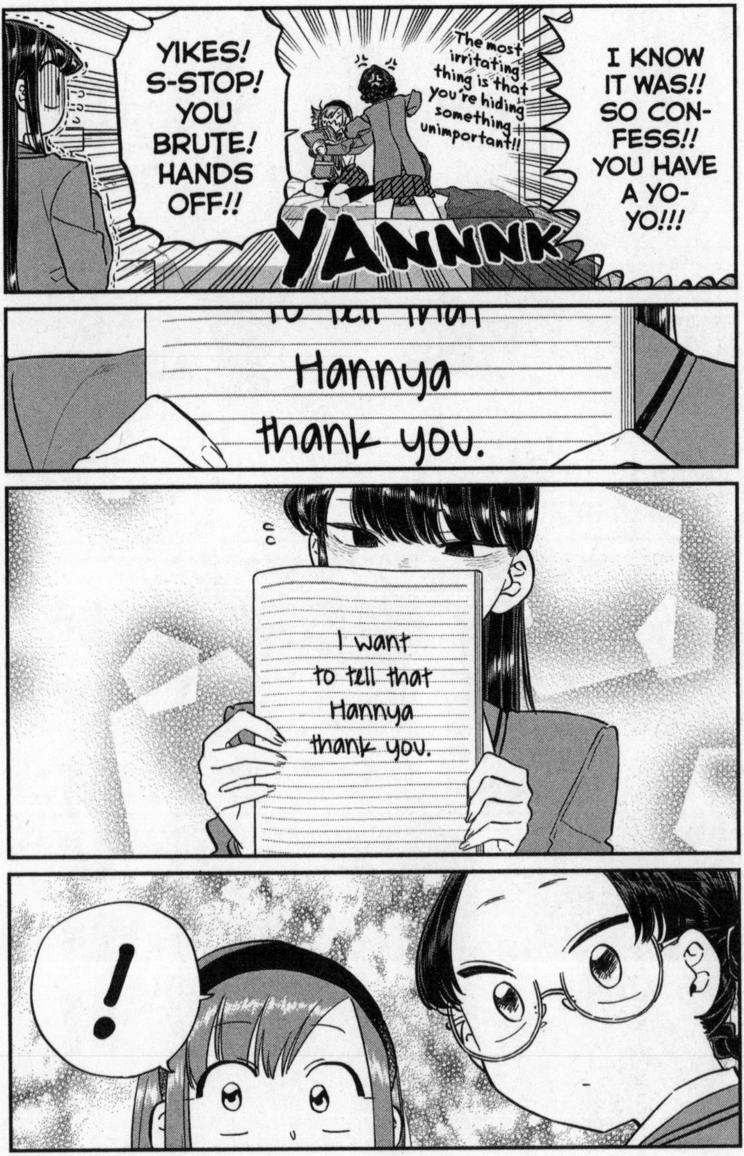
I KNOW IT WAS!! SO CON-FESS!! YOU HAVE A YO-YO!!!
The most irritating thing is that you're hiding something unimportant!!
YIKES! S-STOP! YOU BRUTE! HANDS OFF!!
YANNNK
Hannya thank you.
I want to tell that Hannya thank you.
!

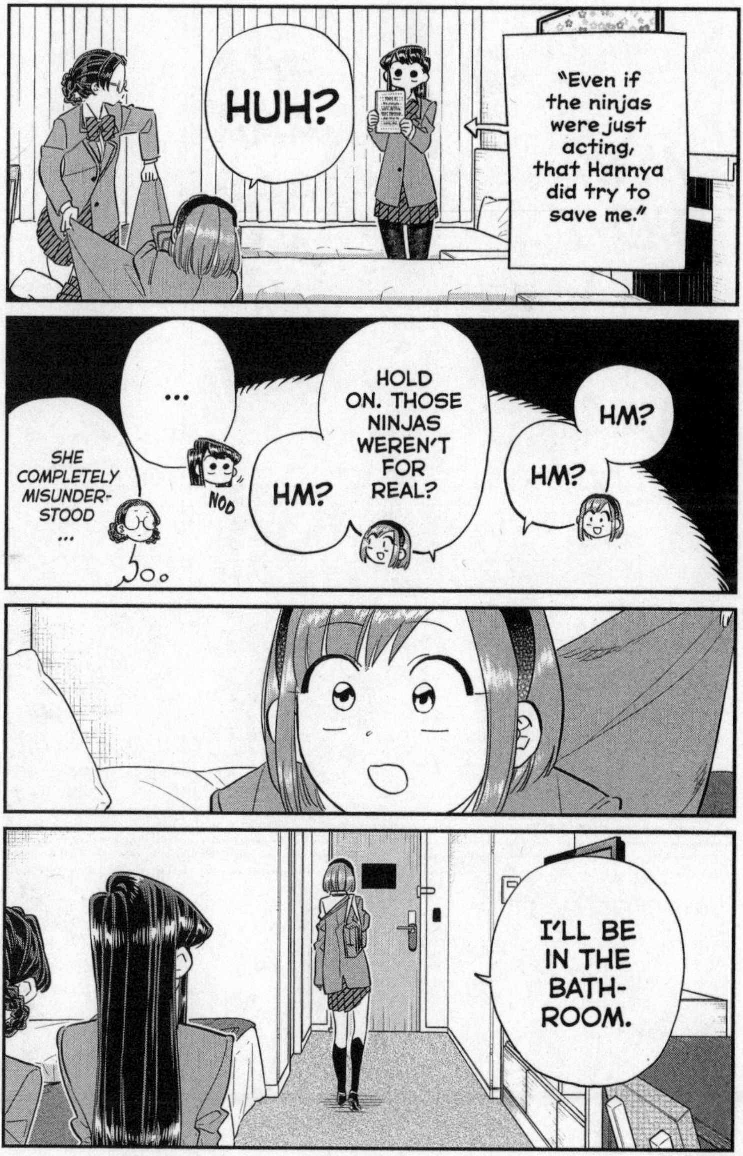
"Even if the ninjas were just acting, that Hannya did try to save me."
HUH?
HM?
HM?
HOLD ON. THOSE NINJAS WEREN'T FOR REAL?
HM?
...
NOD
SHE COMPLETELY MISUNDERSTOOD...
I'LL BE IN THE BATHROOM.

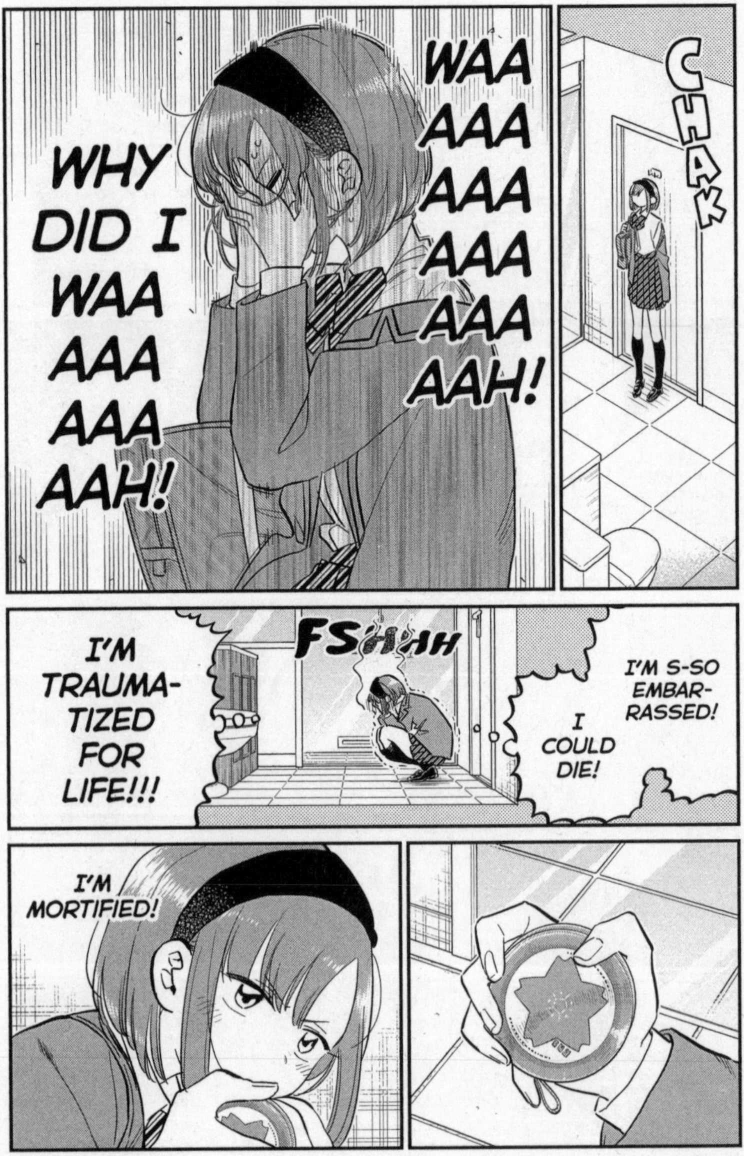
CHAK
WAAAAAAAAAAAAAAAAAAH!
WHY DID I WAAAAAAAAAAH!
I'M S-SO EMBARRASSED!
I COULD DIE!
FSHHH
I'M TRAUMATIZED FOR LIFE!!!
I'M MORTIFIED!

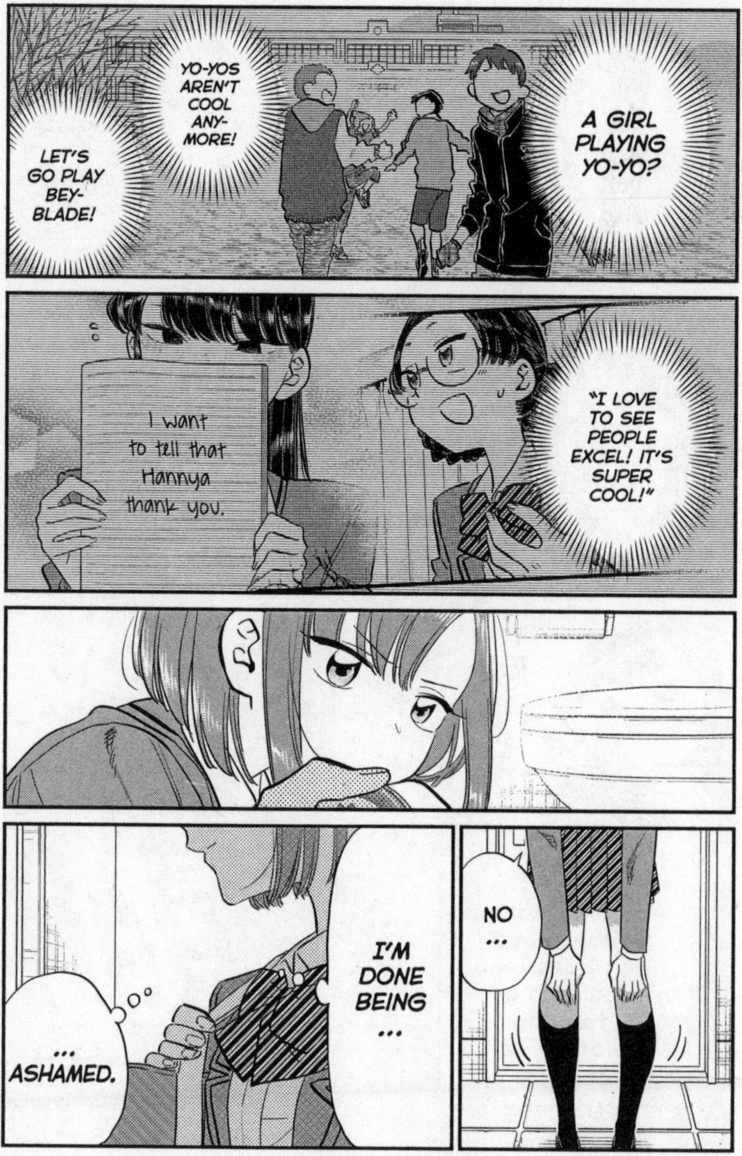
A GIRL PLAYING YO-YO?
YO-YOS AREN'T COOL ANY-MORE!
LET'S GO PLAY BEY-BLADE!
"I LOVE TO SEE PEOPLE EXCEL! IT'S SUPER COOL!"
I want to tell that Hannya thank you.
NO ...
I'M DONE BEING ...
... ASHAMED.

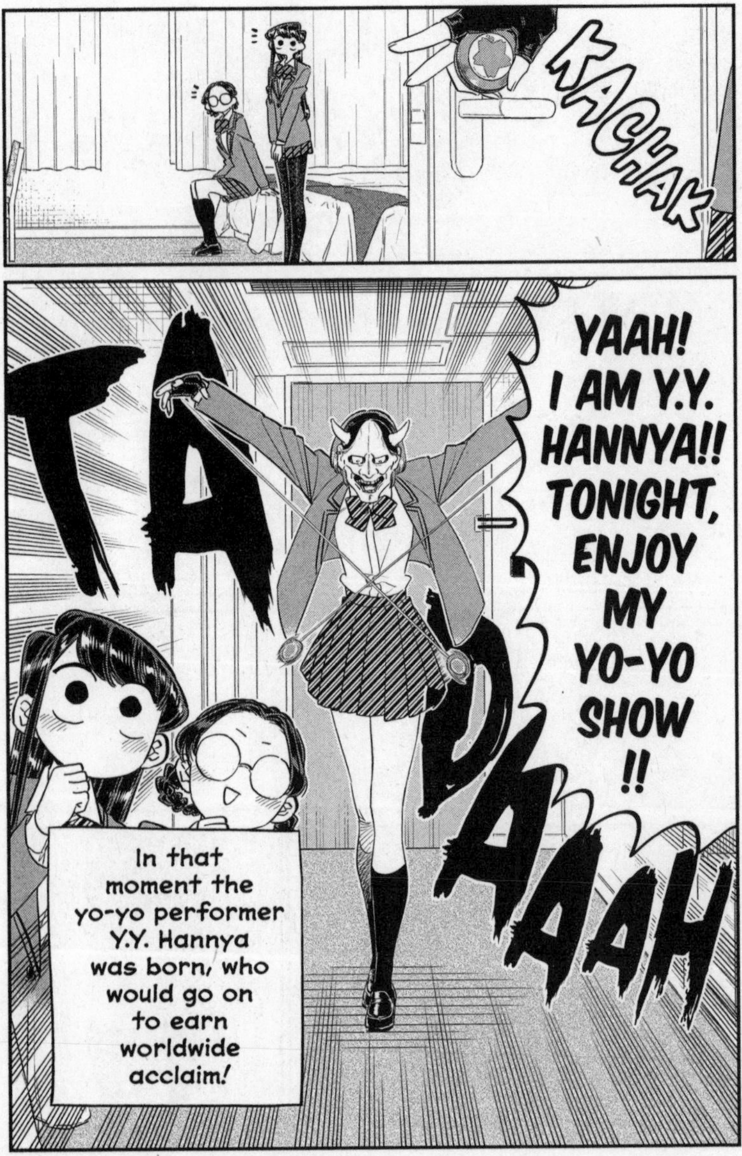
KACHAK
YAAH! I AM Y.Y. HANNYA!! TONIGHT, ENJOY MY YO-YO SHOW !!
TA DAAAH
In that moment the yo-yo performer Y.Y. Hannya was born, who would go on to earn worldwide acclaim!

Communication 111 – The End

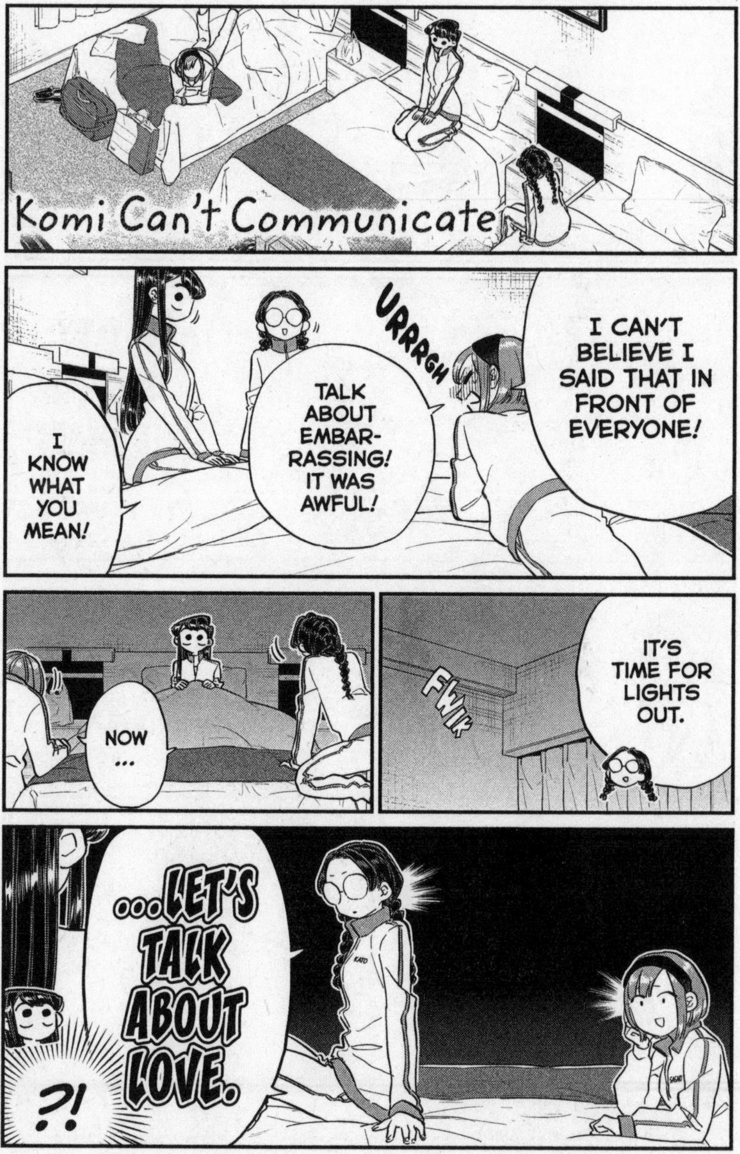
Komi Can't Communicate
I CAN'T BELIEVE I SAID THAT IN FRONT OF EVERYONE!
URRRGH
TALK ABOUT EMBARRASSING! IT WAS AWFUL!
I KNOW WHAT YOU MEAN!
IT'S TIME FOR LIGHTS OUT.
FWIK
NOW...
...LET'S TALK ABOUT LOVE.
?!

Communication 112: The Second Night

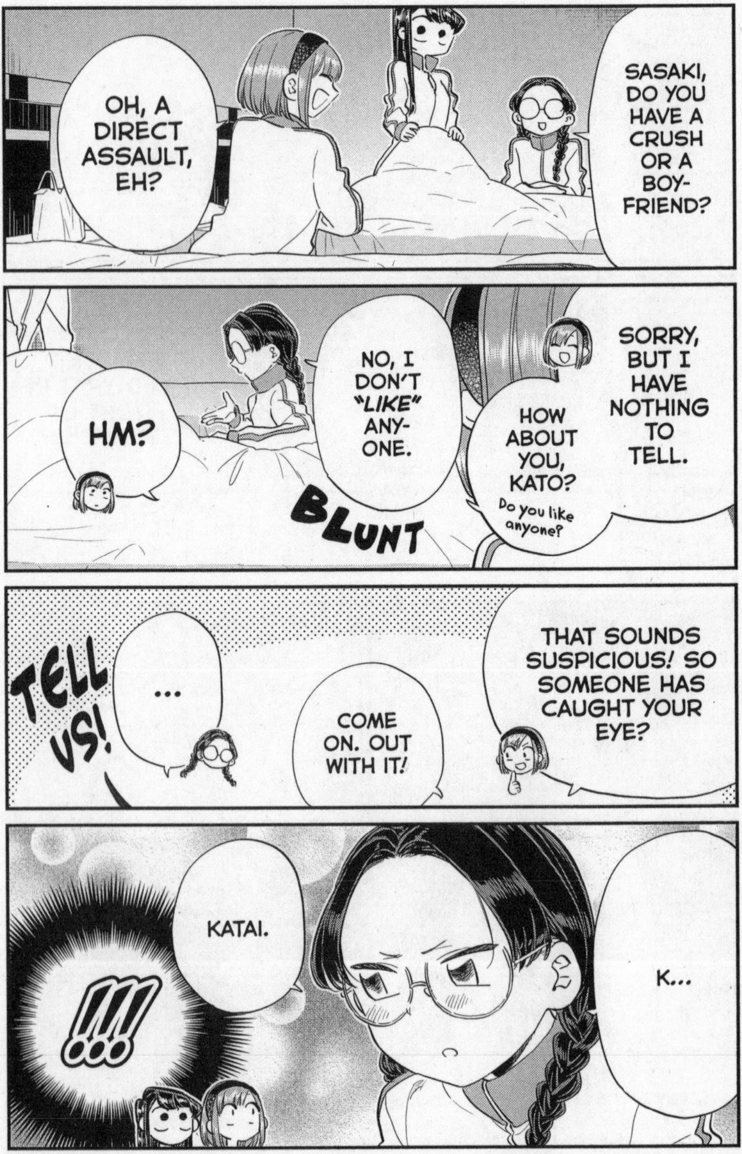
SASAKI, DO YOU HAVE A CRUSH OR A BOY-FRIEND?
OH, A DIRECT ASSAULT, EH?
SORRY, BUT I HAVE NOTHING TO TELL.
HOW ABOUT YOU, KATO?
Do you like anyone?
NO, I DON'T "LIKE" ANY-ONE.
BLUNT
HM?
THAT SOUNDS SUSPICIOUS! SO SOMEONE HAS CAUGHT YOUR EYE?
COME ON. OUT WITH IT!
...
TELL US!
K...
KATAI.
!!!

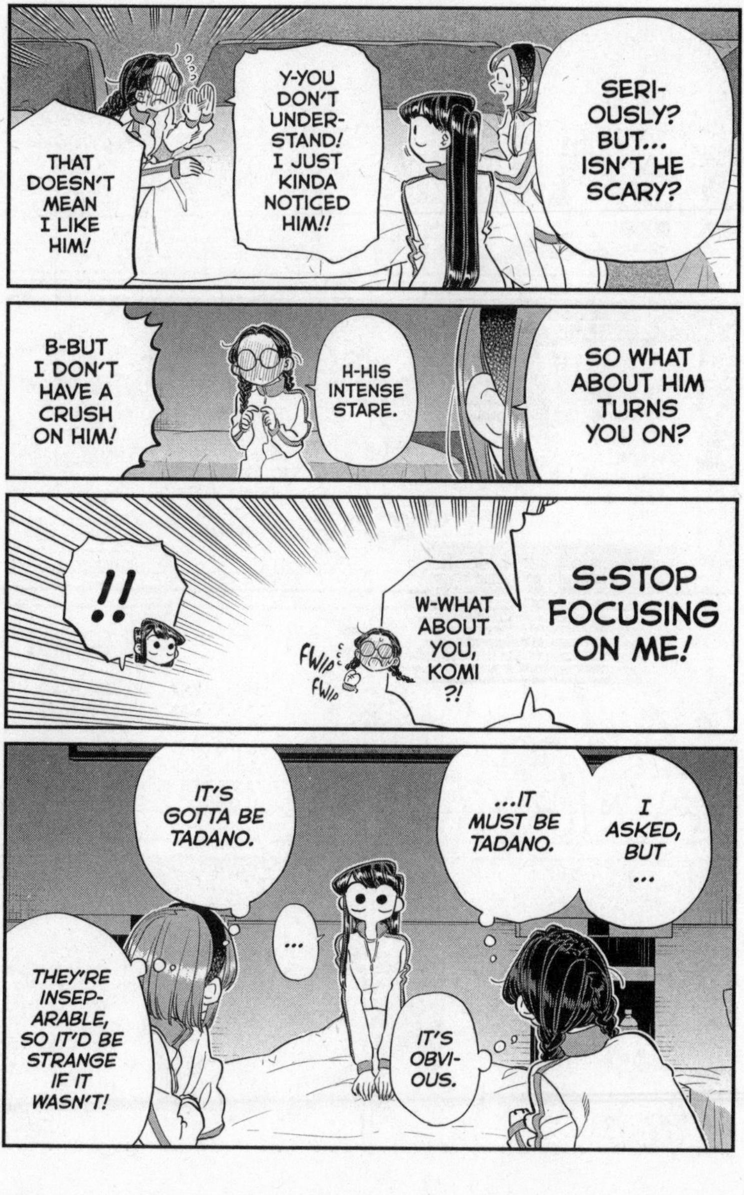
SERIOUSLY? BUT... ISN'T HE SCARY?
Y-YOU DON'T UNDERSTAND! I JUST KINDA NOTICED HIM!!
THAT DOESN'T MEAN I LIKE HIM!
SO WHAT ABOUT HIM TURNS YOU ON?
H-HIS INTENSE STARE.
B-BUT I DON'T HAVE A CRUSH ON HIM!
S-STOP FOCUSING ON ME!
W-WHAT ABOUT YOU, KOMI?!
FWIP FWIP
!!
I ASKED, BUT...
...IT MUST BE TADANO.
IT'S GOTTA BE TADANO.
...
IT'S OBVIOUS.
THEY'RE INSEPARABLE, SO IT'D BE STRANGE IF IT WASN'T!

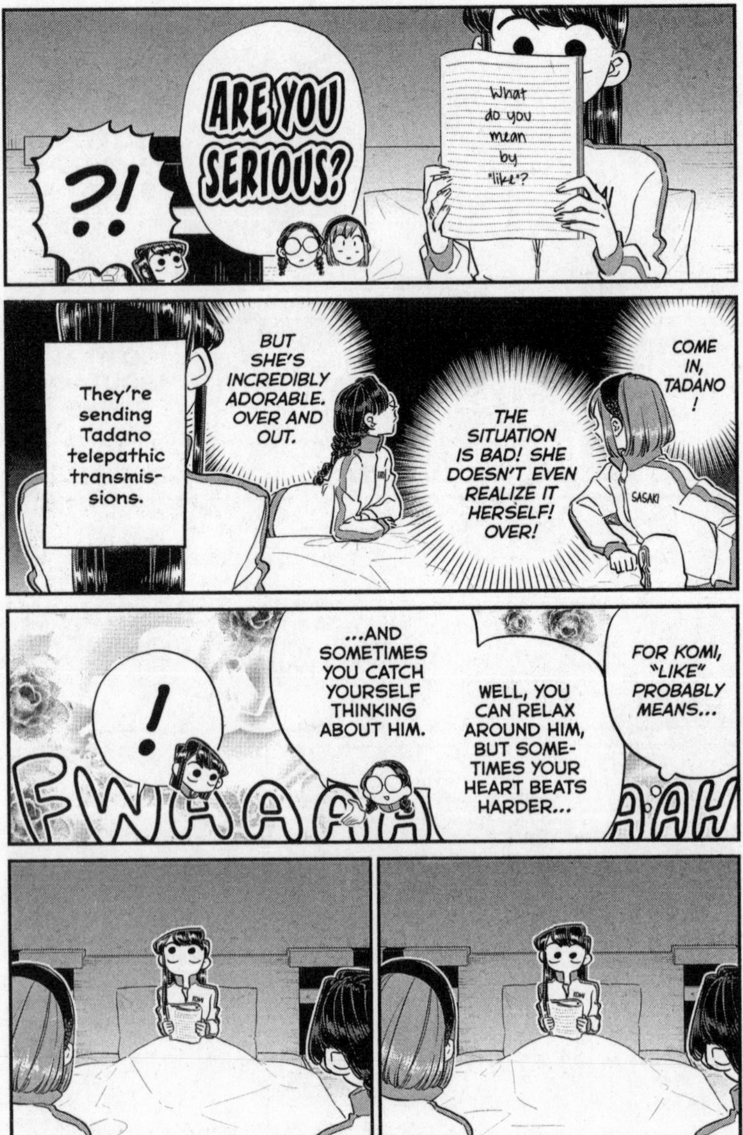
What do you mean by "like"?
ARE YOU SERIOUS?
?!
COME IN, TADANO!
THE SITUATION IS BAD! SHE DOESN'T EVEN REALIZE IT HERSELF! OVER!
SASAKI
BUT SHE'S INCREDIBLY ADORABLE. OVER AND OUT.
They're sending Tadano telepathic transmissions.
FOR KOMI, "LIKE" PROBABLY MEANS...
WELL, YOU CAN RELAX AROUND HIM, BUT SOMETIMES YOUR HEART BEATS HARDER...
...AND SOMETIMES YOU CATCH YOURSELF THINKING ABOUT HIM.
!
FWAAAA AAH

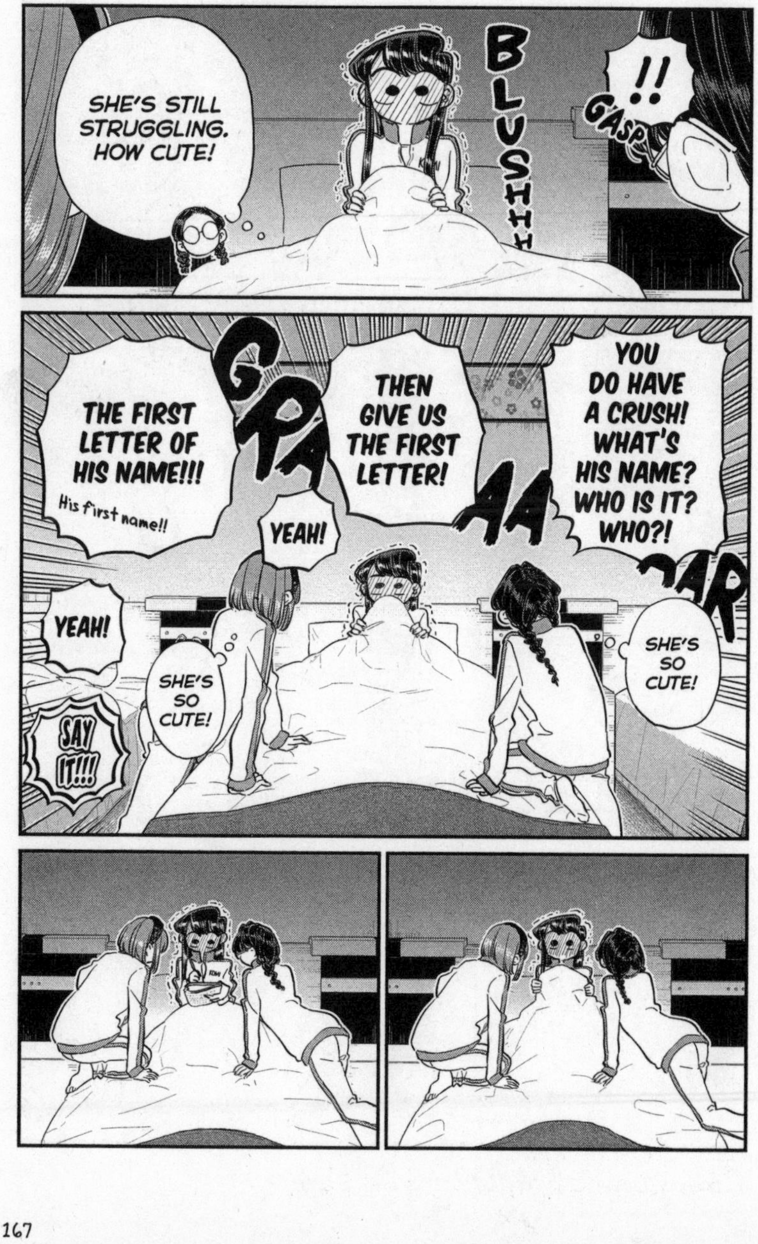
!!
GASP
BLUSHHH
SHE'S STILL STRUGGLING. HOW CUTE!
YOU DO HAVE A CRUSH! WHAT'S HIS NAME? WHO IS IT? WHO?!
GRAAAA
THEN GIVE US THE FIRST LETTER!
YEAH!
THE FIRST LETTER OF HIS NAME!!!
His first name!!
SHE'S SO CUTE!
SHE'S SO CUTE!
YEAH!
SAY IT!!!

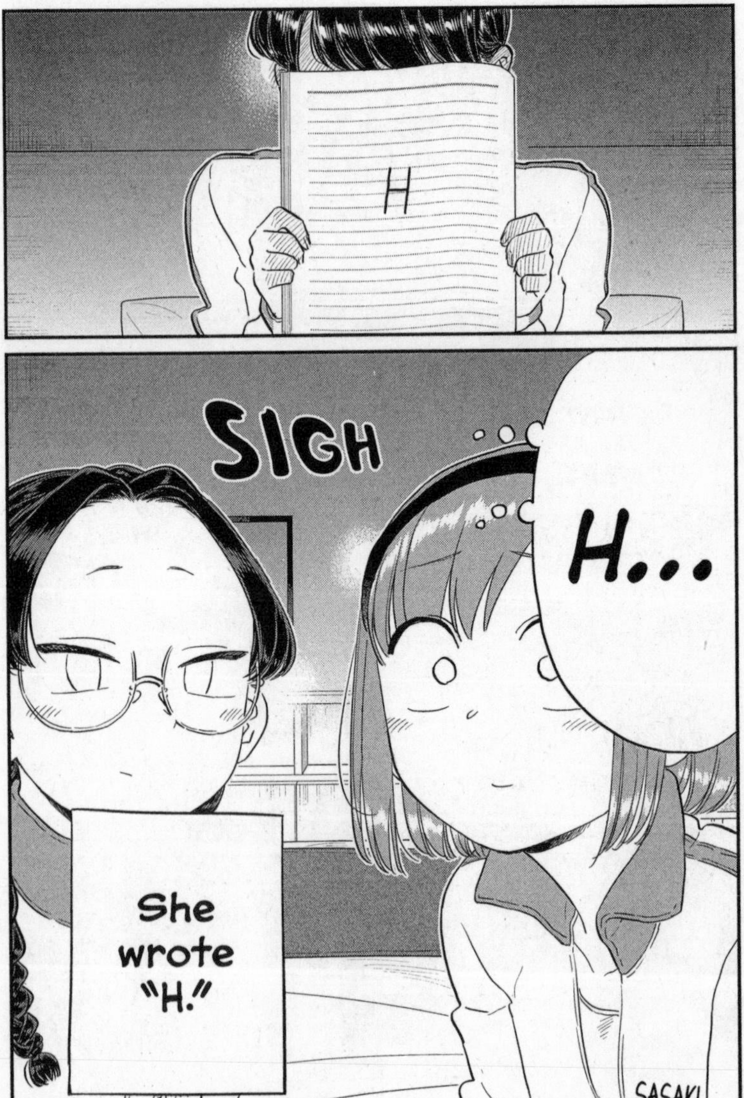
H
H...
SIGH
SASAKI
She wrote "H."

Communication 112—The End

Komi Can't Communicate

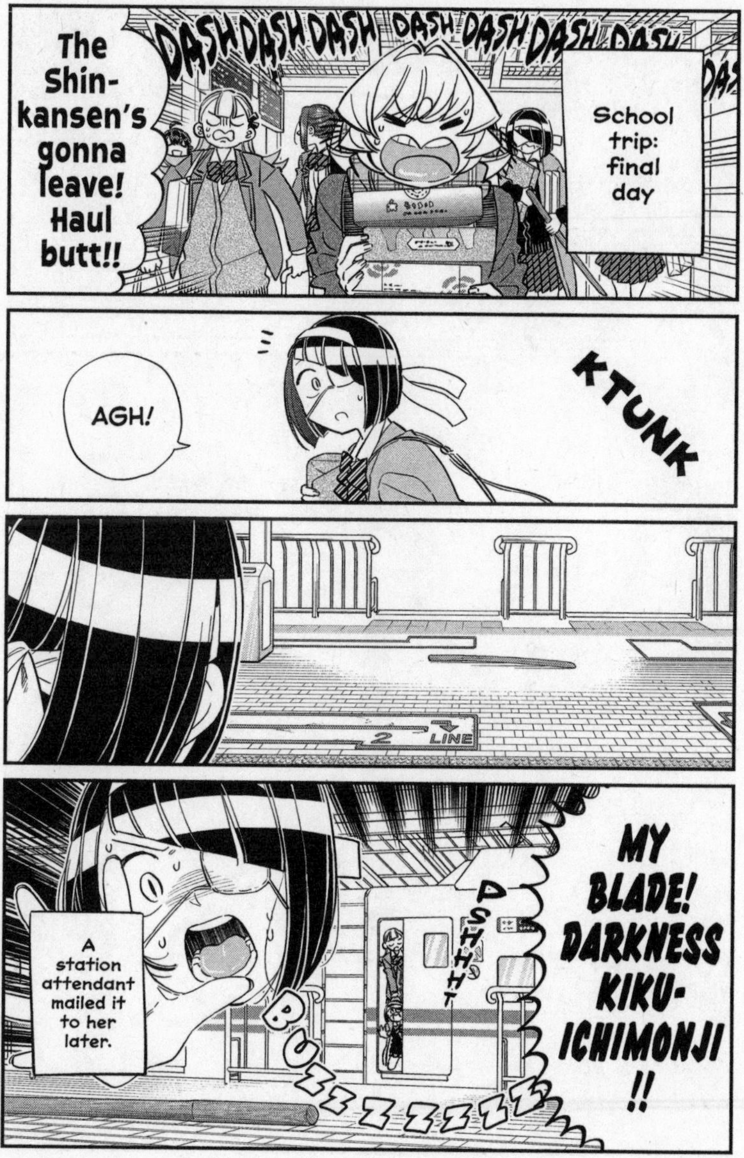
School trip: final day
DASH DASH DASH DASH DASH DASH DASH DASH
The Shinkansen's gonna leave! Haul butt!!
KTUNK
AGH!
2 LINE
MY BLADE! DARKNESS KIKU-ICHIMONJI !!
DASHHHT
BUZZZZZZZZZ
A station attendant mailed it to her later.

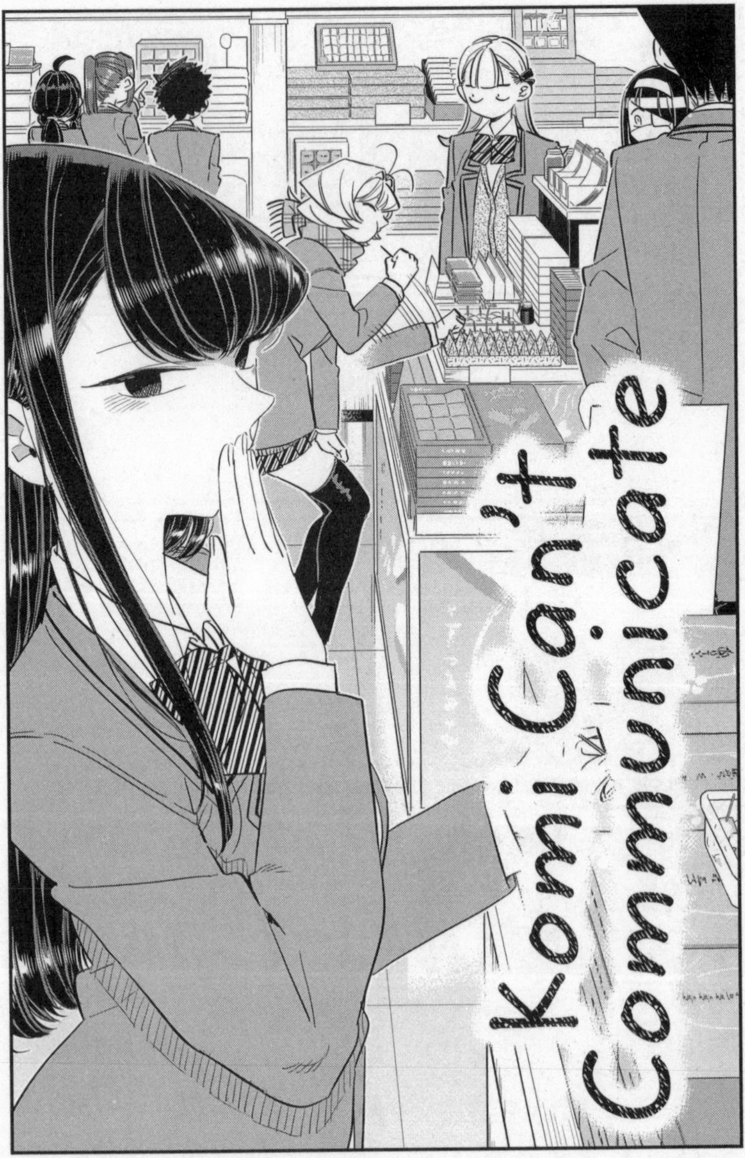
Komi Can't Communicate

Communication 113: The Return Shinkansen

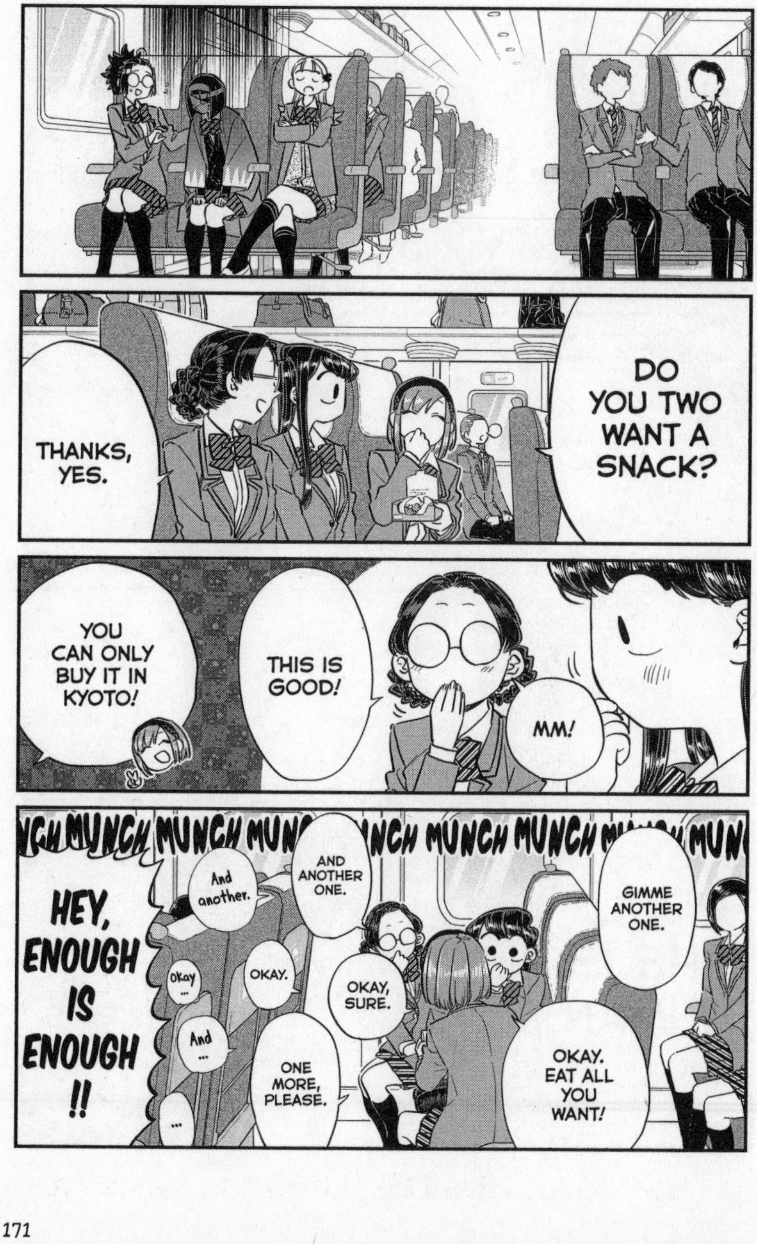
DO YOU TWO WANT A SNACK?
THANKS, YES.
MM!
THIS IS GOOD!
YOU CAN ONLY BUY IT IN KYOTO!
MUNCH MUNCH MUNCH MUNCH MUNCH
GIMME ANOTHER ONE.
OKAY. EAT ALL YOU WANT!
AND ANOTHER ONE.
OKAY, SURE.
OKAY.
ONE MORE, PLEASE.
And another.
Okay ...
And ...
...
HEY, ENOUGH IS ENOUGH!!

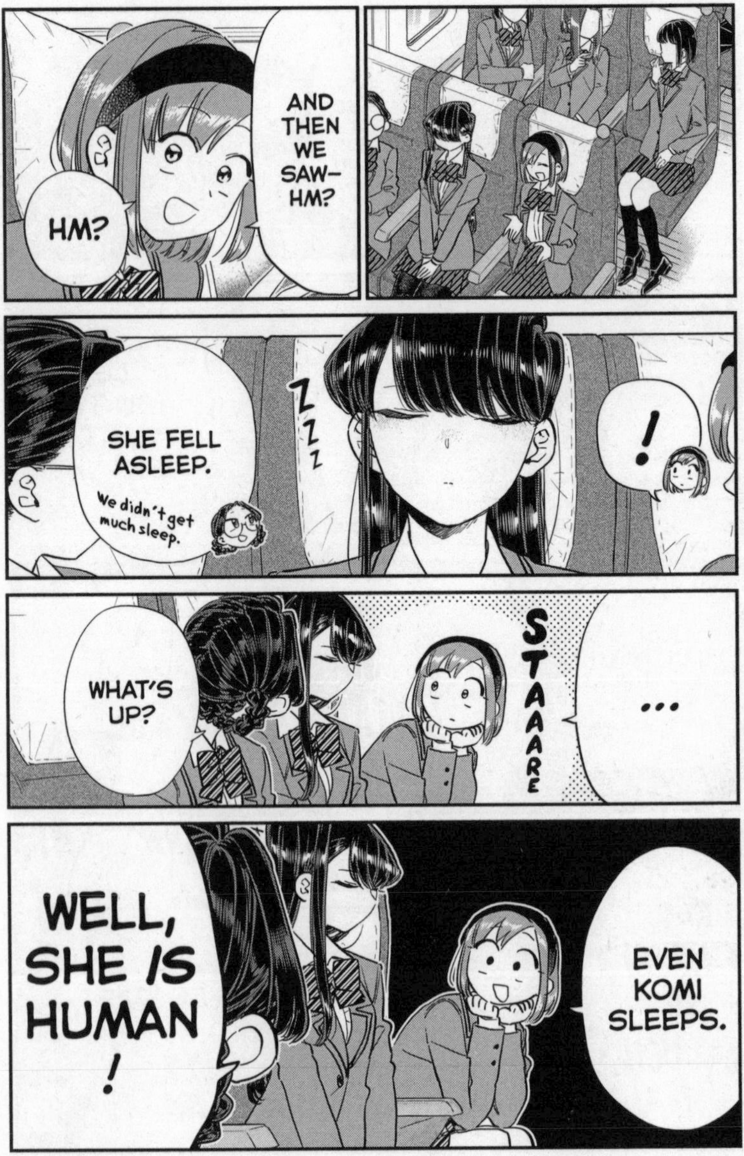
AND THEN WE SAW— HM?
HM?
!
ZZZ
SHE FELL ASLEEP.
We didn't get much sleep.
...
STAAAARE
WHAT'S UP?
EVEN KOMI SLEEPS.
WELL, SHE IS HUMAN!

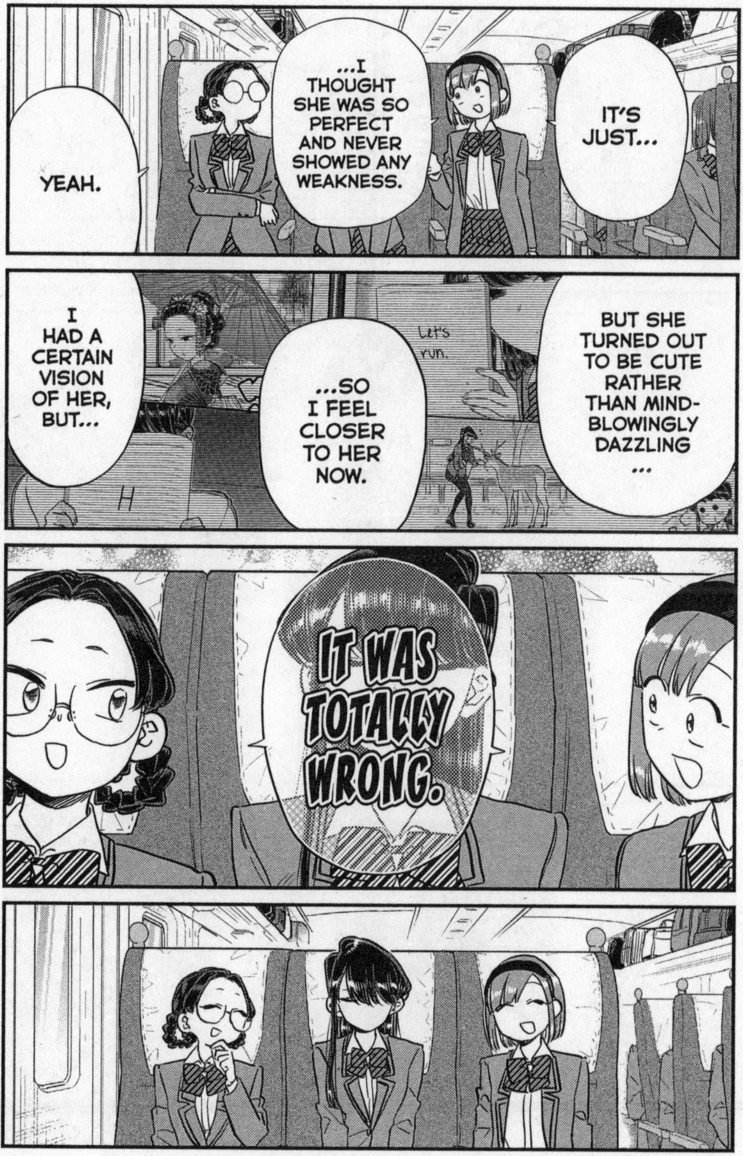
IT'S JUST...
...I THOUGHT SHE WAS SO PERFECT AND NEVER SHOWED ANY WEAKNESS.
YEAH.
BUT SHE TURNED OUT TO BE CUTE RATHER THAN MIND-BLOWINGLY DAZZLING ...
Let's run.
...SO I FEEL CLOSER TO HER NOW.
I HAD A CERTAIN VISION OF HER, BUT...
IT WAS TOTALLY WRONG.

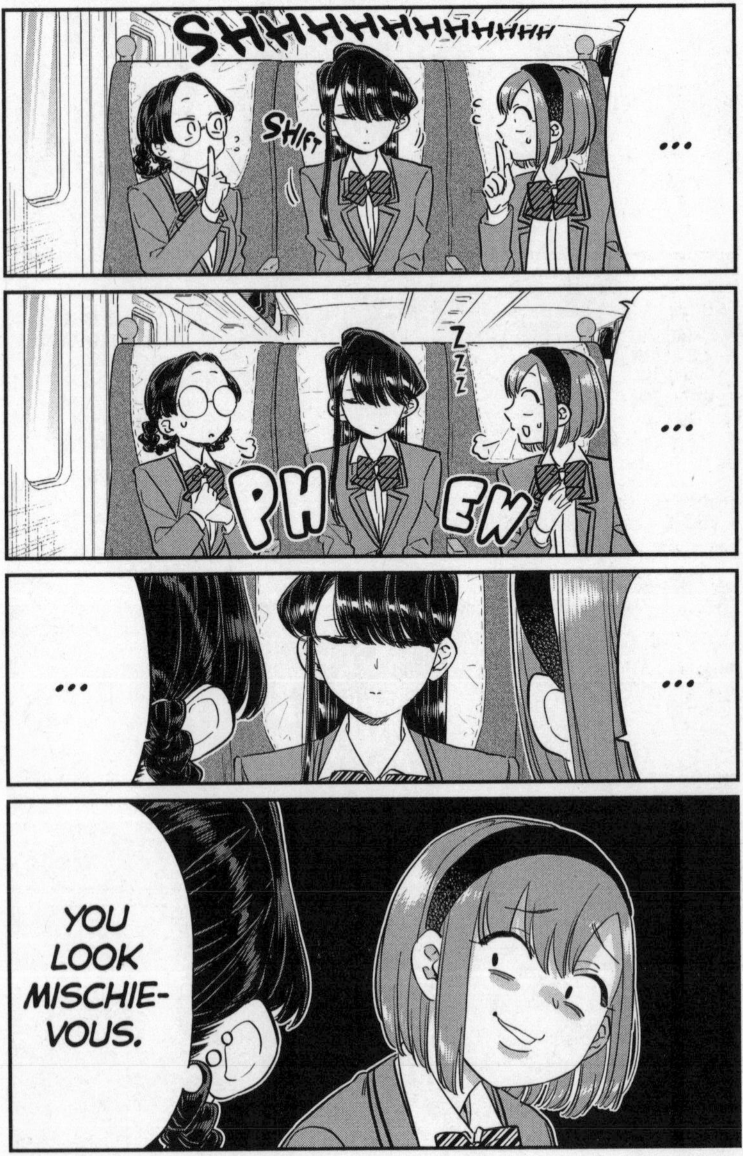
...
SHHHHHHHHHHH
SHIFT
...
ZZZ
PHEW
...
...
YOU LOOK MISCHIE-VOUS.

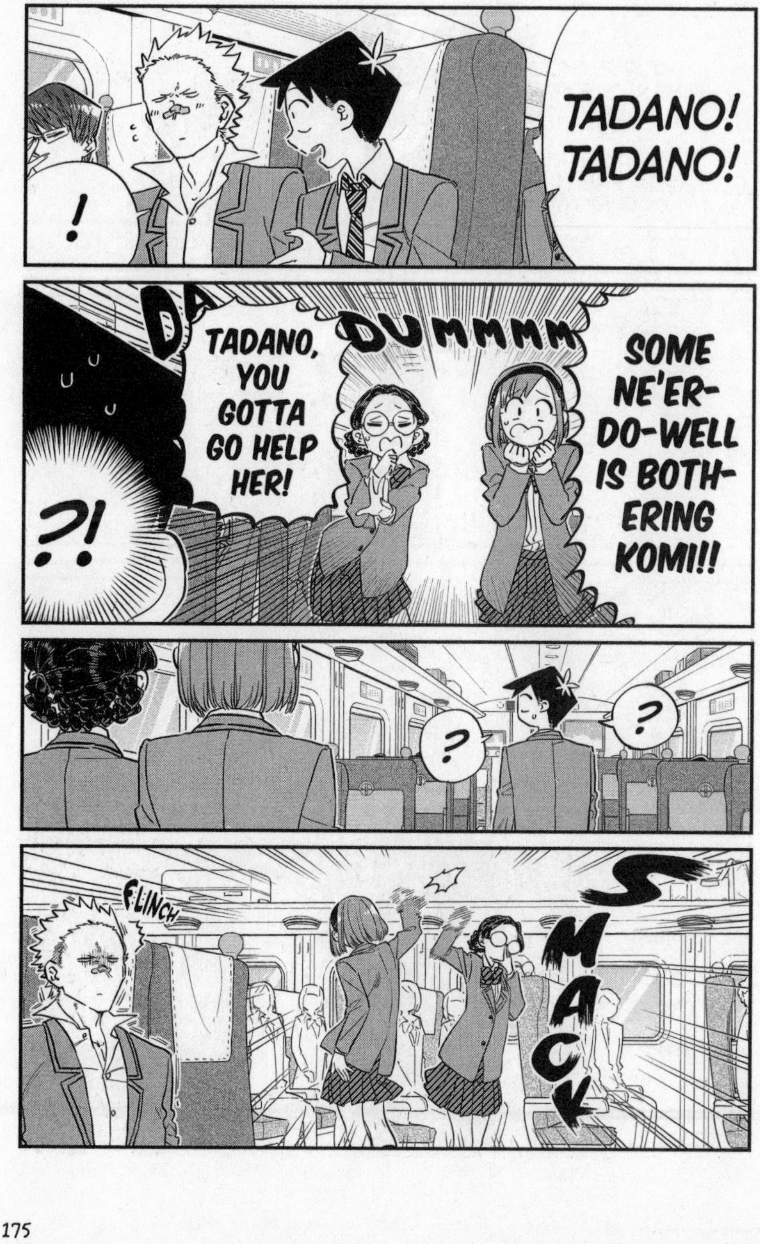
TADANO! TADANO!
!
SOME NE'ER-DO-WELL IS BOTHERING KOMI!!
TADANO, YOU GOTTA GO HELP HER!
DA
DUMMMM
?!
?
?
SMACK
FLINCH

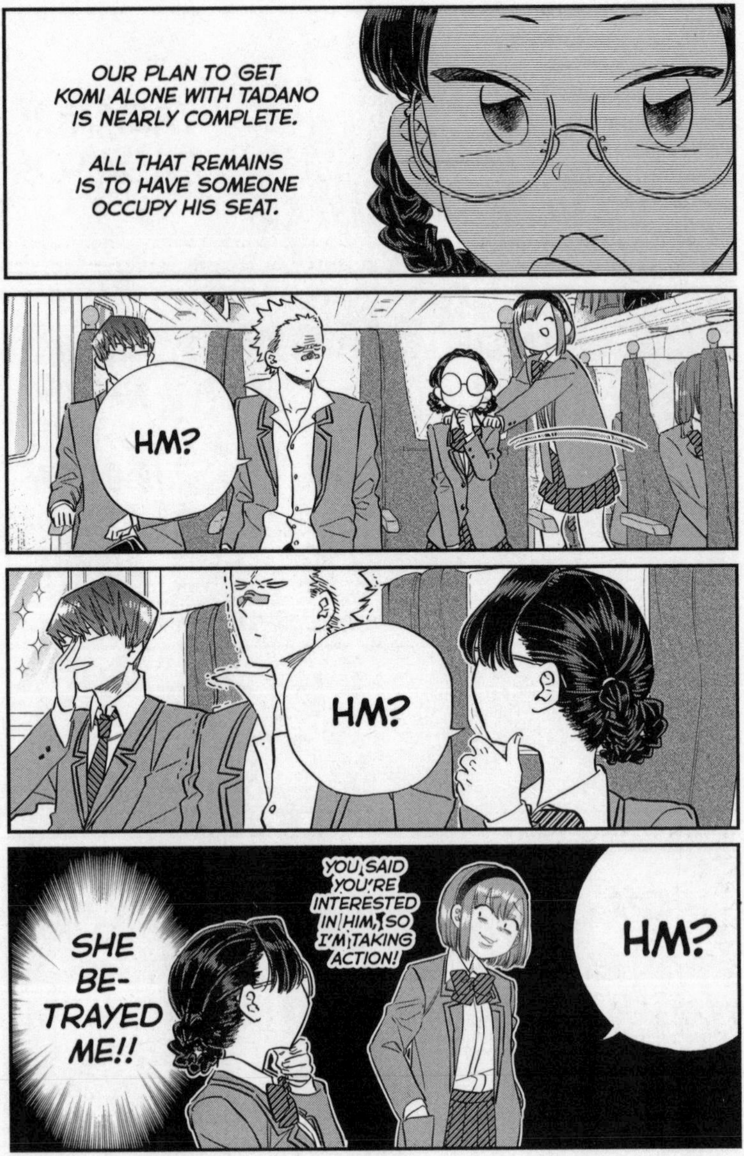
OUR PLAN TO GET KOMI ALONE WITH TADANO IS NEARLY COMPLETE.
ALL THAT REMAINS IS TO HAVE SOMEONE OCCUPY HIS SEAT.
HM?
HM?
HM?
YOU SAID YOU'RE INTERESTED IN HIM, SO I'M TAKING ACTION!
SHE BE-TRAYED ME!!

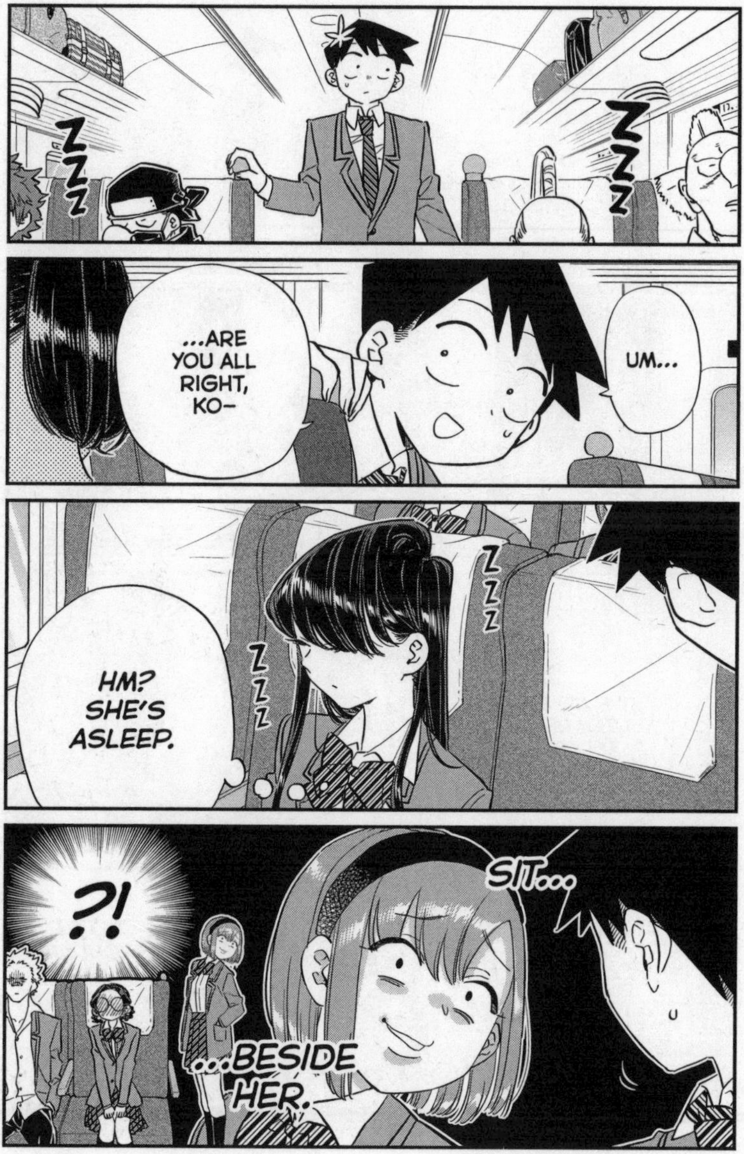
ZZZ
ZZZ
UM...
...ARE YOU ALL RIGHT, KO-
ZZZ
ZZZ
HM? SHE'S ASLEEP.
SIT...
...BESIDE HER.
?!

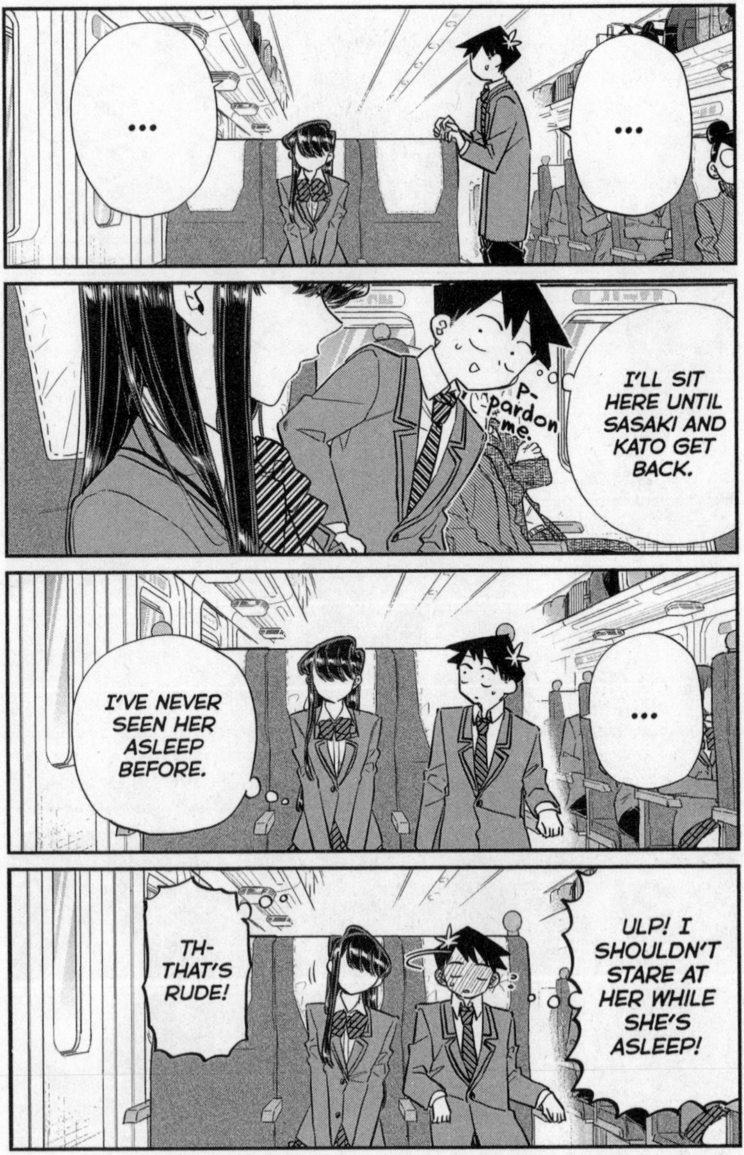
...
...
I'LL SIT HERE UNTIL SASAKI AND KATO GET BACK.
P-pardon me.
...
I'VE NEVER SEEN HER ASLEEP BEFORE.
ULP! I SHOULDN'T STARE AT HER WHILE SHE'S ASLEEP!
TH-THAT'S RUDE!

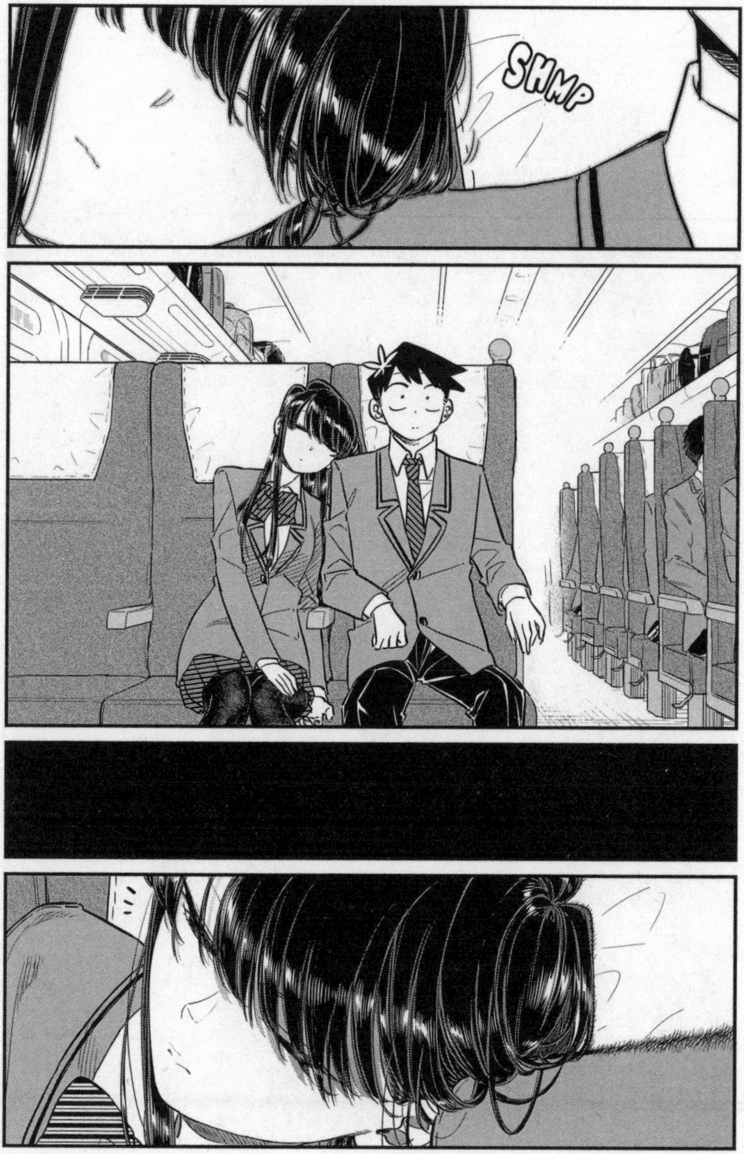
SHMP

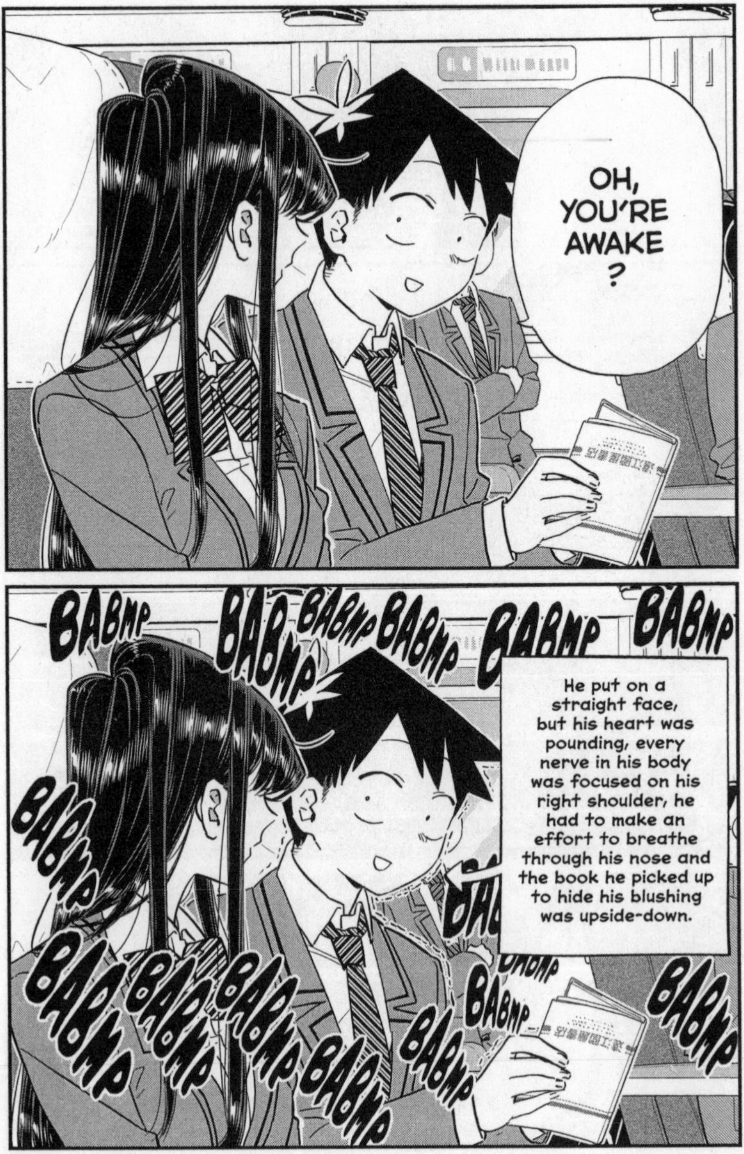
OH, YOU'RE AWAKE ?
BABMP
BABMP
BABMP
BABMP
BABMP
BABMP
BABMP
He put on a straight face, but his heart was pounding, every nerve in his body was focused on his right shoulder, he had to make an effort to breathe through his nose and the book he picked up to hide his blushing was upside-down.
BABMP
BABMP
BABMP
BABMP
BABMP
BABMP
BABMP
BABMP

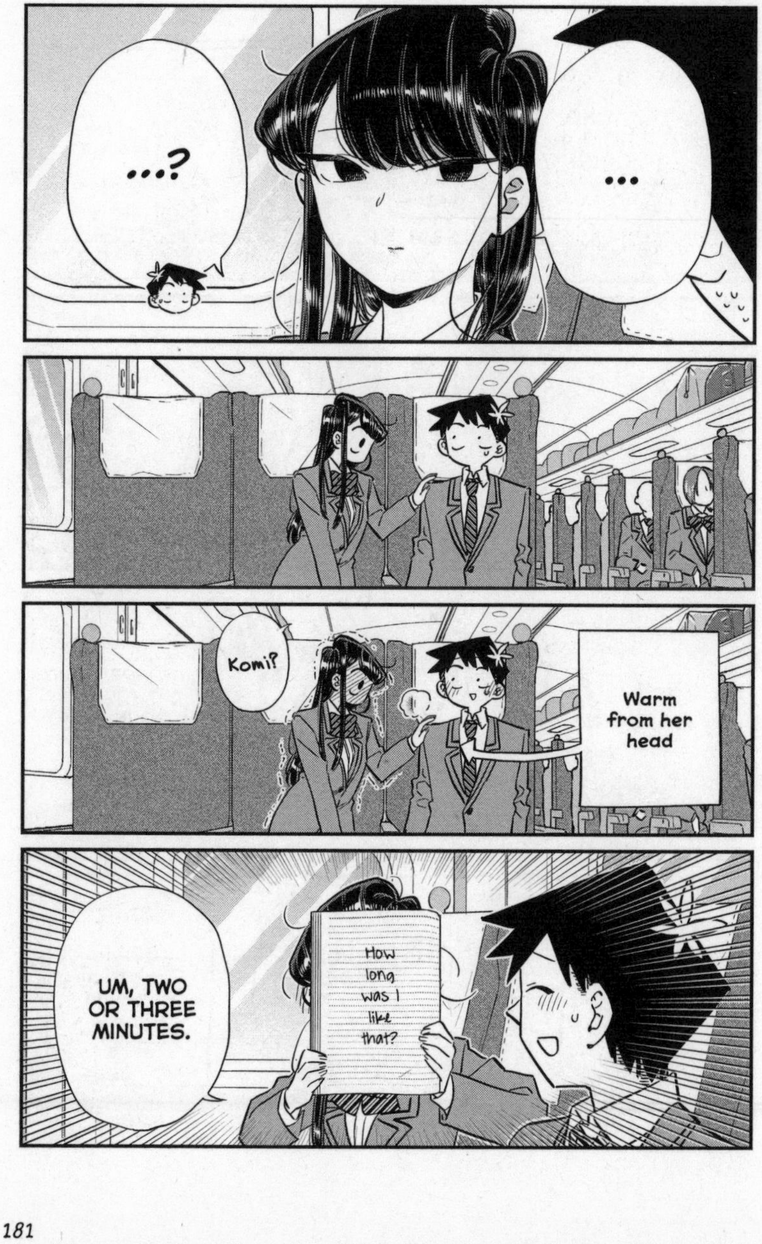
...
...?
Warm from her head
Komi?
How long was I like that?
UM, TWO OR THREE MINUTES.

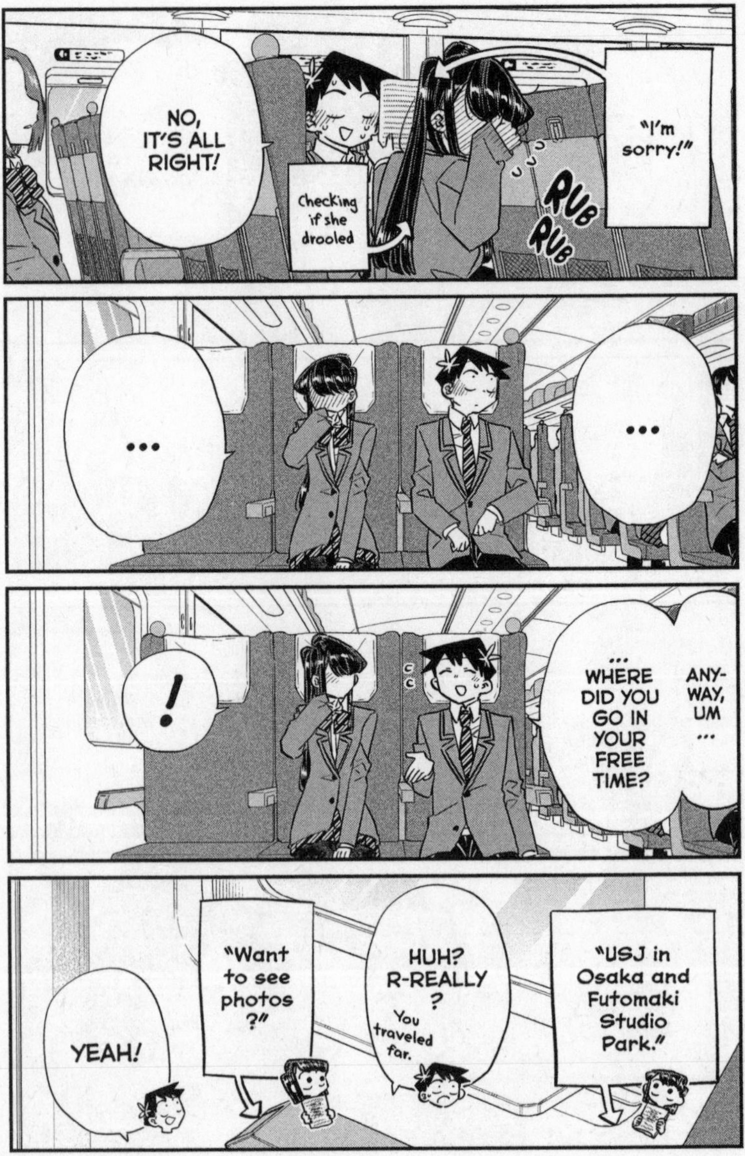
"I'm sorry!"
RUB RUB
Checking if she drooled
NO, IT'S ALL RIGHT!
...
...
ANY-WAY, UM ...
... WHERE DID YOU GO IN YOUR FREE TIME?
!
"USJ in Osaka and Futomaki Studio Park."
HUH? R-REALLY?
You traveled far.
"Want to see photos?"
YEAH!

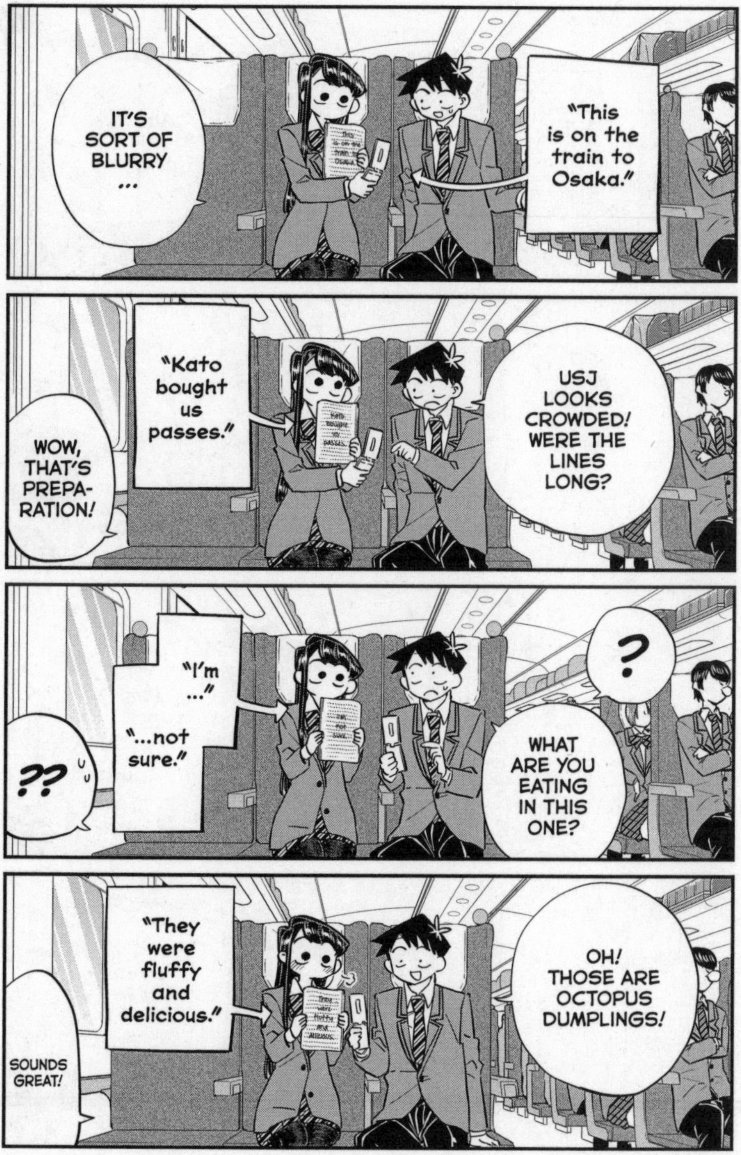
"This is on the train to Osaka."
IT'S SORT OF BLURRY ...
USJ LOOKS CROWDED! WERE THE LINES LONG?
"Kato bought us passes."
WOW, THAT'S PREPARATION!
?
WHAT ARE YOU EATING IN THIS ONE?
"I'm ..."
"...not sure."
??
OH! THOSE ARE OCTOPUS DUMPLINGS!
"They were fluffy and delicious."
SOUNDS GREAT!

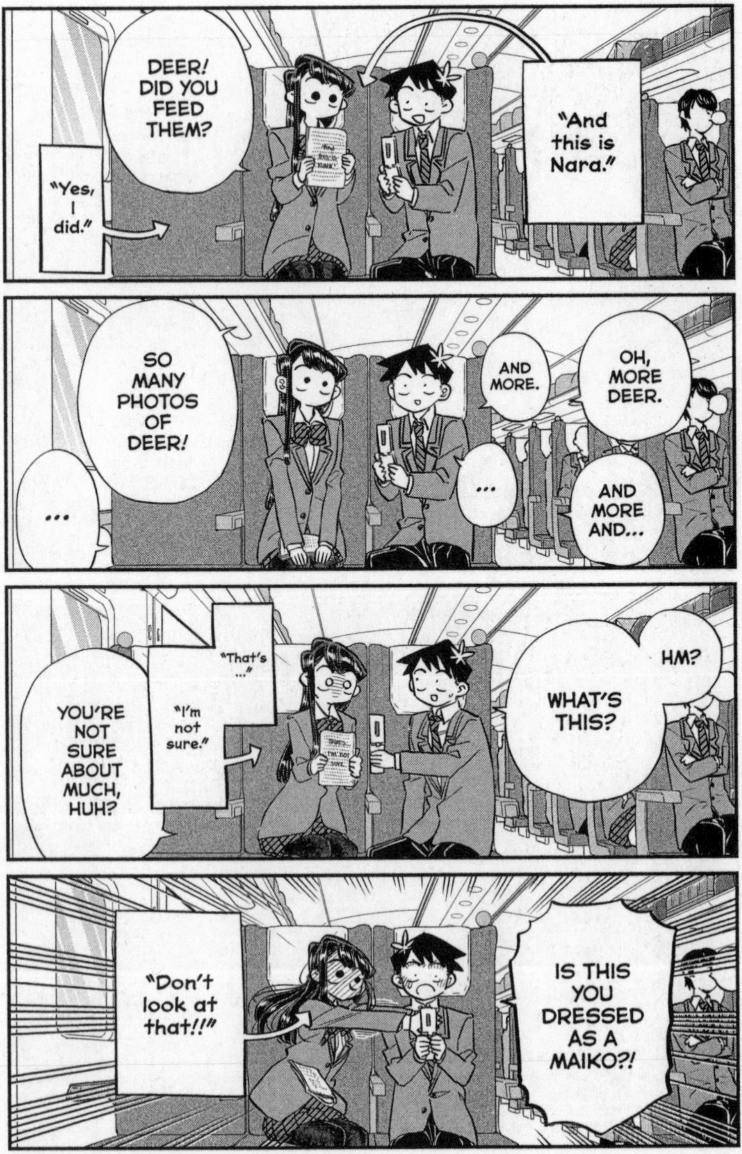
"And this is Nara."
DEER! DID YOU FEED THEM?
"Yes, I did."
OH, MORE DEER.
AND MORE.
AND MORE AND...
...
SO MANY PHOTOS OF DEER!
...
HM?
WHAT'S THIS?
"That's ..."
"I'm not sure."
YOU'RE NOT SURE ABOUT MUCH, HUH?
IS THIS YOU DRESSED AS A MAIKO?!
"Don't look at that!!"

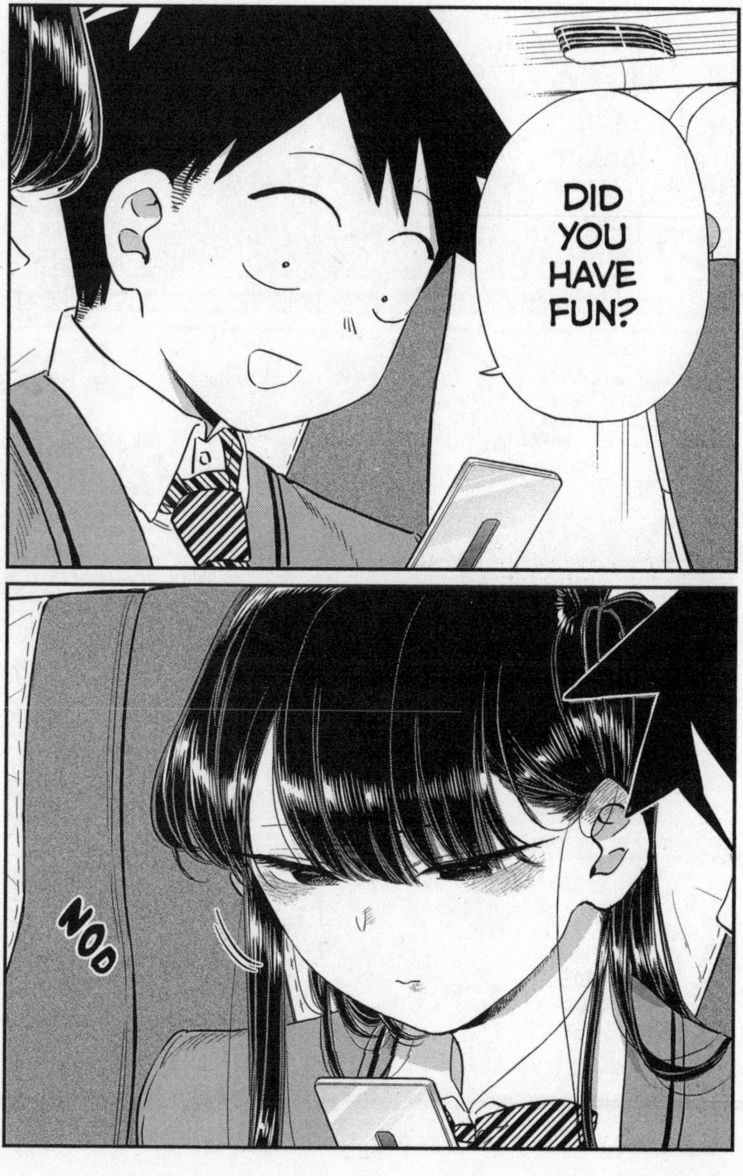
DID YOU HAVE FUN?
NOD

THAT'S GOO–
What're you lookin' at?!
JOLT
?!
There's an open seat! Lucky me!
I'll join you!
We can see your under-wear!
"Um, why did you take a photo of the boys with their shirts off?"
Huh?!
NO, UM...
THAT WAS, UM...
What?! I wanna see!

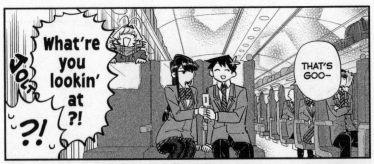

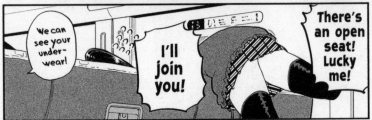

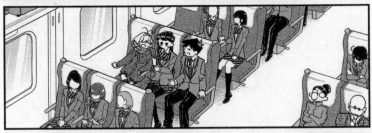

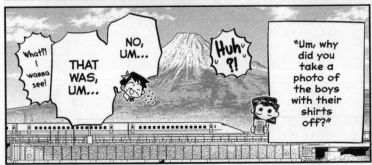

Communication 113 – The End

Komi Can't Communicate

Komi Can't Communicate

Security

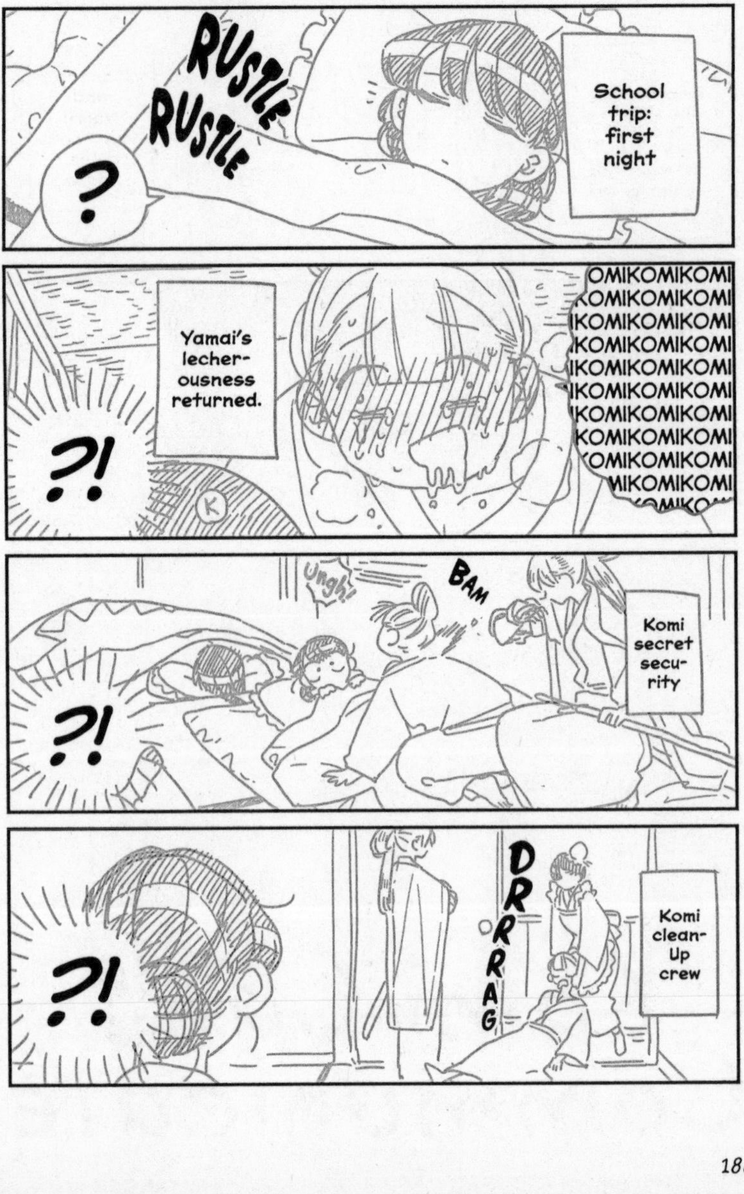
School trip: first night
RUSTLE
RUSTLE
?
KOMIKOMIKOMI
KOMIKOMIKOMI
KOMIKOMIKOMI
KOMIKOMIKOMI
KOMIKOMIKOMI
KOMIKOMIKOMI
Yamai's lecherousness returned.
?!
Komi secret security
BAM
Ungh!
?!
Komi clean-up crew
DRRRRAG
?!

Komi Can't Communicate

Can Komi Make 100 Friends?: A Fun School Trip

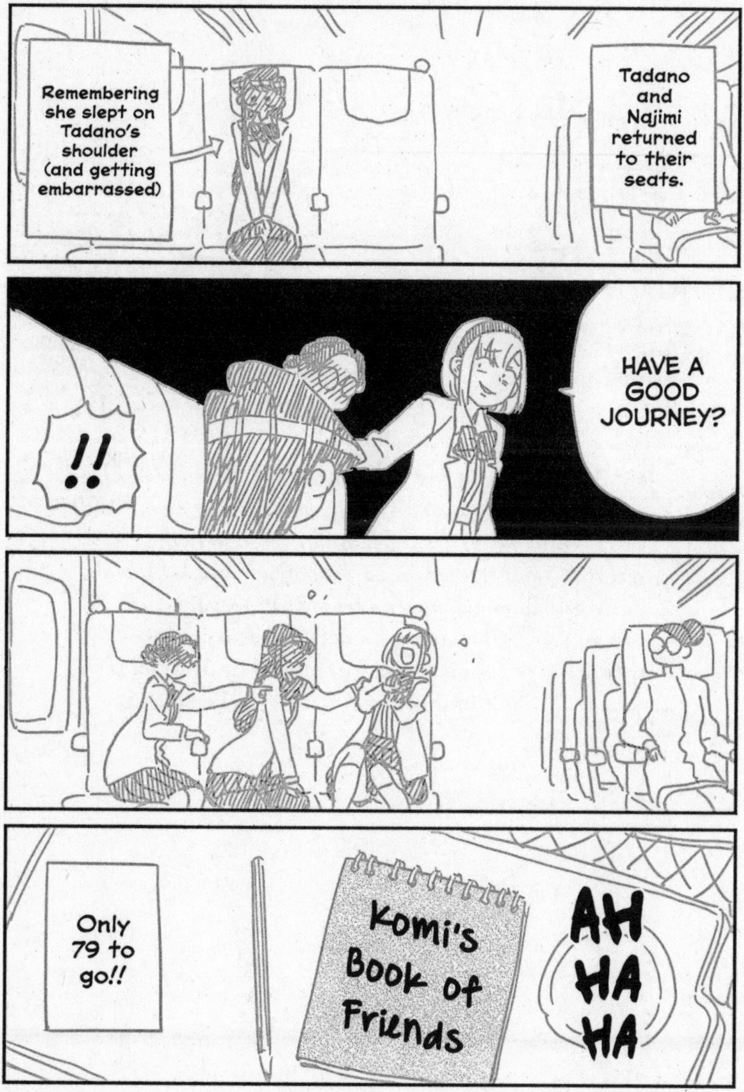
Tadano and Najimi returned to their seats.
Remembering she slept on Tadano's shoulder (and getting embarrassed)
HAVE A GOOD JOURNEY?
!!
AH HA HA
Komi's Book of Friends
Only 79 to go!!

Tomohito Oda won the grand prize for *World Worst One* in the 70th Shogakukan New Comic Artist Awards in 2012. Oda's series *Digicon*, about a tough high school girl who finds herself in control of an alien with plans for world domination, ran from 2014 to 2015. In 2015, *Komi Can't Communicate* debuted as a one-shot in *Weekly Shonen Sunday* and was picked up as a full series by the same magazine in 2016.

Komi Can't Communicate

VOL. 8
Shonen Sunday Edition

Story and Art by Tomohito Oda

English Translation & Adaptation/John Werry
Touch-Up Art & Lettering/Eve Grandt
Design/Julian [JR] Robinson
Editor/Pancha Diaz

COMI-SAN WA, COMYUSHO DESU. Vol. 8
by Tomohito ODA
© 2016 Tomohito ODA
All rights reserved.
Original Japanese edition published by SHOGAKUKAN.
English translation rights in the United States of America, Canada, the United
Kingdom, Ireland, Australia and New Zealand arranged with SHOGAKUKAN.

Original Cover Design/Masato ISHIZAWA + Bay Bridge Studio

Printed in the U.S.A.

Published by VIZ Media, LLC
P.O. Box 77010
San Francisco, CA 94107

10 9 8 7 6 5 4 3 2 1
First printing, August 2020

viz.com

shonensunday.com

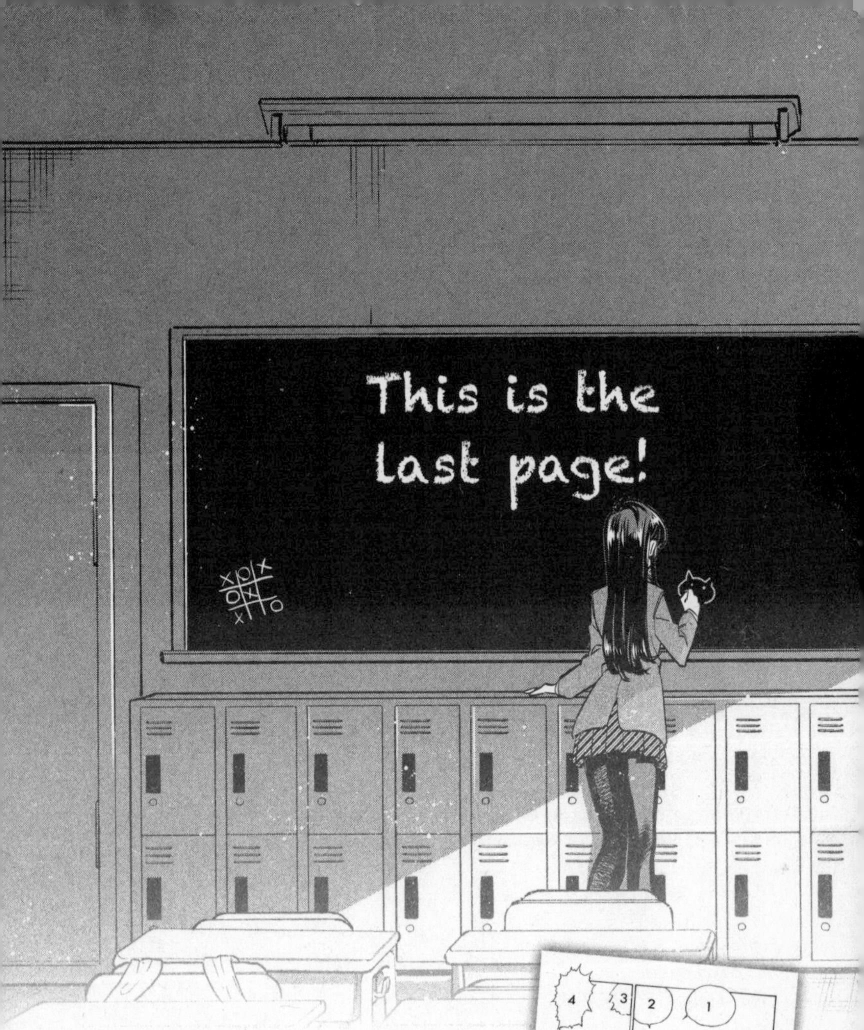
This is the last page!

Komi Can't Communicate has been printed in the original Japanese format to preserve the orientation of the artwork.

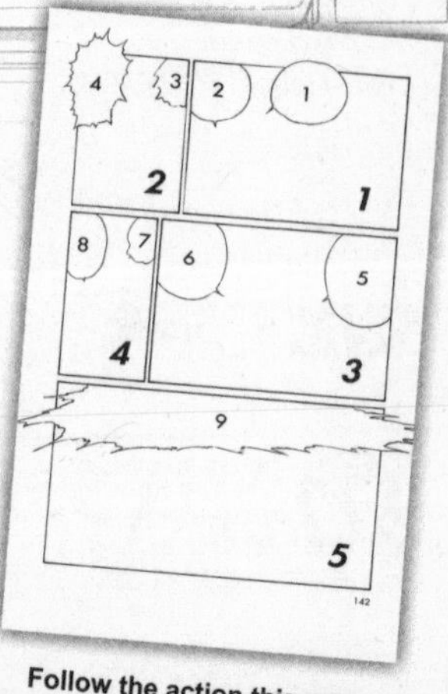

Follow the action this way.